WOMEN

Who

LEAD

*Insights, Inspiration, and Guidance
to Grow as an Educator*

Edited by **JANEL KEATING** *and* **JASMINE K. KULLAR**

Yvette Jackson	Julie A. Schmidt	Jasmine K. Kullar
Carmen Jiménez	Suzette Lovely	Tina H. Boogren
Joellen Killion	Heather Friziellie	Bob Sonju
Janel Keating	Jessica Kanold-McIntyre	Jason Andrews

Solution Tree | Press

a division of
Solution Tree

555 North Morton Street
Bloomington, IN 47404
800.733.6786 (toll free) / 812.336.7700
FAX: 812.336.7790

email: info@SolutionTree.com
SolutionTree.com

Visit **go.SolutionTree.com/leadership** to download the free reproducibles in this book.

Printed in the United States of America

Library of Congress Cataloging-in-Publication Data

Names: Keating, Janel, editor. | Kullar, Jasmine K., 1976- editor.
Title: Women who lead : insights, inspiration, and guidance to grow as an
    educator / Janel Keating, Jasmine K. Kullar.
Description: Bloomington, IN : Solution Tree Press, [2022] | Includes
    bibliographical references and index.
Identifiers: LCCN 2021054342 (print) | LCCN 2021054343 (ebook) | ISBN
    9781951075811 (Paperback) | ISBN 9781951075828 (eBook)
Subjects: LCSH: Women school administrators--United States. | Educational
    leadership--United States.
Classification: LCC LB2831.82 .W67 2022 (print) | LCC LB2831.82 (ebook) |
    DDC 371.20082--dc23/eng/20220316
LC record available at https://lccn.loc.gov/2021054342
LC ebook record available at https://lccn.loc.gov/2021054343

Solution Tree
Jeffrey C. Jones, CEO
Edmund M. Ackerman, President

Solution Tree Press
President and Publisher: Douglas M. Rife
Associate Publisher: Sarah Payne-Mills
Managing Production Editor: Kendra Slayton
Editorial Director: Todd Brakke
Art Director: Rian Anderson
Copy Chief: Jessi Finn
Senior Production Editor: Laurel Hecker
Content Development Specialist: Amy Rubenstein
Acquisitions Editor: Sarah Jubar
Copy Editor: Evie Madsen
Text Designer: Laura Cox
Cover Designer: Kelsey Hoover
Associate Editor: Sarah Ludwig
Editorial Assistants: Charlotte Jones and Elijah Oates

Solution Tree Press would like to thank the following reviewers:

Janna Cochrane
Principal
North Greenville Elementary School
Greenville, Wisconsin

Lori Jeschke
Director of Education
Prairie Spirit School Division
Warman, Saskatchewan

Shan Jorgenson-Adam
Assistant Superintendent—Learning
Battle River School Division
Camrose, Alberta

Visit **go.SolutionTree.com/leadership** to download the free reproducibles in this book.

Table of Contents

About the Editors

Janel Keating is superintendent of the White River School District in the state of Washington. An accomplished educator with more than thirty-five years of experience, she is a former elementary and middle school teacher, elementary principal, director of student learning, and deputy superintendent. For eight years, Janel was principal of Mountain Meadow Elementary School. During her time there, Mountain Meadow was recognized as one of the highest academically performing elementary schools in the state. Mountain Meadow was a finalist for the 2020 DuFour Award and today is the highest performing elementary school of the nearly 180 elementary schools in Pierce County.

Janel has been named Principal of the Year in Pierce County, Washington, and was a recipient of the 2013 Carroll College Alumni Academic Achievement Award. Janel is also the recipient of the 2019 Robert Handy Award for the most effective administrator in Washington State.

As an author, Janel has written four books and numerous articles on leadership and school improvement. She coauthored the lead chapter of *Professional Collaborations in Mathematics Teaching and Learning* (the 2012 National Council of Teachers of Mathematics Yearbook). Janel is past president of the Washington State Association for Supervision and Curriculum Development. She presents at state and national events.

Janel is partnering with the Washington Association of School Administrators and Solution Tree on the Washington State Association of School Administrators

Professional Learning Communities at Work (WASA PLC) Project. This project is ensuring equity districtwide by implementing a guaranteed and viable curriculum; creating a timely and balanced assessment system; removing barriers by implementing additional time, support, and extensions for all students; addressing equity issues through standards-based reporting and grading practices; building an inclusive and healthy district and school culture; and operationalizing the concepts and practices of PLC—from the boardroom to the classroom—as a vehicle to improve leadership and the professional practice of all adults in an effort for all students to learn at higher levels.

Janel earned a master's degree in educational leadership from the University of Idaho and a bachelor's degree in elementary education from Carroll College in Montana. Janel received a superintendent's certificate from Seattle Pacific University.

 **Jasmine K. Kullar, EdD,** is an assistant superintendent of a large metropolitan school district. She is also a faculty member in the College of Professional Studies Educational Leadership Department at Albany State University in Georgia. In addition, she is involved with the Wallace Foundation's University Principal Preparation Initiative (UPPI) and a member of the national UPPI Professional Learning Community (PLC), focused on redesigning university educational leadership preparation programs. Prior to these roles, she was a middle school principal for seven years at two separate schools. With over ten years of school leadership experience, Dr. Kullar has worked at the elementary, middle, and high school levels. She has taught in both Canada and the United States, giving her a variety of experiences in working with schools and school districts. She has expertise in building PLCs as well as school leadership. Her experience with PLCs began in her first year of teaching, when she attended a PLC workshop and heard Richard DuFour. Since then, she has been implementing those tenets. When she became a school administrator, she led her school to Model PLC status—the first school to receive this designation in the state of Georgia. Her school's success as a PLC is featured on AllThingsPLC (www.allthingsplc .info) as "Sample Professional Learning Community Manual." She has published articles with the Association for Supervision and Curriculum Development and presented several workshops at both the state and national levels. She is a lifelong

learner, with her latest certificate from Harvard University in Leading School Systems at the national level.

She earned a doctoral degree from Argosy University in Georgia, a master's degree from Memorial University of Newfoundland, a teaching certificate from Medaille College in Buffalo, and an undergraduate degree from the University of Toronto.

To book Janel Keating or Jasmine K. Kullar for professional development, contact pd@SolutionTree.com.

Foreword

Hannah Treadway

I am an educator's daughter. While other kids were riding the bus home after school, I was in my mother's classroom doing homework, eating snacks from the school vending machine, and playing "teacher" on her blackboard while she attended meetings and finished prepping for the next day. I spent many summer days camped out in an empty classroom or helping in the front office while my mom prepared for the new school year. I became proficient in stapling borders on bulletin boards and drawing smiley faces on graded papers before I had memorized my multiplication tables.

As my mother advanced in her career from novice to lead teacher, from school administrator to world-renowned educational author and consultant, I looked on as if this were a totally normal and natural progression. After all, two of her aunts were leaders in the field of education during a time when many people discouraged women from entering the paid workforce. This is just what women in education do, right? It was not until I grew up that I realized how unique my mother's story was, and how hard she had to work to earn her place in the world of educational leadership.

When Janel Keating reached out to tell me about this book, she shared that each of its authors had been influenced in some way by my late mother, Rebecca DuFour, one of the leading architects of Professional Learning Communities at Work® process. Indeed, I had met some of these women and men while working at or attending PLC at Work institutes. I remember being in awe of the positive impacts they are making on the educators, schools, and districts they serve. While not all of the book's authors worked with my mother in the context of promoting PLCs, she counted them all as colleagues and contemporaries in the important work of transforming school cultures and empowering educators to hold themselves and their students to the highest of standards. Much like my mother did, the authors of this book are blazing trails for a new generation of women in educational leadership!

While reading these chapters, I noticed certain recurring themes—common tenets and practices that guide the incredible women and men who penned these pages. One idea that stood out to me was that of leading with curiosity. Curiosity is heralded as a virtue throughout this book, whether it be when facing change, engaging in difficult conversations, learning from personal mistakes, or approaching one's career as a lifelong learner. Another prevalent piece of advice is the importance of leading with compassion. I was reminded throughout this book that compassion is critical when addressing the needs of those you lead. It can also serve as a connector to one's own purpose. What stood out to me most was the courage of the women whose words I was reading and their insistence that other women must lead courageously. Courage is necessary in tackling one's own insecurities while taking on leadership roles, when making tough decisions in the face of opposition, and while facing and leading change. The honesty with which these authors share personal stories of their leadership journeys speaks volumes about their capacity for courage.

My mom is no longer here to share the stories of her career as an educational leader. However, I remember watching her work and lead with the qualities detailed in this book. My mother was a lifelong learner and the best listener I ever knew. She led with curiosity, always seeking to better understand people and concepts. Her capacity for compassion was immense. She cared deeply about her students, colleagues, and those she was charged with leading. She believed that success in school was the pathway for students to grow and lead productive, fulfilling lives. This end goal—success for *all* students—was her calling, her passion, her moral imperative. Working toward this goal required an enormous amount of courage! My tenderhearted mother learned to cultivate the courage necessary to tackle opposition and face insecurities to ensure the right work was being done on behalf of the students in her care. I heard echoes of my mom's life and career in the words I read in this book.

Since losing my mom in 2018, I've thought a lot about the idea of *legacy*, what it means to leave one, and what legacy she left behind. I've concluded that my mother's legacy does not lie in her individual successes and achievements. Her true professional legacy lies within the educators she influenced, who continue to work tirelessly toward excellence and equity in education. Her legacy is the women and men she mentored, knowing that true leadership means building the capacity of those you lead. Through the words they have written and the work they do, the writers of this book are creating their own legacies of capable, empowered women leading the charge in education. They realize there is no room for competition and divisiveness among women in the field. Rather, there is a need to lift up and challenge one another to lead with curiosity, compassion, and courage. The authors understand there is not only room for more than one woman at the top but also a need for many!

My mom had a habit of gifting books with special notes written inside the front covers. Her grandsons have several books with inscriptions from their "Nanny D." When I started working as an elementary school counselor, she gave me several books to use in my lessons or to further my learning as a professional. *Women Who Lead* is a book she would've gifted *you*, a woman making her way through the path of leadership in her career. I imagine her inscription would have read something like this:

May you always remember your purpose and know you are more capable of effecting positive change than you realize. Our schools need more curious, compassionate, and courageous leaders like you!

Introduction

Janel Keating and Jasmine Kullar

Because high-quality leadership is so central to organizational success, effective leadership characteristics and practices have been the topic of scholarly inquiry for decades. There is no shortage of information about what constitutes effective leadership practices. On the other hand, there is still a lot to learn about the topic of *women in leadership*.

The field of education exhibits a unique disparity in the gender demographics between staff and leadership. In the United States, 76 percent of public school teachers are women (National Center for Education Statistics [NCES], 2021). The gender ratio of educators varies by school level, but women are in the majority throughout (NCES, 2021).

- Eighty-nine percent of elementary teachers are women.
- Sixty-four percent of secondary teachers are women.

By contrast, the majority of educational leaders are men. Women have achieved a slim majority in total principalships in the United States (54 percent; NCES, 2020), but the gender imbalance between elementary and secondary is present at the school leadership level as well. At the elementary level, women make up 68 percent of principals, while 67 percent of high school principals are men (Fregni, 2021). This holds true in Canada as well, with 45 percent of elementary school principals being women, while only 27 percent of high school principals are women (O'Haire, 2004). The same pattern also exists globally. Data show that in Organisation for Economic Co-Operation and Development (OECD) members countries, 68 percent of the secondary school teachers are female, but only 45 percent of the secondary principals are female (Martinez, Molina-Lopez, & Mateos de Cabo, 2020). The gender disparity is the widest in education's top job—the superintendency. Only 24 percent of U.S. public school superintendents are women (Ramaswamy, 2020). While this is a significant increase from the early 1990s, when less than 10 percent of superintendents were women (Glass, Björk, & Brunner, 2000), it remains in stark contrast with the demographics of U.S. educators at large.

So why are women underrepresented in educational leadership? While women are entirely capable of attaining and performing these roles, they have had to overcome many more obstacles than their male counterparts to obtain leadership positions.

The *glass ceiling*—discriminatory barriers that prevent women from advancing or rising to positions of power or responsibility within an organization simply because they are women—is ever present for female educational leaders. One deputy superintendent shared her lived experience.

> I'd spent eight years leading one of the highest-performing schools in the district and state. I re-cultured an entire district in my role as deputy superintendent. I was a knowledgeable point person when the district went through huge budget cuts during the 2008 recession. Yet, when the board of directors promoted me to the top leadership position—superintendent— the outgoing superintendent warned the board that I didn't know anything about the fiscal operations of the school district. How could that be true? How could I be a key person in a districtwide budget-cutting process without knowing anything about the budget and fiscal operations? Maybe his comment said more about him as a mentor than my ability to manage the financial aspects of the district.

Education news outlet *The Hechinger Report* released a report that discusses three major reasons the glass ceiling persists in education: (1) bias and lack of transparency in hiring and promotion, (2) exclusion from formal and informal networks and mentorship programs, and (3) policies that are unfriendly to women with family obligations (Rafal-Baer, 2019).

It starts with the executive-search process and implicit bias. When describing qualities of a potential superintendent, you will find different language about men and women (Bernal, 2020). Men may be called strong, assertive, or directive. Women may be described as good listeners, adaptable, or empathetic. This can set up the interview team members for specific perceptions of the candidates before they even meet them: "Male candidates were perceived as more capable in budgeting and finance, and females were considered by consultants as more likely to allow their emotions to influence their decision making" (Bernal, 2020). These biases are a significant factor in persistent gender inequity.

Women's paths upward in their careers may be less clear and come with fewer guides than men's. The following scenario is representative of many women's experiences—perhaps even yours.

> I was an elementary school teacher with aspirations of becoming an assistant principal. After applying and interviewing for a couple of years—I finally landed the position! Shortly after my experience as elementary school assistant principal, I knew I wanted to move up and become a principal. During this time, I got pregnant with my second child. I went ahead and put my application in and waited and waited—I received no interviews. I tried to ask my principal what feedback he could give me, and he said he didn't really have any. He said maybe it just wasn't my time yet. A few years later, I finally was named principal of an elementary school. I loved it and felt that I was making incredible progress for the students in my school. After five years, I asked if I could expand my experience— maybe another level? I was given another elementary school. After being a principal of another elementary school, I was ready for another change. I knew I wanted to become a superintendent. So, I applied and applied. But I was told that it is difficult to become a superintendent without having had any high school experience. I'm having a hard time getting high school experience because the majority of high school principals I know are men. How do I get that superintendent position?

One of the obstacles for women is the candidate pool from which superintendents are selected; the majority of that pool is made up of secondary school principals. As a result, women, who are mostly elementary school principals, are less likely to get the opportunity (Superville, 2016). Another obstacle is the scarcity of female role models and networking opportunities for women (Ramaswamy, 2020).

Finally, demanding leadership roles can be (or be perceived as) incompatible with family obligations (Kominiak, 2016). Even when they participate in the workforce, women still perform the majority of household chores (Brenan, 2020). Combining all the responsibilities of educational leadership with "keeping home lives running smoothly" is no easy feat (Kendrick-Weikle, 2020). As Kristen J. Kendrick-Weikle (2020), superintendent at McLean County Unit 5 School District in Illinois, illustrates:

While many of our male colleagues have families, some responsibilities tend to fall on us as wives and mothers. We arrange carpooling for extracurricular activities, schedule and attend doctor appointments with kids and parents, ensure supper is on the table, make sure laundry is done and plan birthday parties—all while serving as superintendents.

This scenario from one of our female colleagues describes this barrier.

I remember when my kids were middle and high school age. I would pull up to the house after work and they would be ready with their gear and usually something for both of us to eat and drink (which I would prep on the weekends or late at night). I would take them to practice. Often, I dropped one or another of my sons at the ice rink and then went grocery shopping because I had about forty-five minutes before they got on the ice. I was the only mom at practices usually. About halfway through, the dads would start talking about what their wives were making for dinner, and how hungry they were. I would say, "Well, when I get home, I will be making . . ." And then cleaning up, putting away groceries, and doing the laundry while I oversee my kids' homework. I wouldn't give up that time, but when I look back on it now, I am overwhelmed with how I managed to fit it all into my day.

Hiring bias, lack of networking and opportunities, and the added burdens of household responsibilities are systemic barriers that require systemic solutions. However, we believe women in leadership don't have to wait for systemic changes. While all these barriers are challenges, women can surmount them. There are things women can do individually and together. Imagine a team of women in an organization. They may feel underrepresented; they may find they are frequently being left out and talked over; they may discover credit for their ideas was given to one of their male colleagues. Women can band together to support and amplify one another. Insist on being included in meetings. Once in the meetings, if someone interrupts one woman, another should speak up and say, "I don't think she was finished. I would really like to hear her thoughts." If one woman puts forward an idea or solution, another can repeat it and credit the originator by name. These are all examples of things women can each do to support one another (Landsbaum, 2016).

Our personal experiences as women in leadership positions for the past twenty-five years have included both roadblocks and successes. Now we feel compelled to gather and share lessons our fellow woman leaders, allies, and we have learned in our careers in education. It is our hope that by sharing our collected wisdom with aspiring women leaders, we can help you prepare for leadership, overcome obstacles, and fulfill your potential. We have organized this book into three primary themes.

The theme of part 1 is *effective leadership*. Effective leadership practices are effective leadership practices, regardless of your gender. However, because people all bring their own experiences to the job and there is no denying that men and women bring different experiences to the table, it is important to examine how this impacts women leaders specifically. It does not mean leadership expectations and outcomes are or should be different, but rather, that the execution may not look the same. In the first three chapters, you will have the opportunity to reflect on effective leadership practices and women's relationship to them.

In chapter 1, "Cultivating the Leadership of Confidence," Yvette Jackson and Carmen Jiménez provide insights and practices that will guide women to harness the power of their values and strengths. The future of education requires leadership from women, and especially women of color. The authors will help you discover your purpose and develop the courage and urgency needed as a foundation for successful, equity-conscious school leadership and for enacting the recommendations of later chapters.

In chapter 2, "Facing Change," Joellen Killion addresses the one constant in life—*change*. This chapter discusses the importance of understanding change, how to successfully navigate change, and practical skills for implementing change. Six lessons will prepare you to lead in a constantly shifting environment.

In chapter 3, "Leading With Compassion and Empathy," Janel Keating opens a conversation about supporting others through personal struggles while simultaneously working to improve learning. This is a key role for leaders, but one that does not usually come up in principal prep programs or educational leadership courses. This chapter shows what it is really like to lead in a profession where the line between work and home is often blurry.

The theme of part 2 is *obstacles*. As we noted previously, "women educational leaders—especially women of color—are underrepresented when comparing the male to female ratio of administrators as opposed to the representation of female to male teachers in classrooms" (Arriaga, Stanley, & Lindsey, 2020, p. 54). Although much progress has been made, much is left to be done. Women must face the fact that the playing field is still very uneven. In the next three chapters, you will have the opportunity to reflect on various roadblocks, as well as how to get past them.

In chapter 4, "Looking Out the Window and In the Mirror," Julie A. Schmidt discusses the unique challenges women face when making the decision to pursue a leadership position. This chapter talks about the context of those challenges and how women have confronted that process. While many of the barriers to leadership are out of their control, Schmidt identifies internal strategies women can use to counter those external challenges.

In chapter 5, "Rising Through the Ranks," Suzette Lovely shares the RISE model for career advancement. While women have a different experience climbing the ladder than men, this chapter presents strategies for breaking free of sticky floors and glass ceilings that hold women down and keep them from rising.

In chapter 6, "Braving Difficult Conversations," Heather Friziellie acknowledges that difficult conversations must happen. This chapter will deepen your understanding of what makes these conversations difficult and how to navigate them. The author provides various strategies to ensure women leaders also remain respectful and productive.

The theme of part 3 is *self-growth*. Leaders who stop learning stop growing. No matter what position you hold, you should set aside time for your personal and professional growth. How else do women continue to become better leaders? Leadership experts Jennifer W. Martineau and Portia R. Mount (2019) state that while women are waiting for the glass ceiling to break, they must take charge of their own growth. The journey to being your best means lifelong learning. It means you are always in pursuit of professional and personal self-growth. In the last four chapters, you will have the opportunity to reflect on various ways you can grow as a woman in leadership.

In chapter 7, "Seeking Mentorship and Sharing Your Expertise," Jessica Kanold-McIntyre explores the dual responsibility women have as they move into leadership roles: to seek out trusted mentors for themselves, and to mentor other women. This chapter focuses on those responsibilities, and includes steps mentors can take to build the next generation of women in leadership.

In chapter 8, "Preparing for Promotion," Jasmine K. Kullar helps you mentally prepare and acquire key skills for career advancement. This chapter will guide you to think through some challenges associated with next-level positions and how to best market yourself to get promoted.

In chapter 9, "Taking Care of Yourself," Tina H. Boogren addresses the essential topic of self-care for women in education. Burnout is real. She explains the causes and effects of stress and shares numerous preventative strategies, and also explains the importance of building healthy habits as part of self-care.

In chapter 10, "Learning From Women Leaders," Bob Sonju and Jason Andrews share their perspective as allies. They relay several lessons they have learned from women over the course of their careers in education and recount stories of inspirational women leaders.

Throughout each chapter, you will encounter reflection questions that will guide you to process the authors' wisdom and apply it to your own life. Visit **go.SolutionTree.com/leadership** to access reproducible versions of the reflection prompts for each chapter. Our goal is that reading and reflecting on our book will provide insights, inspiration, and guidance on how to grow as an educator, ultimately closing the gender gap that exists in education's top positions.

References and Resources

Arriaga, T. T., Stanley, S. L., & Lindsey, D. B. (2020). *Leading while female: A culturally proficient response for gender equity*. Thousand Oaks, CA: Corwin Press.

Bernal, C. A. (2020, March). Disrupting the biases inherent in executive searches. *School Administrator*. Accessed at https://my.aasa.org/AASA/Resources/SAMag/2020/Mar20/Sidebar_Bernal.aspx on February 7, 2022.

Brenan, M. (2020, January 29). Women still handle main household tasks in U.S. *Gallup*. Accessed at https://news.gallup.com/poll/283979/women-handle-main-household-tasks.aspx on February 7, 2022.

Buchanan, F. R., Warning, R. L., & Tett, R. P. (2012). Trouble at the top: Women who don't want to work for a female boss. *The Journal of Business Diversity*, *12*(1), 33–46.

Caprino, K. (2015, October 20). The "glass cliff" phenomenon that senior female leaders face today and how to avoid it. *Forbes*. Accessed at https:// forbes.com/sites/kathycaprino/2015/10/20/the-glass-cliff-phenomenon-that-senior-female-leaders-face-today-and-how-to-avoid-it/?sh=3a0fda2779c6 on February 7, 2022.

Fregni, J. (2021, March 1). Working to shatter education's glass ceiling. *One Day*. Accessed at https://teachforamerica.org/one-day/top-issues/working-to-shatter-educations-glass-ceiling on November 21, 2021.

Glass, T. E., Björk, L., & Brunner, C. C. (2000). *The study of the American school superintendency, 2000: A look at the superintendent of education in the new millennium*. Arlington, VA: American Association of School Administrators.

Kendrick-Weikle, K. J. (2020, March). The essence of a support network. *School Administrator*. Accessed at https://my.aasa.org/AASA/Resources/SAMag/2020/Mar20/Kendrick-Weikle.aspx on February 7, 2022.

Kominiak, T. (2016, November 4). There are too few women superintendents—and what we can do about it. *TrustED*. Accessed at https://www.k12insight.com/trusted/women -superintendents-can on February 7, 2022.

Landsbaum, C. (2016, September 13). Obama's female staffers came up with a genius strategy to make sure their voices were heard. *The Cut*. Accessed at https://thecut.com/2016/09/heres -how-obamas-female-staffers-made-their-voices-heard.html on February 7, 2022.

Lok, D. (n.d.). *How leadership differences between men and women are evolving today*. Accessed at https://danlok.com/how-leadership-differences-between-men-and-women-evolving-today on September 27, 2021.

Martineau, J. W., & Mount, P. R. (2019). *Kick some glass: Ten ways women succeed at work on their own terms*. New York: McGraw-Hill Education.

Martinez, M. M., Molina-Lopez, M. M., & Mateos de Cabo, R. (2020). Explaining the gender gap in school principalship: A tale of two sides. *Educational Management Administration and Leadership*, *49*(6), 863–882.

National Center for Education Statistics. (2020). *Characteristics of public school principals*. Accessed at https://nces.ed.gov/programs/coe/pdf/coe_cls.pdf on November 21, 2021.

National Center for Education Statistics. (2021). *Characteristics of public school teachers*. Accessed at https://nces.ed.gov/programs/coe/pdf/2021/clr_508c.pdf on November 21, 2021.

O'Haire, N. (2004). CTF surveys gender composition of Canada's teaching population. *Alberta Teachers' Association (ATA) Magazine*, *85*(3). Accessed at www.teachers.ab.ca/News% 20Room/ata%20magazine/Volume%2085/Number%203/Articles/Pages/Gender%20and %20Leadership.aspx on February 7, 2022.

Rafal-Baer, J. (2019, April 9). How to shatter the education system's glass ceiling: New report outlines 3 steps to help women become top school leaders. *The Hechinger Report*. Accessed at https://hechingerreport.org/opinion-how-to-shatter-educations-glass-ceiling on February 7, 2022.

Ramaswamy, S. V. (2020, February 20). School superintendents are overwhelmingly male. What's holding women back from the top job? *USA Today*. Accessed at https://usatoday .com/story/news/education/2020/02/20/female-school-district-superintendents-westchester -rockland/4798754002 on November 21, 2021.

Superville, D. R. (2016, November 15). Few women run the nation's school districts. Why? *Education Week*. Accessed at https://edweek.org/leadership/few-women-run-the-nations -school-districts-why/2016/11 on February 7, 2022.

Part 1

Effective Leadership

Yvette Jackson, EdD, winner of the 2019 GlobalMindEd Inclusive Leader Award, is adjunct professor at Teachers College, Columbia University, in New York and senior scholar for the National Urban Alliance for Effective Education. Dr. Jackson's passion is assisting educators in cultivating their confidence and competence to unlock the giftedness in all students. She is driven to provide and promote pedagogy that enables students who are disenfranchised and marginalized to demonstrate their strengths and innate intellectual potential. Dr. Jackson's approach, called *Pedagogy of Confidence*, helps educators believe in and value these students and optimize student success, which, for Dr. Jackson, is the basis of equity consciousness.

Dr. Jackson is a former teacher and has served New York City Public Schools as director of gifted programs and executive director of instruction and professional development. She continues to work with school districts to customize and systemically deliver the collegial, strengths-based High Operational Practices of the Pedagogy of Confidence that integrate culture, language, and cognition to engage and elicit the innate potential of all students for self-actualization and contributions to our world. Dr. Jackson has been a visiting lecturer at Harvard University's Urban Superintendents Program, the Stanford Center for Opportunity Policy in Education at Stanford University, the Feuerstein Institute, and Thinking Schools International. In 2012, the Academy of Education Arts and Sciences International honored Dr. Jackson with its Educators' Voice Award for Education Policy/Researcher of the Year. She has applied her research in neuroscience, gifted education, literacy, and the cognitive mediation theory of the eminent cognitive psychologist Dr. Reuven Feuerstein to develop integrated processes that engage and elicit high intellectual performances from students who are underachieving. This work is the basis for her award-winning book, *The Pedagogy of Confidence: Inspiring High Intellectual Performance in Urban Schools*. Dr. Jackson also coauthored *Aim High, Achieve More: How to Transform Urban Schools Through Fearless Leadership* and *Unlocking Student Potential: How Do I Identify and Activate Student Strengths?* with Veronica McDermott, and *Mindfulness Practices: Cultivating Heart Centered Communities Where Students Focus and Flourish* with Christine Mason and Michele M. Rivers Murphy.

Dr. Jackson received a bachelor's degree from Queens College, City University of New York with a double major in French and education, and a master's degree in curriculum design, master of education, and doctor of education in educational administration, all from Teachers College, Columbia University.

To book Yvette Jackson for professional development, contact pd@SolutionTree.com.

Carmen Jiménez is an executive leadership coach and an expert in educational leadership. She supports school systems throughout the United States, public and charter schools, institutions of higher education, and education policy organizations to create sustainable principal leadership development, improve low-performing schools, and build district and school leadership capacity. She works closely with aspiring and practicing superintendents, principals, and assistant principals to enhance their leadership and to develop their coaching and mentoring skills. Carmen's interest and expertise support leaders to bring equity consciousness and social justice to the schoolhouse, district, and community.

Carmen has designed and delivered leadership programs and executive coaching focused on effective management, strategic planning, team building, equity and social justice, emotional intelligence, and proper use and development of fiscal and human resources to transform schools into equitable environments for all students.

A former deputy superintendent, principal, and turnaround specialist of three low-performing schools in New York City, Carmen was a member of the team that developed the New York State standards and examinations for certifying school principals and superintendents.

Carmen served for many years as a member of the faculty at the Harvard Principal's Center summer institutes and as a member of the advisory board for the Harvard Principal's Center. She has also served as adjunct faculty for the Center for Creative Leadership in Greensboro, North Carolina. She has taught graduate level courses at the City University of New York (CUNY).

Carmen earned a professional diploma in educational administration from the Bank Street College of Education and master's degrees from Hunter College. She is a partner at an educational leadership consulting firm.

CHAPTER 1

Cultivating the Leadership of Confidence

Yvette Jackson and Carmen Jiménez

I have learned that as long as I hold fast to my beliefs and values—and follow my own moral compass—then the only expectations I have to live up to are my own.

—Michelle Obama

It takes confidence to lead. To lead confidently, you must "[know] what's expected and [believe] you have what it takes to achieve that" (Jackson, 2011, p. 41). Given the barriers women face in society, the workplace, and educational leadership, they sometimes struggle to develop a sense of surety within themselves and to project that confidence in their leadership. But students need women. The field of education urgently needs women leaders, and women leaders of color in particular, if educators are ever going to achieve true equity for all students. This chapter will share our approach for igniting and enacting the leadership of confidence. You should draw on your purpose, personal experiences, and values to become a confident, equity-conscious leader.

When we started writing this chapter, we had the double goal of developing the confidence of more women of color for leadership positions and supporting women already in leadership roles by expanding their thinking and actions as equity and social justice leaders. Then reality was shaken with the COVID-19 pandemic, virtual schooling, social distancing, and protests for racial justice, and our purpose and our need to write this chapter became crucial. We believe what is needed to lead the transformation of our schools in these turbulent times are confident women, especially women of color. Our goal, therefore, is to remind you of the power of your purpose so you can take on the mantle of confident, equity-conscious leaders in the struggle for a more just society.

Igniting a Leadership of Confidence

A *leadership of confidence* means you fully understand your purpose. Knowing your purpose is the beginning of leadership. Until you know *why* you are a leader, you are only a manager, a supervisor, or a team administrator. Your purpose should be a point of reference for everything you do. Like a North Star, it will guide you to make conscious, deliberate choices—choices more impactful for your work and for the world within which you work. Cognitive psychology and neuroscience substantiate that everyone is wired with the desire to make a difference—albeit negative or positive—to have impact, to be noticed, to have a reason for being (Goleman, 2012; Jackson, 2011; Kabat-Zinn, 2013; Kaplin & Anzaldi, 2015; Winfrey, 2018). Knowing your purpose drives your life, fills you with energy, and enables you to overcome, create, innovate, and take risks. When you know *why*, *how* and *what* become much easier. The stories in this chapter will testify to the power of identifying one's purpose.

Some people have a deep understanding of their purpose early in life. Others may be fortunate enough to have an inspirational moment that ignites their intentions. However, far too many leaders with whom we have worked flounder, never finding the overriding vision to make courageous decisions and take bold actions that would positively affect the students in their charge. These purpose-less leaders end up leaving behind a trail of disillusionment and the squandered potential of broken-hearted students and staff (Jackson & McDermott, 2012).

A powerful purpose comes from paying attention to the *collective lived experiences* of your life: the events and people who have impacted your life positively and negatively, and the situations and experiences that inspire and motivate you (Kabat-Zinn, 2013). Your purpose is wrapped up in this story of you. Thinking about your story, carefully reflecting on how each person or experience has moved you further along a continuum to where you are today helps you bring your purpose into focus. Your purpose is the vital force that animates your leadership of confidence. When your sense of purpose is strong enough, it will propel you to do what others are unwilling to do. This belief enables you to lead confidently and unapologetically, taking the actions that are the evidence of your purpose.

——————————————— *Reflection* ———————————————

What is your purpose?

When was the moment you became conscious of your purpose?

———

Visit **go.SolutionTree.com/leadership** *to access a reproducible reflection guide for this chapter.*

Leading From Belief With an Equity-Conscious Mission and Vision

Regardless of their personal frame of reference, educational leaders must adopt a profound equity consciousness. *Equity consciousness* is a way of educating informed by and situated in the belief that *all* students are innately wired for engagement, high intellectual performance, self-actualization, and personal contribution (Jackson, 2011; Jackson, 2016). Equity consciousness substantiates your purpose as an educator. *Othering practices* spawn a lack of belief in potential because of race, poverty, or ethnicity, squandering the potential of so many students in your care. The only response to this is to confidently and unapologetically generate an equity-conscious mission and vision statement for yourself and your team, school, or district to clearly articulate your purpose.

Creating the mission and vision statement of your purpose affirms and energizes you: "It is the spark that fires up the courage to try something new, to take a risk, to hurl yourself into places you didn't believe you could go" (Jackson & McDermott, 2012, p. 17). From this courage, you confidently profess your commitment to the advent of a new transformative narrative for *all* your students—one that reflects innate value and potential of all students; incorporates the latest research that students can perform at high levels when they have thought-provoking, enriching, intellectually stimulating opportunities; builds their strengths and supports their weaknesses; and develops critical-thinking skills and learning dispositions (Feuerstein, Feuerstein, & Falik, 2010; Hilliard, 1977; Jackson, 2011; Maxwell, 2010; Medina, 2008; Niedenthal & Ric, 2017). An equity-conscious mission and vision statement raises the bar:

> Through an equity-conscious mission and vision statement, you articulate bold goals that indicate the well-defined actions that must be taken to actualize this vision and mission: policies, curricula, programs, pedagogy, assessments, and professional learning experiences reflective of low expectations or othering are no longer permissible. (Jackson, 2011, p. 136)

A mission and vision statement reflective of your purpose paints a picture of possibilities. It indicates the equity-conscious direction that ensures your students' innate potential for high intellectual performances thrives and flourishes. Such a statement achieves the following.

- Affirms belief in and value of students' innate propensity for demonstrating personal strengths, high intellectual performances, and self-determined goal orientation (Jackson & McDermott, 2012)

- Delineates the specific student attributes the system pledges to develop, the commitments it will keep for developing these attributes, and develops the core pedagogy that cultivates these attributes

As an example, consider the equity-conscious mission and vision from Robbinsdale Area Schools (2014), Minnesota:

> The Robbinsdale Area Unified District Vision: High Intellectual Performance through Equity
>
> Robbinsdale Area Schools is committed to ensuring every student graduates career and college ready. We believe each student has limitless possibilities and we strive to ignite the potential in every student. We expect high intellectual performance from all our students. We are committed to ensuring an equitable and respectful educational experience for every student, family and staff member, focusing on strengths related to:
>
> - Race
> - Culture
> - Ethnicity
> - Home or First Language
> - National Origin
> - Socioeconomic Status
> - Gender
> - Sexual Orientation
> - Age
> - Ability
> - Religion
> - Physical Appearance

San Francisco Unified School District (SFUSD; 2008), California, provides another example:

> The San Francisco Unified School District: Beyond the Talk
> The mission of the San Francisco Unified School District is to provide each student with an equal opportunity to succeed by promoting intellectual growth, creativity, self-discipline, cultural and linguistic sensitivity, democratic responsibility, economic competence, and physical and mental health so that each student can achieve his/her maximum potential.

The clear direction and ambition these mission and vision statements demonstrate are "exactly what is needed for a systemic, transformational shift from the traditional focus on weaknesses that leads to low expectations for students of color and other underserved populations to an outcome-directed belief in the intellectual capacities of *all* students" (Jackson, 2011, p. 139).

------------------------------ *Reflection* ------------------------------

How do you define *equity consciousness* for yourself?

Overcoming Inhibitors to Confidence

There is no doubt that working toward equity in education is a challenge—which is why it requires solid, unwavering confidence. For centuries, however, existing cultural norms (for example, the diminutive number of women in leadership positions) that imply women are less capable than men have undermined the confidence of women. For women of color, igniting confidence also requires self-determination of exponential proportions to transcend the very explicit racism they encounter. Racial bias creates cultures of othering within institutions that permeate beyond the explicit practices of inequality affirmative action addresses. This othering is realized in the expressions of prejudice and terminology designed to perpetuate inequality and engender a sense of inferiority (Powell & Menendian, 2016).

In the workplace, women experience a sense of othering through explicit and implicit biases demonstrated in the overt or covert acts of exclusion that make them feel they do not belong. For years, women of color, trying to stay the course in hopes of being recognized for their skills, promoted to leadership positions, and just maybe eventually accepted, have felt restricted to three choices of action in response to othering.

1. Overproducing to prove themselves for validation

2. Accommodating the dominant group by assuming its narrative or views in response to a situation

3. Assimilating into the group by adopting its cultural behaviors and language while repressing or relinquishing their own

Education has long othered students through marginalizing labels such as *minority*, *urban*, *low achiever*, *disadvantaged*, *subgroup*, and *learning gap*. Such labels amplify misperceptions about the abilities of students of color to reach high levels of intellectual performance and perpetuate "a cycle of prejudicing bias, low expectations, and limiting realities" (Jackson, 2011, p. 20).

Igniting the confidence you need to counter and mitigate gender and racial bias and practices of othering for yourself, your colleagues, and your students requires a radical introspection. We say *radical* because it is an introspection in which you must affirm and declare your strengths—which women, especially women of color, have been conditioned not to do. Besides the racial bias that represses such affirmation and declaration in people of color, women have also been culturally conditioned to feel that declaring their strengths is akin to bragging. This is an egregious fallacy. You were born with the propensity to develop strengths so you can make contributions to the world. Being conditioned not to affirm your strengths is like being conditioned not to breathe. And just like not breathing, when you don't affirm your strengths, you deprive yourself of your vital life force, the force that propels you to realize your purpose.

Knowing your purpose calls on you to identify, affirm, and declare your strengths so you can confidently put your purpose into action. Positive affirmations can reprogram negative beliefs, mitigating the effect of disparaging affirmations women receive from stereotypes, negative influences, or the derogatory educational labels that perpetuate a focus on weaknesses and lower self-esteem. Affirming your strengths creates a sense of self that generates confidence and motivates you to apply those strengths more frequently, leading to a cycle of success (Anderson, 2005; Buckingham & Clifton, 2001; Colvin, 2008). Success generates confidence and hope. American journalist, author, professor, and world peace advocate Norman Cousins (1989) illustrates that there is an authentic biology to the effect of hope; this same biology applies to the effect of recognizing your strengths for acting on your purpose (Chopra & Tanzi, 2012; Kabat-Zinn, 2013).

Enacting the Power of Purpose

Knowing your purpose is the catalyst to confidently moving into action. But if taking action feels like too big a leap, there are steps you can take to activate your confidence. Remembering how you got to where you are helps you gain perspective about the influences that give power to your purpose. Reflecting on the urgency of change helps you rekindle your motivation. Discovering *your edge*—your fearlessness—helps you take bold action even when it is not easy. Finally, shepherding your team and bringing people along with you builds critical mass. This power propels the enactment of your purpose and gives you the fuel to make difficult decisions and take bold action with equity consciousness.

———————————— *Reflection* ————————————

Think of a time when a situation or an experience propelled
you to enact your purpose with edge. What happened?

Remembering the Source of Your Purpose

What drew you into education to begin with? Do you remember your commitment and passion to employ practices to elicit your students' desire to learn and their potential to achieve? When you remember your first concrete evidence of student success and the confidence you felt from using your gifts to unlock your students' gifts, you remember your purpose. You know this is your purpose because these memories make you feel an energizing glow. This "glow" is actually a neurological response to your acting on your purpose, and it literally fuels your ability to achieve your purpose. Confidence generated from experiencing competence stimulates your brain, causing it to burn glucose and "glow" from the released energy (Jackson, 2011; Jensen, 1998). The stimulation releases neurotransmitters including endorphins that cause euphoria. When you feel competent, the brain also releases fewer catecholamines (chemicals related to stress). The effect of competence on your body is the same whether you are actively engaged in an experience of competence or remembering one (Jackson, 2011; Jensen, 1998).

Remembering how you arrived at your purpose reignites those feelings. Then, you'll recognize that the actions you take are the manifestation of your purpose. To illustrate remembering the source of your purpose, Carmen shares the following story.

> On March 17, 1987, the superintendent came to the middle school where I had been assigned interim supervisor to inform me that I was now the acting principal for the school. Before I knew it, it was June and we were making plans for graduation. Two weeks before the ceremony, the guidance counselor came to see me to discuss what to do about students who would not be attending graduation because they had nothing appropriate to wear. Compelled by the force of equity consciousness, we came up with a plan to provide our most needy students with clothes for the event. We even arranged for their teachers to take the students to lunch and provide a gift for them after the ceremony. On the morning of graduation, I took a female student into my office to help get her ready and time stood still.
>
> I had this flashback of being back in sixth grade, with my own graduation approaching. I remembered plotting to avoid the ceremony by pretending to be sick, as I knew it was an expense that my mother could not afford. On the Saturday before the graduation, I was walking with my mom, when we saw a neighbor whose daughter was in the other sixth-grade class. The woman launched into a flustered monologue about how she was still shopping for Monday's graduation. My mother glanced at me, and I just held my head down. My mom asked me if it was true that there would be a graduation ceremony on Monday. I told her yes, but that I did not want to go. She walked over to a fabric store and bought a beautiful white fabric with eyelets and a wide piece of white satin. My mother, who owned a

sewing machine but was not a seamstress, had decided she would sew a graduation dress for me. She spent the entire night and all of Sunday into the wee hours of Monday morning sewing. A few hours later, she dressed me, combed my curly hair and even put a little pink lipstick and a bit of rouge on me. As I proudly looked into the mirror, I thought my dress was beautiful. But when I walked into my classroom and saw so many puffy, store-bought dresses, I deflated and lost my pride and my confidence. My teacher, Mrs. Herman, was my champion. I remember how she exclaimed how beautiful I looked and what a beautiful dress I was wearing. I remember how she put her hand on her cheek, and with a big smile, just gushed over me. As we lined up, other teachers came by to look at us and many of them made a point to single me out and comment how beautiful I looked. Right before going to the auditorium, the principal came over to our line and singled me out to say what a beautiful dress I had—and I told her, beaming, that my mom had made it for me. By this time, I was strutting down to the auditorium. It was a glorious day!

Then I was back in the present day. As I looked at the young lady I was helping look her best for her special day, I realized that I had come full circle and face-to-face with my purpose. All of a sudden, I knew why I was there! Every experience in my working life and every person I had met along the way who had influenced or impacted my life had in some way prepared me for leading, to ensure that this young lady and all future students would see their potential and not allow their economic circumstances define who they could become. I was living proof. And at that very moment, I realized what had really transpired on that day of my own graduation. Mrs. Herman, the principal, and all my other teachers did not allow the way I looked in my homemade white dress with the white satin sash to erode my confidence in who I really was. I could not see it then, but their gesture ensured that I would have the self-confidence to walk into that auditorium with my head held high and proud my mother made my dress. Their kindness helped me realize how important it was for me to feel confident and proud and not allow my appearance to influence how I valued myself. They would not let me compare myself to all those other girls whose circumstances were so different from mine. Their gesture would influence me unconsciously, and then consciously and deliberately, to develop a keen sense of empathy and fairness, and to understand the power I would have to transform the lives of students whose circumstances might send a message that they were not valuable, or smart, or would never overcome those circumstances. I cried that day at the school where I was now the principal, finally understanding the powerful meaning of that day in sixth grade and vowed that I would

be an equity warrior like Mrs. Herman and all those teachers who guided
me. I would dedicate my leadership to ensuring all students would reach
for the best in themselves regardless of their circumstances! It was on
that graduation day that I became the real leader of the school and the
cheerleader of the students. I was formally appointed on June 26, 1987,
and never looked back.

Your story, which is the source of *why* you do what you do, is also about developing your confidence. You need confidence to be a transformational leader who takes the time to remember your purpose and assesses the culture of your school or organization and the manner in which your staff values or devalues the potential of the students in your charge. And where and when needed, it takes a leader with confidence to boldly articulate the gap between the students' innate potential and what they are achieving, and to take a stand against the debilitating beliefs that create the inequitable education that renders the underachievement of students (Jackson, 2011). It is possible. Some of you may already have a disposition to take up the challenge; others may need to develop theirs. It is never effortless to take on this kind of challenge; it requires a level of courage that builds confidence and lets you stand for what is just, true, and moral.

———————————— *Reflection* ————————————

Who are the inspiring figures—the "Mrs. Hermans"—in your life?
What from their impact has remained with you to this day?

Reflecting on the Urgency of Change

Educators have long been facing turbulent times in education. However, the COVID-19 pandemic turned all notions of normal schooling on its head. Our experiences working in inner-city schools have made it clear to us that the traditional model of schooling, which has never treated students of color fairly, became even more inequitable overnight. Those educators who have long been engaged in the battle for equity and social justice understand that the only difference between before March 2020 and after is that the needed shift to virtual schooling made the number of students who never had access to technology blatantly visible, and educators could no longer ignore it. The pandemic widened the gap between the haves and have nots; no community has been spared.

To make matters worse, it appears that, sadly, educators are still seeking only technical solutions to what leadership authority Ronald A. Heifetz (1994) calls *adaptive challenges*—challenges with no easy answers or even current solutions. Racial prejudice, intolerance, and injustice are all rooted in challenges with no technical solutions. To move forward in education, educators must let go of the old idea that schooling for Black and Brown students, as well as for poor White students, was ever fair or equitable. This reality makes reflecting on and navigating from your purpose as an equity-conscious leader even more urgent. You need more courage than ever before, more edge, more intuition, more intention, and more deliberate actions to free your classroom, school, or district from the status quo of underachievement and the squandered potential of students. You should embrace the idea that equity consciousness is an adaptive strategy to face adaptive challenges in education. The answers you search for will force you to challenge your own beliefs, biases, and values, and why you do this work in light of all the entrenched racism and unfairness in the systems of education. And they are *deeply* entrenched, as Carmen shows in this story.

> As another graduation drew near in a school where I was the principal, the school leadership team sat down to discuss awards and student speakers for the ceremony. I noticed the entire population of English learners was absent from every list of award nominees and potential speakers. I asked, "Why?" One teacher answered that the bilingual children were not included because staff did not expect them to reach the same standard of achievement as monolingual children. I asked, "Why not?" She informed me this was because they spoke limited English. I responded, "What makes you believe that speaking or not speaking English is an indicator of intelligence or academic, social, or emotional success? Are we giving awards using the ability to speak English as the only criterion of academic success?"
>
> Stepping away from that conversation, I started to think how deeply this judgment of students based on their ability to speak English permeated the entire school. But as I reflected on this situation, I knew instinctively that this situation was just a symptom of something deeper, more ignorant, and fully entrenched in the school's culture. I needed to turn around this thinking. As I faced the reality of the debilitating beliefs that manifested in the poor teaching and learning that were rampant throughout the school, I realized that acting from my moment of purpose in June 1987 was crucial. It stoked my confidence and it provided me with the emotional energy to step boldly onto the path of equity consciousness.

By reflecting on, navigating from, and leading with equity consciousness, you open the space to create, innovate, and transform the status quo.

Discovering Your Edge

The commitment to your purpose inspires a critical edge in your leadership. *Edge* is the fearless ability to make difficult decisions even when everyone else is comfortable with the status quo. It means having the courage to make the unpopular choice, but also to help others understand the process for making those decisions. Edge happens when you stand firm in your values and beliefs when confronted with difficult and challenging decisions. You find your edge when you act on your purpose from a sense of confidence; when you take a bold stand on what you believe, your confidence intensifies. The confidence in who you are, why you do this work, and the values that drive your decisions ensures the edge you muster will always be in alignment with your purpose, galvanizing you with the emotional energy to unapologetically act for the good of your students and staff.

Summoning the emotional energy to fuel and fearlessly use your edge is a challenge for many leaders, especially women of color, because it often requires the leader to take an unpopular position, make arduous decisions, and negotiate or consciously confront uncomfortable or "undiscussable" issues and practices. However, many women have not had the latitude, opportunities, or guidance to develop their edge. For women of color, using their edge can come with labels like "the feisty Latina" or "the angry Black woman." In the following story, Carmen recalls how she initially struggled with confidence, but eventually found her edge.

> My culture taught me women did not really speak up or take a stand on certain issues. I was taught girls don't talk back or "act like a man." My mother would often say, "Men belong to the streets and women to the home." So I struggled with edge during my early career. I knew I was smart but whenever I spoke up, it was with great effort, hiding my finely tuned fear. My hands became sweaty, my heart rate increased, and I flushed and even stuttered sometimes. I tried very hard to avoid conflict, sometimes using humor to feel brave. Quite often I said nothing—and later regretted not speaking up. That was until I found my Lola (Adler & Ross, 1955)!
>
> When I was assigned to my first principalship, it was in a very difficult, underperforming school in one of the poorest and most dangerous neighborhoods in New York City. The former principal had been sick for a long time and during the lapse in leadership, the staff had descended into chaos. All the adults in the building, except a small cadre of hardworking teachers and staff, were out to get what was in it for them. There was even a small group of staff whose only agenda was to make sure I did

not stay permanently. They were incessantly insidious in their unsubtle demonstrations of defiance and passive aggression. When I was on the verge of giving up, I went to the superintendent to inform him that I would only lead the school to the end of the school year. After that, I wanted to return to my former position. He listened to me deliver my monologue about the subterfuge I was enduring, and then told me a story about Lola.

The superintendent recounted his first day as a new teacher, waiting for the principal to arrive for the first faculty conference of the year. The staff all awaited her arrival with excitement and fear, as she had a reputation in the district as being a formidable leader like no other. Then, into the room walked two tall men dressed in black suits, and between them was a small-framed woman, neatly dressed in a suit and heels. She confidently walked into the middle of the gym, and then turning to each section of the gym, she pointed her finger at each staff member and said, "Whatever Lola wants, Lola gets, and I'm Lola!" The superintendent said his jaw dropped. She was intimidating! When he finished recounting his story, he turned to me and said, "I want you to be like her!"

What? I didn't understand and left a bit confused, but I adamantly decided, right there and then, that at the end of the school year I would just resign. I was finished trying to get anything done at that school. I had no energy, no motivation. I was trying so hard and yet at every single step, that small group of staff members, who had strong connections to politicians, union leaders, and school board members, continued to try to derail me. I just wasn't cut out to be a principal, I thought. I felt I did not have the courage or the edge to stand up to that group.

As I returned to the school from my visit with the superintendent, the dean of the school approached me. She wanted to alert me that the antagonistic group was taking bets as to my last day and were planning a party to celebrate my departure. They had decided among themselves which of them would become principal after I left and what they were going to do with the teachers and staff who had supported me. I asked the dean how they knew I was falling apart and ready to leave—I had consciously tried to conceal my lack of confidence. She said that the group had designated a couple of teachers to watch for signs of defeat and it seems that I was showing a lot of them. I felt defeated. I had never been one to give up, but I went into the office and sat there crying for myself.

As I drove home, I thought about my conversations with the superintendent and the dean and reflected on what this all meant. I cried and prayed. I asked for guidance and peace. All of a sudden, I felt this anger rise up in *me that started at the soles of my feet and shot through me as if someone had plugged me into an electrical socket. I thought, "Really? You don't plan a party to celebrate defeating this Latina!" I thought of all the struggles in my life, sacrifices made, obstacles overcome. I said aloud, "Don't they know who I am?" And in that moment, I discovered my inner Lola!*

The next day when I arrived at school, I announced an emergency meeting for the end of the day. I could feel the anticipation in the building. I was certain some people thought I was going to announce my resignation. At the time of the meeting, I went into the cafeteria and addressed the staff, channeling my own version of what I thought Lola would have said, making it up as I went along. As I spoke, I looked at each person and said I wanted to announce that I had accepted the honor of being appointed as the permanent principal of the school and that the rumors of my departure were premature to say the least. I proceeded to tell them I had never really told them about myself, and I wanted to do so now since it was important for them to really know the leader of their school. I said I ran with the "big boys" downtown. I said I was Lola, and whatever Lola wants, Lola gets. I told them for those who chose to stay, they needed to understand there was only one Lola in the building and if Lola wasn't happy, nobody would be happy! With that, I left the room. I went to my office to await the call from the superintendent firing me. I had already told my secretary I was prepared to be fired. Sure enough, a call came! It was the deputy superintendent.

She said, "I heard you had quite a meeting!"

I responded, "Yes, I did."

She told me she and the superintendent just wanted me to know they had my back. I could hear the superintendent laughing in the background. He was proud that I had finally taken control of the situation.

From that day on, I had the staff's respect. The group that had worked against me not only attended my appointment announcement but also spoke about all my wonderful leadership qualities and how they were happy I had gotten the job. The out-group—staff members who had felt oppressed and mistreated—knew I was there to support them and became a collegial team to be reckoned with! Together, we moved that school to heights never seen in that area, and my reputation preceded me to my next assignment. The rest was history.

Lola inspired me to reach for my purpose and stand on it. She was the personification of my edge. Years later, I heard Beyoncé talk about Sasha Fierce—her alter ego who came out when she went on stage to perform. I could relate to that feeling of not feeling totally confident. Like her Sasha Fierce, my Lola was able to say and do things I could not. She became my strongest ally and confidant. She was me, and I was her.

There is a Lola in each of you just waiting to be discovered. But you can only activate that edge when you deeply understand your purpose and have confidence in your sense of equity consciousness. So, remember and reflect on your purpose and you will discover your Lola. She will enable you to be the fearless transformational leader your team needs.

─────────────── *Reflection* ───────────────

Do you have a "Lola?" If so, who is it and why? If not, why not?

───

Shepherding Your Team: Moving From Your Purpose to Our Purpose

When you lead with confidence, you look for ways to shepherd students, staff, and the community to share in your mission and vision. *Leading like a shepherd* means leading from the back, always tending, spurring, and protecting the "flock." For teachers and educational leaders, this means guiding students and staff in the right directions and urging them to be their best. Often, however, we find staff who come to school merely to "get the job done." These staff members engage coworkers in what author and founding director of the Principals' Center at Harvard University Roland S. Barth (2006) refers to as *congenial relationships,* or acting friendly toward and even socializing with coworkers outside the school grounds. But these staff members never have deep, vital conversations about students' strengths or needs, challenge colleagues about the best ways to support students, or have conversations that deal with the *undiscussables* (for example, deficit thinking, othering behaviors, or racism) that impede student achievement. Many staff members have fears related to such conversations—fears of being exposed as prejudiced or bias, challenged about their values, or questioned about their teaching practices. Congenial relationships and the unwillingness to have brave conversations thwart the communal investment it takes to actualize progress.

As a confident leader who appreciates the power of distributed leadership, you must intentionally and explicitly cultivate a safe, supportive environment that transitions staff from congenial relationships to collegial relationships. *Collegial relationships* are built on trust, honesty, fairness, and knowledge. Collegial teams can struggle through difficult and unpopular issues because they feel safe—members allow themselves to become vulnerable so they can mature and grow together professionally. Shared leadership is the conduit for enacting equity consciousness and the vital ingredient in the transformation process (Drago-Severson & Blum-DeStefano, 2018; Jackson, 2011). When you lead with confidence, you inspire and empower others to own the new direction, shifting the description of the mission and vision from *your purpose* to *our purpose*. This shift is seismic, enabling a *re-culturation* of awareness for proliferating equity consciousness. In the following story, Carmen describes what this looks like in action.

> One principal I worked with was the epitome of a confident leader who knew and led from her purpose. I was struck by her personal journey and how it influenced her clarity of purpose (the strong moral compass that guided her commitment to equity and social justice). My role in the school was to support her as she shepherded her building leadership team from her purpose to our purpose. As we worked together, the team reached a revelatory moment. The principal presented the current student achievement data, prompting the team to examine why so many students were not reaching proficient levels. Since we had already spent time developing collegial relationships, the conversation shifted from placing the blame on factors over which students have no control (that is, their race, socioeconomic status, and language) to realizing and accepting that their teaching practices were keeping students from achieving. What the team began to recognize and take responsibility for follows.
>
> 1. Their debilitating beliefs about the potential of students
>
> 2. The inequities in practices perpetuating these debilitating beliefs and creating a culture of failure
>
> It was a moment to freeze in time. This leader's confidence and commitment to her purpose inspired the team members to leap onto a path of genuine equity consciousness, taking a systemic perspective, reflecting on and owning the impact of their deficit-focused practices, and searching for practices that would enable their students to thrive and flourish. At this point, I informed the team members that: (1) there was no getting off this path; (2) the journey ahead was unknown and they had a lot of learning to do; (3) the journey would also be difficult, as we were embarking on erasing the deeply entrenched inequities of the larger deficit-focused education system; but (4) together they would create a new oasis for our students.

Conclusion

Throughout this chapter, we emphasized the importance of starting the journey toward a leadership of confidence by remembering and reflecting on your purpose, discovering the power of your purpose, and fearlessly leading from a strong stance of equity consciousness. From this stance, you can embolden others to do more than they think they can do, and motivate students, colleagues, and community members to see the long-range picture without discouragement or disillusionment. To women—especially women of color—we wrote this to give you faith in your purpose, for "faith is the substance of things hoped for, the evidence of things not seen" (*King James Bible*, 1769/2017, Hebrews 11:1). The struggle for a just society depends on you deliberately and consciously enacting your purpose and leading with confidence, so all students in all situations thrive and reach their innate potential for high performance and personal contribution. This is the outcome of cultivating a leadership of confidence.

Reflection

In what ways does reading this chapter affirm the relationship between your purpose and leading for equity consciousness?

What do you want your legacy to be as a confident, equity-conscious leader?

References and Resources

Adler, R., & Ross, J. (1955). Whatever Lola wants, Lola gets [Recorded by G. Verdon]. For *Damn Yankees* [Musical]. Burbank, CA: Warner Bros.

Anderson, E. (2005). Strengths-based educating: A concrete way to bring out the best in students—and yourself. *Education Horizons, 83*(3), 180–189.

Barth, R. S. (2006). Improving relationships within the schoolhouse. *Educational Leadership, 63*(6), 8–13.

Buckingham, M., & Clifton, D. (2001). *Now, discover your strengths.* New York: Free Press.

Chopra, D., & Tanzi, R. E. (2012). *Super brain: Unleashing the explosive power of your mind to maximize health, happiness, and spiritual well-being.* New York: Three Rivers Press.

Colvin, G. (2008). *Talent is overrated: What really separates world-class performers from everybody else.* New York: Penguin.

Cousins, N. (1989). *Head first: The biology of hope.* New York: Penguin.

Drago-Severson, E., & Blum-DeStefano, J. (2018). *Leading change together: Developing educator capacity within schools and systems.* Alexandria, VA: Association for Supervision and Curriculum Development.

Elmore, R. F. (2004). *School reform from the inside out: Policy, practice, and performance.* Cambridge, MA: Harvard University Press.

Feuerstein, R., Feuerstein, R. S., & Falik, L. H. (2010). *Beyond smarter: Mediated learning and the brain's capacity for change.* New York: Teachers College Press.

Gladwell, M. (2008). *Outliers: The story of success.* New York: Little, Brown.

Goleman, D. (2012). *Emotional intelligence: Why it can matter more than IQ* (10th anniversary ed.). New York: Bantam Books.

Heifetz, R. A. (1994). *Leadership without easy answers.* Cambridge, MA: Belknap Press.

Hilliard, A. (1977). Classical failure and success in the assessment of people of color. In M. W. Coleman (Ed.), *Black children just keep on growing: Alternative curriculum models for young Black children.* Silver Spring, MD: Black Child Development Institute.

Jackson, Y. (2011). *The pedagogy of confidence: Inspiring high intellectual performance in urban schools.* New York: Teachers College Press.

Jackson, Y. (2016). Transformational pedagogy: Cashing the promissory note of equity for marginalized students and all students. *Equity-centered capacity building: Essential approaches for excellence and sustainable school system transformation.* Accessed at https://capacity buildingnetwork.org/article8 on February 8, 2022.

Jackson, Y., & McDermott, V. (2012). *Aim high, achieve more: How to transform urban schools through fearless leadership.* Alexandria, VA: Association for Supervision and Curriculum Development.

Jensen, E. (1998). *Teaching with the brain in mind.* Alexandria, VA: Association for Supervision and Curriculum Development.

Kabat-Zinn, J. (2013). *Full catastrophe living: Using the wisdom of your body and mind to face stress, pain, and illness* (Rev. and updated ed.). New York: Bantam Books.

Kaplin, A. I., & Anzaldi, L. (2015). New movement in neuroscience: A purpose-driven life. *Cerebrum.* Accessed at www.researchgate.net/publication/282038769_New _Movement_in_Neuroscience_A_Purpose-Driven_Life on February 1, 2022.

Kegan, R., & Lahey, L. L. (2009). *Immunity to change: How to overcome it and unlock the potential in yourself and your organization.* Cambridge, MA: Harvard Business Press.

Khalifa, M. A. (2018). *Culturally responsive school leadership.* Cambridge, MA: Harvard Education Press.

King James Bible. (2017). King James Bible Online. Accessed at www.kingjamesbibleonline.org on April 25, 2022. (Original work published 1769)

Maxwell, L. A. (2010). Turnaround funds flowing to the state coffers. *Education Week, 29*(29), 1, 28.

McDermott, V. (2017). *We must say no to the status quo: Educators as allies in the battle for social justice.* Thousand Oaks, CA: Corwin Press.

Medina, J. (2008). *Brain rules: 12 principles for surviving and thriving at work, home, and school.* Seattle, WA: Pear Press.

Mysoon, A. (2017, February 2). The science behind intuition and how you can use it to get ahead at work. *Forbes*. Accessed at https://forbes.com/sites/alexandramysoor/2017/02/02/the -science-behind-intuition-and-how-you-can-use-it-to-get-ahead-at-work/#965b78b239fe on February 2, 2017.

Niedenthal, P. M., & Ric, F. (2017). *Psychology of emotion* (2nd ed.). New York: Routledge.

Piaget, J. (1950). *The psychology of intelligence*. New York: Routledge.

Powell, J. A., & Menendian, S. (2016). The problem of othering: Towards inclusiveness and belonging. *Othering and Belonging*. Accessed at https://otheringandbelonging.org/the-problem -of-othering on February 8, 2022.

Robbinsdale Area Schools. (2014). *Unified district vision: High intellectual performance through equity*. New Hope, MN: Author.

San Francisco Unified School District. (2008, June). *Beyond the talk: Taking action to educate every child now. SFUSD strategic plan, version 1*. Accessed at https://docplayer.net/152003 80-Beyond-the-talk-taking-action-to-educate-everychild-now-sfusd-2008-2012-strategic -plan-version-1-published-june-2008.html on February 8, 2022.

Sinek, S. (2011). *Start with why: How great leaders inspire everyone to take action*. New York: Penguin Books.

Whyte, D. (2002). *Clear mind, wild heart: Finding courage and clarity through poetry* [CDs]. Boulder, CO: Sounds True.

Winfrey, O. (Host). (2018, September 24). Jon Kabat-Zinn: Mindfulness 101 [Audio podcast episode]. In *Super Soul*. Accessed at https://oprah.com/own-podcasts/jon-kabat-zinn -mindfulness-101 on February 1, 2022.

Joellen Killion champions educator learning as the primary pathway to student success. She serves school systems, schools, and regional, state, and national agencies in the United States and abroad as a consultant and learning facilitator. She is senior advisor and former deputy executive director of Learning Forward. Joellen leads, facilitates, and contributes to initiatives related to examining the link between professional development and student learning. She has more than thirty years of experience in planning, design, implementation, and evaluation of professional learning at the school, system, state, and international levels.

Joellen is a frequent contributor to education publications and the author of multiple books, numerous chapters, and papers on the design, implementation, and evaluation of professional learning, coaching, and teacher leadership. Her particular interests are collaborative learning teams, coaching educator success, change leadership, evaluation and program audits, standards for professional learning, policies to support professional learning, and comprehensive planning and implementation of high-quality, standards-based, results-focused professional learning. Joellen works with teachers, coaches, teacher leaders, principals, district leaders, educational consultants, and education agency staff to support the practices of continuous learning and development for all educators.

Joellen earned a bachelor's degree from the University of Michigan and a master's degree from the University of Colorado. She has also completed advanced studies at the University of Colorado.

CHAPTER 2

Facing Change

Joellen Killion

> Stepping onto a brand-new path is difficult, but not more difficult than remaining in a situation, which is not nurturing to the whole woman.
>
> —Maya Angelou

Change is daunting and inevitable. Because it is constant in organizations and in leadership, effective leaders understand change, know how to engage in it, and know how to lead it, both personally and in their organizations. Over the decades, leaders in both public and private organizations have grappled with understanding and leading change. Leaders still often take a single approach, typically focusing on implementing a process for change rather than looking at the multiple dimensions of change, including the scope of the change and how people respond to change. Implementation and improvement sciences have emerged as fields of knowledge and practice to guide change initiatives, but deep and sustained change in any system is both challenging and too often unsuccessful. Reports of failed change efforts abound in the literature. As the urgency for continuous improvement persists, leaders seek a way to effect change.

This chapter explores how leaders face change. *Facing change* means understanding the two dimensions of change: (1) how leaders cope with their own personal and professional changes and (2) how leaders lead change in their organizations. *Being a savvy leader of change* means understanding its multiple dimensions, both personal and professional. This chapter does not advocate a single approach to change leadership or argue that traditionally feminine leadership archetypes are more or less effective than traditionally masculine ones. Scholars and practitioners have examined the impact of gender in leading change, and they suggest leadership practices—the context in which change exists, the people involved in change, and the change itself—often matter more than gender-specific leadership (Beard, 2017; Deprez, Van den Broeck, Cools, & Bouckenhooghe, 2012; Eagly & Johnson, 1990; Helgesen, 1990, 1995; Kise & Watterston, 2019).

As an emerging female leader in education, I noticed a striking pattern: women, even in predominantly male-led education systems, often initiated, facilitated, and implemented change. It was the female middle managers who proposed, organized, and enacted change. It was the teachers and teacher leaders—mostly female—who implemented change. Male leaders managed, monitored, directed, and inspected change efforts. Throughout the early roles I held in education, it was clear that expectations of me as a female leader were more about carrying out someone else's (often a male leader's) vision of excellence and less about being a visionary. As a woman, I was expected to follow others' plans for change rather than creating the plans. In the systems where I worked early in my career, I observed that considering the *human factor*—people's response to change and adapting actions to address the responses—was neither a concern nor a component of most change efforts. As more women leaders emerged within those systems, my experiences shifted.

In contrast to my early experience, successful women leaders in the 21st century cultivate a deep understanding of change and how to manage, facilitate, and implement change in their personal and professional lives. At the heart of this chapter is my own experience leading, supporting, and engaging in change. Experience, I find, yields hard-earned insight. Throughout my career, I have served in the roles of manager, facilitator, and implementer of change. Each role, different in scope, responsibilities, and tasks, brought difficulties and rewards. The change initiatives across the education system ranged from curriculum and assessment design and implementation, leadership and supervision development programs, instructional programs, professional learning programs, coaching programs, and state, local, and ministerial policy development. At the same time, I experienced personal changes in areas such as health, work-life balance, and relationships. Each change allowed me to become more than what I was. And each change, personal and professional, was a source of learning—because I chose to take that view. To meet the challenges and grow as leaders, women must continuously analyze their leadership beliefs and practices, and how their leadership identities influence the management, facilitation, and implementation of change. From my experiences and study of change, I offer six fundamental lessons about facing change.

1. Change is constant and unavoidable.
2. Managing, facilitating, and implementing change are not equivalent.

3. Everyone experiences change differently.

4. Change is a journey.

5. Assumptions influence how people face change.

6. Certain skills are useful for facing change.

Lesson 1: Change Is Constant and Unavoidable

"Change is the only constant," acknowledged the Greek philosopher Heraclitus (as cited in Kahn, 1981). Changes of all sizes and forms are an inexorable part of life, from the cycle of the seasons to personal growth, and to mundane changes like redecorating a room. Some small changes are nearly imperceptible, but deliver as many unexpected challenges and complexities as the more significant ones. Furthermore, the world does not present one major change at a time. Nearly every aspect of your personal and professional life is evolving at the same time.

Adopting a stance that life is about becoming more than you are currently is a healthy way to manage the reality of constant change. Social psychologist and writer Daniel Gilbert (2006), in his book *Stumbling on Happiness*, says people too often assume they are finished changing once they reach adulthood. In reality, human beings are works in progress. At this very moment, Gilbert (2006) proposes, no one is what he or she has the potential to become. Similarly, Maria Popova (2014), the writer of *Brain Pickings*, says:

> By calling ourselves beings, we deny our ever-unfolding becomings.... once forced to figure out who we want to be in life, most of us are so anxious about planting that stake of being that we bury the alive, active process of our becoming. In our rush to arrive at who we want to be, we flee from the ceaseless mystery of our becoming.

Being open to *becoming* at every stage of life is a way to manage the frenetic pace of change in all aspects of life. For leaders, the inability to adapt or develop is a major cause of career derailment (Leading Effectively Staff, 2020). Being flexible and adaptable requires the capacity to do the following.

- Be aware of the changing environment.
- Adapt leadership practices to shifting circumstances.
- See the positive aspects of change.
- Adjust plans and strategies as needed.
- Appreciate and respond to others' concerns.

In addition, educational leaders grapple with the rapid changes in education, leadership, and their environment. The rapidity of change and the multidimensional conditions within which organizational and personal change occur complicates these changes. Author, speaker, and organizational consultant William Bridges (2016) notes:

> The hardest thing to deal with is not the pace of change but change in the acceleration of that pace. It is the acceleration of the pace of change in the past several decades that we are having trouble assimilating and that throws us into transition. Any change in the acceleration of change—even a deceleration—would do that: if change somehow suddenly ceased today, people would have difficulty because the lack of change would itself be a change and would throw them into transition. (pp. 112–113)

Managing multiple changes requires understanding and navigating the big picture and the intersection of the changes, and maintaining coherence among the changes. Recognizing and tapping into the intersection between personal and organizational change require leaders to blend process-oriented and human-response approaches to change. When leaders examine how they experience the changes they face in their personal and professional lives, they can better understand and adapt their leadership approaches to meet the needs of their staff during change.

──────────────── *Reflection* ────────────────

When facing multiple changes at once, what can you learn from each experience that will enrich and extend what you can do in other experiences?

How is what you are doing and feeling the same or different in each change initiative? What contributes to the variance, and how does it influence how you experience and support change?

Visit **go.SolutionTree.com/leadership** to access a reproducible reflection guide for this chapter.

Lesson 2: Managing, Facilitating, and Implementing Change Are Not Equivalent

Not all leadership skills are the same. Facing change involves multiple roles, such as change manager, facilitator, and implementer. *Change managers* conduct the "orchestra." *Change facilitators* lead rehearsals, coach orchestra members to hone their talents, contribute to the musical arrangement to highlight talent in the orchestra, and support the conductor. *Change implementers*, the orchestra members, use their mastery and skillfulness to contribute to a harmonious product worthy of a dedicated audience and a beautifully tuned orchestra hall. These roles and responsibilities may be independent, interdependent, or simultaneous.

Change managers hold positions of authority within an organization and use their power to direct, oversee, and coordinate the actions of others. They may initiate the change or lead collaborative processes to make decisions about the change itself and the overarching strategy for implementing change. They do not often directly engage in the efforts to implement the changes. They are vision and goal driven; they seek to advocate the change. They monitor the progress of change and address barriers that may interfere with the change. They have responsibility for creating and maintaining structural supports including policies, material resources, finances, and staff. In education, change managers are often superintendents, assistant superintendents, principals, and program managers.

Change facilitators are directly involved in the change work, perhaps enacting specific tactics and interventions associated with the change; designing tools, processes, and structures; building a culture to support those who will implement the change; facilitating professional learning in preparation for the change; and coaching implementation. Change facilitators interact closely with change implementers to meet their needs. They may contribute to shaping the structural components of an organization or community to support the change effort. Their work is simultaneously responsive, calculated, and planned, requiring a broad range of skillfulness in the facilitation of teams, process and task management, training and development, measurement and assessment, and intervention design, diagnosis, and communication. Directors, teacher leaders, or program directors often serve as change facilitators, although in some organizations (particularly smaller ones), change managers act as change facilitators in addition to their change-manager roles.

Change implementers are those responsible for the behavior changes associated with the innovation. In other words, they are beneficiaries of change facilitators' efforts and share responsibility for enacting the change. Implementers exhibit varying degrees of investment in and levels of effort toward the change. Their own beliefs and how others—especially change managers and facilitators—perceive and treat them shape their agency and efficacy. If viewed as end-of-the-line recipients and expected to comply with the change, implementers are less willing to invest in it. On the other hand, when treated as cocreators or partners in constructing the process, change implementers are more likely to engage and commit to the end results. Implementers require differentiated, personalized attention related to their concerns, needs, and stages of implementation. They seek recognition for achievements and progress, and want to engage with feedback about what is working and what is not. They want to be involved in conceptualizing the change and contribute to decisions about the scope and pace of the change. Their degree of success also influences their ongoing investment (Guskey, 2020). When they experience success in their practice, their attitude about the change becomes more positive, thereby influencing their commitment and level of effort. Teachers and noninstructional staff are the primary change implementers, although anyone working in a system experiencing change can be a change implementer.

Coauthors Gene E. Hall and Shirley M. Hord (2020) acknowledge that while responsibilities differ and overlap, complex change requires people with various roles (such as managers, facilitators, and implementers) to work in sync to orchestrate change. They recommend a team approach to leading change in which the various agents work in a coordinated fashion to undertake their unique and overlapping responsibilities. Leaders naturally have different styles, status, power, and influence, and a team can build on the strengths of each leader to accomplish all the essential tasks. Each role weaves together with the others to contribute to change success. In some situations, a single leader assumes all three roles; in other situations, two or more people take on the various roles. By delineating the responsibilities within each role and who serves in each one, leaders can orchestrate the design, implementation, and support necessary to achieve results and build their staff's capacity to face change.

Reflection

Thinking of a specific change initiative, what is your role?

How do you use your role to build others' commitment to and investment in the change initiative? How do you use your role to advocate for your own, others', and the initiative's success?

Lesson 3: Everyone Experiences Change Differently

While change is somewhat predictable, individual responses to change are less so. For some, change is exciting and enticing; for others it is abhorrent. Some people may be ready and even eager for change, yet others may not. Occasionally, the same person demonstrates a dualistic response to change—delighted one day and defeated the next. Individuals' life circumstances, sense of efficacy and agency, mental models, experiences, and organizational context affect how they experience change. Leaders cannot presume to know how people will respond to change, and as a result, they must simultaneously keep their eyes on future goals while addressing present behaviors.

Communication theorist and sociologist Everett M. Rogers (2003) studies the *diffusion of innovations*—what it takes to spread new ideas, practices, and technology within cultures. He identifies five categories of innovation adopters, which explain how people respond to change (see table 2.1). His work provides a lens through which to understand why some people are more comfortable with change and others are less eager or more resistant (Rogers, 2003). Change leaders can use this information to proactively address these types of responses as they are planning for and implementing change. Researchers apply Rogers's (2003) diffusion of innovation theory in adoptions of change when implementing evidence-based practices in nursing (Mohammadi, Poursaberi, & Salahshoor, 2018), tourism (Dibra, 2015), and online gaming (Cheng, Kao, & Lin, 2004).

Table 2.1: Levels of Innovation Adopters

Categories of Adopters	Description
Innovators	Innovators are risk takers. They are quick to innovate and connect with science and data, and they often associate with other innovators. Innovators are mostly young, have high social status, and are financially stable.
Early adopters	Early adopters are opinion leaders. They make discrete decisions about each innovation. They are mostly young and educated, have high social status, and are financially stable.
Early majority	The early majority follows previous groups in adopting innovations. Members of this group are not opinion leaders, but have social status and are connected to early adopters.
Late majority	The late majority adopts innovations well after the majority and with some skepticism. Members of this group have little opinion leadership, lower social status, and less financial stability.
Laggards	Laggards are the last to adopt an innovation if they do at all. They are change averse and seek to maintain tradition and the status quo. They have lower social status and limited connections beyond family and friends.

Source: Adapted from Rogers, 2003.

Later adopters may actively resist change. Resistance to change is a continual challenge for leaders. Multiple change models begin with building awareness and rationale for the change to minimize resistance. Inspirational speaker and author Simon Sinek (2020) calls this the *why* in his golden circle model. Change thought leader, professor, and author John P. Kotter (2012) describes this early stage as *creating urgency* in his eight-step process for planning, initiating, and implementing change. Organizational change experts and coauthors Richard Beckhard and Reuben T. Harris (1987) find that those implementing change are more likely to be ready and willing for change when they perceive its urgency, benefits, and practicality. Any change, they suggest, requires a level of dissatisfaction with the current situation, a sense that the proposed change is desirable or attractive, and a belief that the change will be feasible and practical (Beckhard & Harris, 1987). If any element is missing, there is likely to be resistance to change. Hall and Hord (2020) describe the stages of change, beginning with *self-concerns*—those concerns related to the personal impact of the change. Once change implementers understand how the change impacts them personally, they move to *task concerns*—those concerns about how to carry out the change. For example, in implementing new curricula or instructional practices, it is important for teachers to understand how the new curricula or instructional practices benefit and affect them first before they can appreciate how the change will benefit students.

It is crucial that leaders stay open to legitimate resistance, rather than dismiss it. People are inherently wary of or resistant to change; the brain "interprets change as a threat" (Pennington, 2018). According to Patricia Roy (2013), senior consultant with Learning Forward's Center for Results:

> Resistance is a natural part of the change process. . . . Resistance can take many forms, from indifference to active sabotage. To support ongoing and continuous change, leaders and facilitators need to understand why resistance occurs and develop strategies to overcome resistance. (p. vi)

Michael Fullan (2001), global leadership director of New Pedagogies for Deep Learning, advocates, "Respecting resistance is essential, because if you ignore it, it is only a matter of time before it takes its toll, perhaps during implementation, if not earlier" (p. 42). Fullan (2001) also recommends leaders listen to resisters as sources of learning—they may have different, unexamined perspectives.

Similarly, Catherine Adenle (2011), founder of Catherine's Career Corner, advises leaders to change their attitude about resistance and view it "as a signal that there are ways in which the change effort should be modified and improved." She recommends the following strategies to address resistance (Adenle, 2011).

- Communicate in a timely, straightforward, and consistent manner.
- Lead by example rather than only talk about the change.
- Apply emotional intelligence to support employees the change affects.
- Listen openly and seek authentic, honest input often.
- Work side by side with employees.
- Be realistic when setting goals.
- Clearly express the reasons for the goals often.

Leaders who initiate or buy into a change may fail to comprehend how difficult that change may be for those responsible for implementing it. Leaders cannot change how people react to change; leaders must learn to adjust their own responses. Rather than deflect, disregard, or judge people or their reactions, a leader accepts the response as those individuals' reality, seeks to understand their worries or concerns and what is behind them, and provides appropriate supports that align with the expressed concerns.

--- *Reflection* ---

Reflect on a time when you were skeptical of or resistant to change. How did the leaders of that change respond? What would you do similarly or differently if met with resistance to a change you are leading?

Lesson 4: Change Is a Journey

While leaders may desire for change to be easy, it is a human process and requires a journey through both smooth and rapid waters. It can be unpredictable and volatile (Fullan, 1999). Historically, most change theorists, researchers, and practitioners viewed change as a linear process that follows a predictable pathway. In the 21st century, experts view change more as a recursive, emergent, evolutionary, and exploratory process that incorporates cycles of initiation, implementation, and discovery, with frequent adaptations to refine and accelerate the change (Clemente, Durrand, & Roulet, 2016; Hernes, Hussenot, & Pulk, 2021; Tsoukas, 2021). Improvement science suggests that small-scale changes in rapid cycles lead to more contextually appropriate results and facilitate greater engagement and less resistance from change implementers (Bryk, Gomez, Grunow, & LeMathieu, 2015).

Leaders of change understand the best-laid plans often require revision. Each aspect of the change process opens the door to potential shifts, interruptions, or new discoveries. This is what makes the journey both exciting and frustrating. The uncertainty about how implementers adjust to change requires leaders to be aware of implementers' needs and flexible in responding to them; what works for some may not work for others. For example, consider the following change process (Kotter, 2012).

1. Create urgency.
2. Form a powerful coalition.
3. Create a vision for the change.
4. Communicate the vision.
5. Remove obstacles.
6. Celebrate short-term wins.
7. Build the change.
8. Anchor the change in organizational culture.

Though listed as steps, change is not a linear process. Leaders may find that some steps need more attention, or that they need to circle back to earlier steps. When implementing a curriculum change, for example, leaders may find while they are striving to remove obstacles, it is necessary to revisit the urgency for the change and recommunicate the vision. As they celebrate short-term wins, leaders may discover new obstacles to remove to achieve the next wins. The change process is a journey with detours and interruptions.

Leaders must understand that change takes time, particularly when it involves human behavior. Knowing the core components of change and multiple approaches to them allows change leaders to be ready to grapple with unexpected interruptions and equips leaders to take action to adjust their plans and even the desired outcomes. Because organizations and humans are living systems, any unexpected personnel, organizational, or natural interruptions can derail a change effort. Even the best-conceived plans can be interrupted without notice. When leaders take time to respond personally in direct alignment to identified needs, they are able to dismantle barriers to progress.

Reflection

Consider a change journey you have experienced.
What prompted the detours, backtracks, or interruptions?
How did you address them? What other responses might you use?

Lesson 5: Assumptions Influence How People Face Change

How people cope with change is deeply rooted in the assumptions they hold about change, themselves, and their place in the world. Assumptions influence what you think, say, and do (Schön, 1983, 1987; Senge, 2006). The mental models people hold, sometimes invisible, have a powerful influence. These *mental models* are the beliefs that drive actions, thoughts, and words. Harvard Graduate School of Education Professor Emeritus Robert Kegan and lecturer on education Lisa Laskow Lahey (2001, 2009, 2016) call these *big assumptions*:

> Not so much as the assumptions we have, but the assumptions that have us. Our big assumptions come close to naming an ineffable, hard-to-grasp thing: something like the meaning-regulative principles by which we shape the world in which we live. (2001, p. 68)

They add that big assumptions are "uncritically taken as true. They may be true, and they may not be, but as long as we simply assume they are true, we are blind even to the question itself" (Kegan & Lahey, 2009, p. 58). These big assumptions often become guiding principles, yet can be altered through reflection if one analyzes actions and grows increasingly aware of those hidden assumptions. Professor of philosophy at the University of Massachusetts Amherst Hilary Kornblith (2012) notes, "Without reflection, there is no justified belief; and without justified belief, there is no knowledge" (p. 11).

Assumptions are powerful and manifest themselves in how people act, think, and speak. Consider a school principal who is required to hold an active-shooter drill. She questions her superior about the disruption to instruction. The principal conveys the rationale for the drill to staff and ensures they have guidance and access to information on the correct procedures. Internally, the principal feels irritable and comes down hard on staff who do not follow procedures correctly. In the debriefing meeting with district supervisors, the principal lashes out and complains about her staff. What lies at the root of her irritability is her complete frustration about the state of the world that necessitates active-shooter drills. She is angry, not with her staff, but at the weight of her responsibility to make schools a safe place for students and staff. The drills conflict with her belief about schools being safe places for students and staff. Until she acknowledges her big assumptions and alters them, she will continue to be irritable whenever she must face issues related to safety and her role in them.

Your mental models also influence how you approach change and introduce new behaviors associated with change. A leader's mental model about change is a unique blend of assumptions, personality characteristics, and experiences with change, both positive and negative. One learning theory that applies in educating both adults and students is *social learning theory* (Bandura, 1977; Cherry, 2021; Western Governors University, 2020). Social learning theory has three elements:

> First is the idea that people can learn through observation. Next is the notion that internal mental states are an essential part of this process. Finally, this theory recognizes that just because something has been learned, it does not mean that it will result in a change in behavior. (Cherry, 2021)

If leaders follow social learning theory, their efforts will focus on helping people become aware of their current behaviors before introducing new ones. Through these actions, leaders can use modeling and reflection to guide the adoption of new behaviors.

Another approach to change depends on a different set of assumptions about how change happens. Coauthors Richard T. Pascale, Jerry Sternin, and Monique Sternin (2010) posit the *positive deviance* approach, which emphasizes implementing the change practices *before* shifting assumptions and beliefs. If leaders follow this approach, they focus on getting people to act their way into a new way of thinking by realizing the benefits of the new behaviors as the means to shift their assumptions.

Differing assumptions can also cause conflict in change. The assumptions some people hold and those that others hold may be at odds. For instance, a new principal who worked her way up through the system faced her first major decision and it went terribly wrong, causing a breach of trust with staff. She made the decision alone with no staff input. The staff members expected her to ask for their input as the former principal had. When a facilitator engaged the principal and staff in unpacking the root of the issue, it was clear their assumptions were at odds. The new principal, who worked her entire career for a position of authority, exerted what she presumed to be her right and responsibility as the principal. The staff members, who previously had been involved in collaborative decision making, assumed the principal would continue to ask for their contribution.

Self-awareness is a key characteristic of a strong leader (Leading Effectively Staff, 2021). Without deeply examining and analyzing assumptions, it will be difficult to adapt or change leadership behaviors. Leaders identify and grapple with their own assumptions. They examine disturbing or discomforting experiences and analyze what is at work. They seek perspectives from trusted colleagues, supervisors, and those they supervise to uncover blind spots. They seek out knowledgeable others to coach them about, unpack, and test assumptions. Leaders' mental models about change influence how they face change. Those who are logical and have a strong need for a detailed plan approach change differently from those who are more spontaneous.

Reflection

What fundamental assumptions do you hold about change, and how do they influence your actions as a manager, facilitator, or implementer of change?

Lesson 6: Certain Skills Are Useful for Facing Change

Facing change in the role of manager, facilitator, or implementer requires numerous skills and behaviors, a broad body of knowledge, and positive dispositions about change. While some leaders are successful because they embody effective leadership characteristics such as self-awareness, integrity, empathy, and courage, it is the behaviors associated with those traits that matter in change. *Behaviors* are manifestations of traits, so leaders want to hone those behaviors that convey leadership.

Of the multiple skills leaders employ when facing change, two are particularly important to sharpen. Listening fully and being deeply curious to understand are the primary leadership skills for change (Covey, 2020; Stanier, 2020).

Listening

"Listening is a vital and overlooked tool and the cornerstone of leading across differences in race, gender, culture, and socioeconomic status, language, and age, among other factors," notes writer, coach, and facilitator Shane Safir (2017, p. xxvii). Listening makes neither judgments about the speaker nor holds preconceived notions about what the speaker *should* say. It means avoiding the desire to change, fix, alter, rescue, or judge, in favor of appreciating and valuing the message and the speaker. Listening requires silence and space for formulating and processing thoughts. It may be serendipitous, yet it is true that the same letters spell both *listen* and *silent*. *Listening* means turning off the voice generating messages in your own head to fully receive and appreciate the voice of the speaker.

Listening also requires silencing your internal critics—the ones that say, "We don't have time for dissenters; if you are not on board, get out" or "How can you not understand when we have talked about this so many times?"

Listening means giving over control of the situation (a difficult task for many leaders) and letting others drive the conversation while you follow to capture meaning. It means letting go of self-interests to grasp the speaker's interests, what the speaker cares about, or what the speaker wants. It means seeing the other person and having the person feel seen and understood. It means discovering the speaker's assumptions and the foundation for the message, with the hope of seeing the world from the speaker's perspective.

Listening to your own internal messages may even be harder than listening to others, but it is also important. Noticing the tight knot in your gut, the sudden burst of acid reflux, the tenseness around your jaw, or the feeling of uneasiness, anxiety, or apprehension is the first step in listening to yourself. These are physical and emotional signals. When ignored, these signals can create significant negative effects. Listen to them with an openness to understand. Acknowledging these signals exist is a first step; finding meaning in them is another. By listening internally to their own signals and externally to signals from others, leaders can understand how change affects them and others, and use that understanding to adapt and respond as needed to mitigate interruptions, resistance, or conflicts and move forward to achieve results.

Listening, though seemingly simple, is one of the most challenging leadership skills. It is often easier to speak, give advice, take control, ask leading questions, and direct the conversation. Safir (2017) notes, "Listening Leadership extends beyond the act of listening; it is also an orientation toward collegiality, shared leadership, personal growth, and equity" (p. xxvii). Practice improves this skill, and the real work comes in shifting your assumptions about what a leader is. You must let go of the misconceptions that purport leadership means having all the answers, taking control, giving advice, and being solely responsible. Replace these misconceptions with the power of empathy. Listening deeply and fully demonstrates empathy.

Curiosity

Curiosity is a cousin of listening and means remaining open rather than being certain. A desire to search, inquire, find meaning, discover, and understand drives curiosity. It is rarely satiated. It abandons the need to presume. Commitment to learning and inquiry is how leaders demonstrate and model curiosity. According to psychiatrist, executive coach, and consultant Mark Goulston (2010):

> The more interested you are in another person, the more you narrow the person's mirror neuron receptor deficit—that biological hunger to have his or her feelings mirrored by the outside world. The more you do that, the more grateful the person is toward you in return, and the more empathy the person feels toward you. So, to be interesting, forget being interesting. Instead be *interested*. (p. 57)

The secret to being curious is to be genuine about it—to want to know the stories of the other person more than you want to tell your own story. It is not about fact-finding or looking for an opening to tell your own story or one-upping the other person's story. Curiosity requires the patience and sense of anticipation that allow stories to unfold rather than rush them or interrupt their flow. The delivery of the story is as revealing as the plot line. Where are the moments of emotion? What causes a pause? Curiosity is fed with coaching thought leader Michael Bungay Stanier's (2016) famous *AWE question* (that is, *And what else?*). By asking this question, a leader invites additional information, demonstrates interest, and refrains from quick judgments.

Curiosity helps leaders stay flexible when facing change:

> Lifelong inquiry is the generative characteristic needed because postmodern environments themselves are constantly changing. We are probably never exactly right in the first place, but in any case, we need the checks and balances of inquiry because in changing times our initial mental maps "cease to fit the territory." (Fullan, 1993, p. 15)

Shifting political, sociological, physiological, fiscal, technological, and environmental circumstances continually impact the field of education. These constant shifts require leaders to forecast and read the emerging trends, adapt their leadership practices, and initiate changes to meet the shifting landscape. Leading Effectively Staff (2020) at the Center for Creative Leadership note that more than ever:

> Adaptability is a requirement. Because change is constant and inevitable, leaders must be flexible to succeed. Our research confirms this imperative to adapt. Adaptability is about having ready access to a range of behaviors that enable leaders to shift and experiment as things change.

Being curious about your own responses, feelings, and tensions is as important as being curious in conversation with others. *Mindfulness*, a deep sense of inner awareness, is a tool you can use to explore how you interact with change. Being mindful represents curiosity toward what is occurring and gives you permission to acknowledge and accept the reasons for your response. Mindfulness gives you time to consider and decide how you want to respond, rather than reacting emotionally. When facing change, remain curious about how the change affects you, ask questions, stay open, and learn to appreciate the gift of ambiguity.

Curiosity requires a shift in assumptions about leadership. If leaders believe their responsibility is to rescue others from any form of discomfort, curiosity will be difficult. On the other hand, if leaders hold the belief that their primary role is to empower, engage, and extract the expertise that resides in others, curiosity is easier.

―――――――― *Reflection* ――――――――

What are the roles of listening and curiosity in leading change?
How are you using listening and curiosity as a change leader? Of the two skills, which is a stronger one for you? How will you continue to develop both?

Conclusion

Leaders grapple with change daily, particularly in the modern climate of rapid and dramatic changes. The six key lessons in this chapter guide leaders to understand how change affects them and how it affects others.

1. Change is constant and unavoidable.
2. Managing, facilitating, and implementing change are not equivalent.
3. Everyone experiences change differently.
4. Change is a journey.
5. Assumptions influence how people face change.
6. Certain skills are useful for facing change.

Each lesson, drawn from my personal experience with change in various roles throughout my career, offers opportunities for other leaders to reflect on and learn from their own experiences as change managers, facilitators, or implementers. Use the lessons to understand your own assumptions, beliefs, and approaches to change as a precursor to leading and understanding others' experiences with change. Apply the skills of listening and curiosity in everyday conversations and experiences as vehicles to construct knowledge about facing change and serving as a leader in change. Interrogate your own experiences in change for lessons learned and compare them to those of other leaders. When leaders face their own change with open eyes and an intent to learn, they gain knowledge about themselves, those they lead, and the change process, and can be flexible and adaptive for the ever-changing landscape in education.

———————————— *Reflection* ————————————

What are the lessons you are learning about leading change as change manager, facilitator, or implementer? How do you respond to your own change, and how is your response different when you lead others? How can the lessons in this chapter contribute to your practice as a change leader?

References and Resources

Adenle, C. (2011, July 26). 12 reasons employees resist change in the workplace. *Catherine's Career Corner*. Accessed at https://catherinescareercorner.com/2011/07/26/12-reasons-why-employees-resist-change-in-the-workplace on January 19, 2022.

Bandura, A. (1977). *Social learning theory*. Englewood Cliffs, NJ: Prentice Hall.

Beard, M. (2017). *Women & power: A manifesto*. London: Profile Books.

Beckhard, R., & Harris, R. T. (1987). *Organizational transitions: Managing complex change* (2nd ed.). Reading, MA: Addison-Wesley.

Brauer, J. R., & Tittle, C. R. (2012). Social learning theory and human reinforcement. *Sociological Spectrum, 32*(2), 157–177.

Bridges, W. (2016). *Managing transitions: Making the most of change* (4th ed.). Boston: DaCapo Lifelong Books.

Bryk, A. S., Gomez, L. M., Grunow, A., & LeMathieu, P. G. (2015). *Learning to improve: How America's schools can get better at getting better*. Cambridge, MA: Harvard Education Press.

Cheng, J. M. S., Kao, L. L. Y., & Lin, J. Y.-C. (2004). An investigation of the diffusion of online games in Taiwan: An application of Rogers's diffusion of innovation theory. *Journal of American Academy of Business, 5*(1/2), 439–445.

Cherry, K. (2021, July 28). How social learning theory works. *VeryWellMind*. Accessed at https://verywellmind.com/social-learning-theory-2795074 on January 19, 2022.

Clemente, M., Durrand, R., & Roulet, T. (2016). The recursive nature of institutional change: An Annales school perspective. *Journal of Management Inquiry, 26*(1), 17–31.

Covey, S. R. (2020). *The 7 habits of highly effective people: Powerful lessons in personal change* (30th anniversary ed.). New York: Simon & Schuster.

Deprez, J., Van den Broeck, H., Cools, E., & Bouckenhooghe, D. (2012). *Gender differences in commitment to change: Impacted by gender?* [Working paper]. Accessed at https://wps-feb .ugent.be/Papers/wp_12_775.pdf on April 20, 2020.

Dibra, M. (2015). Rogers theory on diffusion of innovation: The most appropriate theoretical model in the study of factors influencing the integration of sustainability in tourism businesses. *Procedia: Social and Behavioral Sciences, 195*, 1453–1462.

Eagly, A. H., & Johnson, B. T. (1990). Gender and leadership style: A meta-analysis. *Psychological Bulletin, 108*(2), 233–256.

Fullan, M. (1993). *Change forces: Probing the depths of educational reform.* Bristol, PA: Falmer Press.

Fullan, M. (1999). *Change forces: The sequel.* Bristol, PA: Falmer Press.

Fullan, M. (2001). *Leading in a culture of change.* San Francisco: Jossey-Bass.

Gilbert, D. (2006). *Stumbling on happiness.* New York: Knopf.

Goulston, M. (2010). *Just listen: Discover the secret to getting through to absolutely anyone.* New York: American Management Association.

Guskey, T. R. (2020). Flip the script on change: Experience shapes teachers' attitudes and beliefs. *The Learning Professional, 41*(2), 18–22.

Hall, G. E., & Hord, S. M. (2020). *Implementing change: Patterns, principles, and potholes* (5th ed.). Upper Saddle River, NJ: Pearson Education.

Helgesen, S. (1990). *The female advantage: Women's way of leadership.* New York: Doubleday Currency.

Helgesen, S. (1995). *The web of inclusion: A new architecture for building great organizations.* New York: Currency/Doubleday.

Hernes, T., Hussenot, A., & Pulk, K. (2021). Time and temporality of change processes: Applying an event-based view to integrate episodic and continuous change. In M. S. Poole & A. H. Van de Ven (Eds.), *The Oxford Handbook of Organizational Change & Innovation* (2nd ed., pp. 731–750). Oxford, England: Oxford University Press.

Huberman, A. M., & Miles, M. B. (1984). *Innovation up close: How school improvement works.* New York: Plenum Press.

Kahn, C. H. (1981). *The art and thought of Heraclitus: A new arrangement and translation of the fragments with literary and philosophical commentary.* Cambridge, England: Cambridge University Press.

Kegan, R., & Lahey, L. L. (2001). *How the way we talk can change the way we work: Seven languages for transformation.* San Francisco: Jossey-Bass.

Kegan, R., & Lahey, L. L. (2009). *Immunity to change: How to overcome it and unlock the potential in yourself and your organization.* Boston: Harvard Business Press.

Kegan, R., & Lahey, L. L. (2016). *An everyone culture: Becoming a deliberately developmental organization.* Boston: Harvard Business Review Press.

Kise, J. A. G., & Watterston, B. K. (2019). *Step in, step up: Empowering women for the school leadership journey.* Bloomington, IN: Solution Tree Press.

Kornblith, H. (2012). *On reflection.* Oxford, England: Oxford University Press.

Kotter, J. P. (2012, November). Accelerate! *Harvard Business Review.* Accessed at https://hbr .org/2012/11/accelerate on February 9, 2022.

Leading Effectively Staff. (2020, November 24). Adapting to change requires flexibility. *Center for Creative Leadership.* Accessed at https://ccl.org/articles/leading-effectively-articles /adaptability-1-idea-3-facts-5-tips on January 19, 2022.

Leading Effectively Staff. (2021, August 23). What are the characteristics of a good leader? *Center for Creative Leadership.* Accessed at https://ccl.org/articles/leading-effectively-articles /characteristics-good-leader on February 9, 2022.

Mohammadi, M. M., Poursaberi, R., & Salahshoor, M. R. (2018). Evaluating the adoption of evidence-based practice using Rogers's diffusion of innovation theory: A model testing study. *Health Promotion Perspectives, 8*(1), 25–32. Accessed at https://ncbi.nlm.nih.gov/pmc /articles/PMC5797305 on January 19, 2022.

Pascale, R. T., Sternin, J., & Sternin, M. (2010). *The power of positive deviance: How unlikely innovators solve the world's toughest problems.* Boston: Harvard Business Press.

Pennington, C. (2018, April 3). We are hardwired to resist change. *Emerson Human Capital.* Accessed at https://emersonhc.com/change-management/people-hard-wired-resist-change on January 19, 2022.

Popova, M. (2014). Being vs. becoming: John Steinbeck on creative integrity, the art of changing your mind, the humanistic duty of the artist. *The Marginalian.* Accessed at https://brainpickings.org/2014/12/15/john-steinbeck-integrity-lettuceberg on October 13, 2021.

Prochaska, J. O., & DiClemente, C. C. (1983, June). Stages and processes of self-change of smoking: Toward an integrative model of change. *Journal of Consulting and Clinical Psychology, 51*(3), 390–395.

Rogers, E. M. (2003). *Diffusion of innovations* (5th ed.). New York: Free Press.

Roy, P. (2013). *School-based professional learning for implementing the Common Core: Unit 1— Managing change.* Oxford, OH: Learning Forward. Accessed at https://learningforward.org /wp-content/uploads/2017/09/school-based-professional-learning-unit-1-packet.pdf on January 19, 2022.

Safir, S. (2017). *Listening leader: Creating the conditions for equitable school transformation.* San Francisco: Jossey-Bass.

Scharmer, C. O. (2018). *The essentials of Theory U: Core principals and applications.* Oakland, CA: Berrett-Koehler.

Schön, D. A. (1983). *The reflective practitioner: How professionals think in action.* New York: Basic Books.

Schön, D. A. (1987). *Educating the reflective practitioner: Toward a new design for teaching and learning in the professions.* San Francisco: Jossey-Bass.

Senge, P. M. (2006). *The fifth discipline: The art and practice of the learning organization* (Rev. and updated ed.). New York: Doubleday/Currency.

Sinek, S. (2020). *The golden circle presentation.* Accessed at https://simonsinek.com/commit /the-golden-circle on May 16, 2020.

Stanier, M. B., (2016). *The coaching habit. Say less, ask more & change the way you lead forever.* Toronto, Ontario, Canada: Box of Crayons Press.

Stanier, M. B. (2020). *The advice trap: Be humble, stay curious, & change the way you lead forever.* Toronto, Ontario, Canada: Box of Crayons Press.

Tsoukas, H. (2021). The performative "picture": Thinking about change as if change mattered. In M. S. Poole, & A. H. Van de Ven (Eds.), *The Oxford handbook of organizational change & innovation* (2nd ed., pp. 847–856). Oxford, England: Oxford University Press.

Western Governors University. (2020, May 15). *A guide to social learning theory in education* [Blog post]. Accessed at https://wgu.edu/blog/guide-social-learning-theory-education2005 .html#close on January 19, 2022.

CHAPTER 3

Leading With Compassion and Empathy

Janel Keating

When you lead with compassion, you invest time into people and set them on a path for success.

—Lionel Valdellon

In July 1998, I accepted the position of principal at Mountain Meadow Elementary School. After more than a dozen successful years as an elementary and middle school teacher, I signed on to lead a school of over five hundred students and sixty-plus staff members. Armed with enthusiasm, my goal was to create a school where all students were safe, felt special, and learned at high levels—in every classroom, with every teacher, and during every lesson—a school good enough for my own child. After all, accompanying me to this new community was my eight-month-old daughter. Effective instruction and a caring, encouraging classroom culture have always been my leadership comfort zone. Place me in a classroom co-teaching or working alongside a teacher to design an intervention for a student struggling with behavior, and it would be the highlight of my day. I felt prepared to apply my deep understanding of this work in my new role, where I would be responsible not just for the students in my own classroom but also for the students in every classroom in my school.

I soon realized I had a lot to learn when it came to leading adults and adult learning. Honestly, the staff issues and life challenges that came through my office door surprised me. There were days when I thought I must have missed a course in my educational leadership degree. Naïvely, I had expected all the difficulties of my position would concern academics, since less than 50 percent of students were meeting grade-level expectations. It simply had not occurred to me that staff members would bring their personal issues to me or that as a thirty-three-year-old, first-year principal, I was supposed to have answers, give advice, or solve their personal issues.

As a new principal and new mother, I understood the challenges and needs of my teachers who were also young mothers—their experience mirrored my own, and I was good at nurturing them. I was familiar with their home responsibilities and their duties at work, and I knew their two worlds would come crashing together on more than one occasion. In many instances, I could see the collision coming and clear the way before a wreck occurred because I understood it. Their lives reflected my life. But young mothers were only a fraction of my staff. In my staff of more than sixty, only three were male—the plant supervisor, the physical education teacher, and one classroom teacher. The rest were women, but women whose personal lives I often could not relate to at the time. I didn't understand my teachers who were struggling to take care of teens and aging parents. I didn't know how to support my teachers who were dealing with divorce. I didn't understand my teachers who were going through menopause! I was ill-equipped to respond to teachers whose family members had passed away or were struggling with mental health issues and addiction.

All of life's challenges eventually find their way to the principal's office. I felt like I needed a leadership course called leading through life. The educators who sat in front of me in staff meetings or in my office presented an intricate and difficult leadership issue: failing to understand the needs and circumstances of the people I was leading would have an impact on student learning. People can talk about leaving their personal problems at the door when they come to work, but that does not actually happen. People all have "real lives" that impact their "work lives" occasionally, and a career in education is one where the lines between home and work are blurred in the best of times. I had always prided myself on my ability to solve problems, but I did not know how to fix my staff's personal struggles.

What I really didn't understand then was that often the most important thing I could do for my staff was simply listen without judgment. As Marilou Ryder (2020), a professor in the doctoral program for organizational leadership at the University of Massachusetts Global, shares, "Listening with authenticity gains admiration and trust." However, people in leadership positions tend to be problem solvers and jump to action first, often bypassing listening. Despite the best of intentions, this can leave staff members feeling frustrated and unheard. Leaders need to show their staff they are able to listen with an open mind and without judgment by focusing on the person speaking, asking questions, and not contradicting (Ryder, 2020). When a staff member walked into my office and asked, "Do you have a few minutes to discuss an issue?" it helped to start the conversation by asking about her expectations. Some staff members needed me to just listen. Others needed me to help them problem solve. Yet others needed me to solve the problem for them.

Before continuing, I need to make a point. Trust and compassion aren't always standard in the workplace. Teachers are not going to sit down and bare their souls to you if you have not established a foundation of trust with your staff. Effective leadership coach, consultant, and facilitator Charles Feltman (2021) writes in *The Thin Book of Trust*, "Trust is defined as choosing to risk making something you value vulnerable to another person's actions" (p. 9). Once you establish trust, you can employ compassion and empathy to guide staff members through common personal challenges.

Compassion

According to coauthors Rasmus Hougaard, Jacqueline Carter, and Marissa Afton (2021), "It is helpful to consider the two distinct qualities of compassion: understanding what another is feeling, and the willingness to act to alleviate suffering for another." Many people think you need to say or do something to be helpful when someone brings you a problem. But it is worth remembering that those experiencing difficulty also just need someone to be there, listen, and demonstrate compassion. Sweet Institute (2017) recommends "just showing up," being present, letting the other person lead the conversation, and offering space for that person to process the challenge. Compassionate, empathetic listening is an important skill for leaders when it comes to supporting the people who work for them. Author and science journalist Daniel Goleman (2021) states, "Supervisors and coworkers with strengths in empathy and teamwork are more likely to provide social support at work," which is essential to employees' work-life balance and overall mental health.

Treating others with compassion also includes being sensitive to the lasting effects of prior experience and trauma. Most educators are aware of the impact of *adverse childhood experiences* (ACEs) on the students in the classroom (Felitti et al., 1998). What educators talk about less often is that many staff come to work with their own ACE histories, which can continue to affect staff throughout their lives. According to the Centers for Disease Control and Prevention (2019), 61 percent of adults have had at least one ACE, and 4 percent have had four or more. Women and certain ethnic minorities, including Black and Indigenous people, are at greater risk of experiencing four or more ACEs. In addition, various challenging life events bring additional stress. Recognizing and addressing the challenges that families and individuals face, providing a supportive environment, and destigmatizing asking for help are some of the things leaders can do to support staff.

Listening to staff and being aware of the struggles they may be experiencing in their lives can also help leaders support students. If a student has been sent to the principal's office because she is having a fight-or-flight reaction or other emotional outburst, the principal's goal is to help her calm down enough to return to class. However, if the principal knows the teacher in that classroom is going through personal trauma and is, therefore, less emotionally resilient, the principal might decide to keep that student a little longer than usual to prevent any chance of escalation and irreparable damage to the teacher-student relationship. After all, the mission is to ensure high levels of learning for every student. As leaders extend compassion to staff, they also need to remember students' needs and design solutions that support everyone—staff and students alike. The emotional health of staff affects student learning in each classroom.

Compassion requires you to do personal work. It does not ask you to fix first, but rather to begin by connecting. American Buddhist nun Pema Chödrön (2018) writes:

> Compassion is not a relationship between the healer and the wounded. It's a relationship between equals. Only when we know our own darkness well can we be present in the darkness of others. Compassion becomes real when we recognize our shared humanity. (p. 41)

You cannot be more accepting of others than you are of yourself. If you are not open and aware of your own emotions and feelings, it is difficult to hear and understand someone else's.

Reflection

Can you think of a time when you didn't respond to a staff member with compassion? What might you do differently next time?

Visit **go.SolutionTree.com/leadership** *to access a reproducible reflection guide for this chapter.*

Empathy

While it is clear gender does not determine one's ability to effectively lead the work essential for school success, all leaders have different life experiences that influence how they approach the tasks at hand. Simply put, women have experiences unique to their gender that shape the lens through which they view both students and adults. Because of their life experiences, women in leadership positions are likely to be adept at understanding and putting themselves in the position of other women. Clearly, this is beneficial for leading teachers, who are predominantly women. Women can naturally resonate with aspects of womanhood that men might have difficulty relating to.

Of course, true leadership requires supporting and understanding people whose experiences are different from your own, whether those differences relate to religion, ethnicity, LGBTQ+ communities, and so on. When working with people who are different from yourself, it is always helpful to be aware of *implicit bias*, or "bias that occurs automatically and unintentionally, that nevertheless affects judgments, decisions, and behaviors" (National Institutes of Health, 2021). People all have implicit biases that can affect how they react to others who need help or care. Our brains even process members of out-groups differently than people whom we perceive as similar to ourselves (Sapolsky, 2017). You might be able to notice a strong negative response to certain extreme out-groups, but most are much more subtle—and it can be hard to admit to these subconscious reactions, especially when they go against your conscious views. Perceiving someone as different or other typically results in feeling bad for that person's pain but not actually doing anything to help, unless you work to overcome the brain's *us versus them* wiring (Sapolsky, 2017). Fortunately, you can mitigate your implicit biases with strategies for compassionate listening, as well as by working to identify and be mindful of your own implicit biases. Consider taking the Implicit Association Test (https://implicit.harvard.edu/implicit/take atest.html) that social psychologists Anthony Greenwald, Mahzarin Banaji, and Brian Nosek at Project Implicit Health first developed.

Your physiological state also affects your unconscious and automatic reactions to people. Neuroendocrinology researcher and author Robert M. Sapolsky (2017) says, "People become more conservative when tired, in pain or distracted with a cognitive task, or when blood alcohol levels rise" (p. 448). Judges are much more likely to grant parole to prisoners just after lunch (60 percent) than just before lunch (0 percent; Sapolsky, 2017). If you are having a potentially difficult conversation with a staff member when you are also tired, hungry, or upset, you may not be approaching it with the best version of yourself. You are likely to react badly, despite your best intentions. It would be better to ask that person to reschedule for a time when you can be more present. If you are interested in reading more about the role of biology in compassion and empathy, I recommend Sapolsky's (2017) book, *Behave: The Biology of Humans at Our Best and Worst.*

Even under the best circumstances, it can be hard to feel empathy for someone when you struggle to understand what that person is feeling and why. You might feel a more emotionally distant *sympathy*, but that is not enough to spur action. *Empathy* means reaching to find the places where you connect with the other person and being able to imagine what the emotions at hand feel like for that person. In her book *Atlas of the Heart*, Brené Brown (2021), research professor, lecturer, author, and podcast host, writes, "We can respond empathically only if we are willing to be present to someone's pain. If we are not willing to do that, it's not real empathy" (p. 122). Of course, it is possible to go too far, to slip into the emotionally raw state of feeling someone else's pain as if it were happening to you, rendering you unable to help. Empathy is the sweet spot.

New leaders often wonder how to show empathy to people with different challenges than themselves. First, strive to bring curiosity, transparency, and compassion to every conversation (McRaney, 2022). Curiosity is a genuine interest in what the other person is saying. Transparency means that you are honest about what is going on in your own head. Compassion, as we discussed in the previous section, is a recognition that the other person is a human with her own perspective (McRaney, 2022). Second, realize that many diverse experiences have underlying emotions in common. Feelings like "joy, hurt, heartbreak, shame, grief, love" and so on transcend cultures and individual experiences (Brown, 2021, p. 125). You can empathize with people different from yourself if you connect to the basic emotion—even if you haven't been in their shoes (Brown, 2021). You don't have to experience the same thing to be compassionate and empathetic, but doing so will require more from you if you don't already have some understanding of the experience. It will require you to make an intentional, effortful connection. Finally, Hougaard and colleagues (2021) suggest five key strategies for using empathy as a catalyst for leading with more compassion and kindness.

1. **Empathize, then mentally step back:** Avoid becoming overwhelmed by other peoples' pain. Staying above the turmoil will help you act as a guide when emotional colleagues need a calmer perspective.

2. **Ask what they need:** Make suffering people feel heard and allow them to define the desired outcomes to their problems.

3. **Remember the power of non-action:** Sometimes people just need someone to listen to them and understand, rather than take action to solve their problems.

4. **Coach people so they can find their own solutions:** Guide people and help them face challenges themselves. This growth will benefit them more in the long term.

5. **Practice self-care:** Listening to, empathizing with, and mentoring people who are struggling is emotional labor, which can be draining. Ensure you recharge your own batteries with healthy physical and mental practices.

Hougaard and colleagues (2021) also note, "A leader without empathy is like an engine without a spark plug—it simply won't engage. Empathy is essential for connection and then we can leverage the spark to lead with compassion." Additionally, leaders can proactively familiarize themselves with common challenges their staff may deal with. These challenges will vary by location and culture, but the following sections describe several categories of personal difficulties teachers in any school might experience. Awareness and understanding of these topics—especially if you have not experienced them yourself—can help you show compassion and empathy to others.

--- *Reflection* ---

Have you thought about implicit biases you might hold?
What are some things you can do to prep yourself for a
conversation where your implicit biases might play a role?

Common Challenges

As mentioned previously, when I first became a principal, I did not feel prepared to support my teachers whose personal struggles were so different from my own. It took me time and life experience to prepare. Simultaneously, with the challenges of their jobs, people working in schools may be balancing the challenges of parenting, menopause, and divorce, as well as other human challenges. Teachers might deal with any of these issues themselves, or they may need to support family members who are struggling with these life events. Here, I share information about these common challenges from experts and my own experience so that you might be more prepared than I was when you take on your first leadership role.

Parenting

Many teachers are parents. Being a teacher is their "second shift"—when they arrive in the classroom, they have already put in a full day of work. They made breakfast, packed lunches, loaded backpacks, and shuttled the kids to daycare or the bus stop before coming to work. Perhaps they were up early grading a stack of papers or thinking through the lesson plans for the day. A quick stop at the store for that last-minute item for a classroom party or art project might be for their own children or for their students. Once they arrive at work, they are not only teaching, but also attending team meetings, providing interventions, participating in professional development, meeting with parents, and much more.

These teachers are *double burdened*, "a term used to describe the workload of people who work to earn money, but who are also responsible for significant amounts of unpaid domestic labor" (Hochschild, 1989). Importantly, most teachers are women, and women still take on a disproportionate amount of childcare, household chores, and care for sick family members due to traditional gender roles (Moen, 1989). Despite women's increasing role in the workforce, this continues to be the case in many countries. Researchers and coauthors Lyn Craig and Killian Mullan (2011) examine this question in four countries—Australia, Denmark, Italy, and France: "In all four countries, mothers spent more time performing childcare than did fathers, with fathers averaging between 35 percent (Denmark) and 25 percent (France) of household care time" (p. 846).

The COVID-19 pandemic exposed and amplified long-standing systemic social problems, including gendered divisions of labor. With many schools and childcare facilities closed, households faced parents leaving their paid positions (voluntarily or not) and trying to juggle paid work with childcare and at-home schooling. Women took on even more unpaid labor (Lyn & Churchill, 2020). At the same time, women's paid employment was disproportionately affected, which will have long-term effects on job prospects, lifetime earning potential, and even retirement for women (Fry, 2022). In both the paid and unpaid sectors, the pandemic increased gender disparities.

In my school district, we use the question, "Is it good enough for my own child?" to remind ourselves of our dedication to create rich learning environments and amazing opportunities for students. But it's important to recognize that educators also have children in schools and should not be excluded from participating in the opportunities that schools offer other families. Ask yourself the following questions.

- "Are my school or district policies family friendly?"
- "Does my school or district have unspoken norms that exclude educators from participating in their children's field trips?"
- "Are conferences, concerts, and other events scheduled on the same days across the district so teachers must choose between their children and their students?"
- "Have I set norms for teachers bringing their children to work with them before or after school?"
- "Do teachers have the skills to navigate peer-to-peer discussions where the roles of coworker and parent are blurred?"

Understanding parents' challenges and making the workplace accommodating for them is an important consideration for educational leaders.

Menopause

According to the Organisation for Economic Co-operation and Development (OECD; 2019) *Teaching and Learning International Survey (TALIS),* the average age of teachers is forty-three in the United States and forty-four across all countries in the survey. Combined with the fact that two-thirds of teachers are women (OECD, 2019), this means it is very likely that a given school will include women who are perimenopausal or menopausal. Leadership expert Jeneva Patterson (2020) explains:

> Menopause often intersects with a critical career stage. It usually occurs between ages 45 and 55—which is also the age bracket during which women are most likely to move into top leadership positions. Since menopause generally lasts between seven and 14 years, millions of postmenopausal women are coming into management and top leadership roles while experiencing mild to severe symptoms such as depression, anxiety, sleep deprivation, and cognitive impairment, to name a few. If we want to continue to move the needle on the number of women in leadership roles and maintain their valuable contributions to a company's bottom line, we need to be more open about what menopause is and how it affects both individuals and organizations.

Symptoms women find most bothersome during menopause include the following (Macdonald, 2021).

- Fatigue
- Hot flashes
- Difficulty concentrating
- Anxiety
- Insomnia
- Problems with memory recall

Certain aspects of work can exacerbate these symptoms. These factors include the following (Macdonald, 2021).

- Workspaces that are warm, poorly ventilated, or humid
- Workspaces that are noisy with no access to a quiet or restful space
- Long hours
- High workloads or short and changing deadlines
- Negative interactions with customers, patients, or clients

Clearly, women need compassionate support to manage the stresses of teaching when dealing with symptoms like fatigue and difficulty concentrating. Leaders should be responsive to these needs both because they care about their teachers as people and because the symptoms of menopause may hamper the delivery of education to students.

In my first year as principal, I really started to make this connection when I noticed I was dealing with too many low-level discipline referrals from a certain classroom. Students were being sent to my office for minor instances of blurting out, being out of their seats, or coming to their reading group without a pencil. The teacher should have easily managed these issues in the classroom. It turned out the teacher was exhausted from menopause-related insomnia, and thus she did not have the emotional reserve to handle minor discipline issues appropriately. She lost her patience. I knew I needed to intervene to prevent damage to the relationship between this teacher and her students. My response was to use my physical presence. I went into her classroom and tried to give her a break when I knew she really needed it. She needed my help, and it was not a major departure from my usual duties—I was just going to be in that classroom more than other classrooms that day.

A classroom of students presents challenges for anyone on a good day, but for a woman in the throes of menopause, it can be almost overwhelming. There is a need to foster a workplace culture where staff members feel empowered to speak up about difficulties they encounter. This may include finding a way to open the conversation about menopause and build awareness and understanding around this natural phase in a woman's life. It can be hard for women to approach their leaders about issues related to menopause—many even hesitate to bring it up to their own doctors. Creating a supportive and flexible work environment and talking openly about the subject are big steps in the right direction. I found that focusing on my own birthday and discussing all the things I had to look forward to in my forties (including the potential onset of menopause) was an approachable way to open this conversation. You cannot eliminate the symptoms menopause causes, but you can make school better for teachers and the students they serve.

Divorce

Divorce is an everyday reality. Almost half of all first marriages in the United States and Canada end in divorce (American Psychological Association, n.d.; Winnipeg Divorce, Child Custody and Family Lawyer, 2020). One in three marriages in Australia ends in divorce (Makela, 2020). There are very few people who have not felt the sting of divorce—if not in their own marriages then in those of their parents, children, relatives, or close friends.

Divorce can have a devastating effect on people. For most, divorce is more than legal action. It's an emotional journey—one that often takes years. Even amicable divorces take time and are draining as couples divvy up assets, work out custody of children, and wade through the emotional fallout. Stephen Ministry (2000b) explains:

> Many people describe divorce as a wound that never really heals. Even after the marriage ends, matters such as children, property, money arrangements continue to need attention. For many people, it is simply impossible to cut all ties to the ex-spouse to get on with work. Instead, the former couple must continue to deal with each other, reopening the wound again and again. (p. 593)

As staff members navigate their divorce journey, they may be oblivious to the larger impacts of their actions or inactions. All-consuming emotional tragedies can make something like being late to work feel like a meaningless issue. And issues can spiral—being tardy can become missing days of work, which leads to periods of poor performance. Even though staff members may be physically present at work, they're often absent mentally, emotionally, and creatively. It can become a struggle for day-to-day survival.

One of my staff members who went through a divorce shared with me that she was struggling to get out of bed in the morning, as were her children. She was their emotional support and she also desperately needed emotional support herself. As sympathetic as I was to her situation, her candidness also set off my alarm system. As a leader, I had decisions to make. Her students deserved a well-rested, prepared, and attentive teacher. They deserved to learn grade-level standards and have their own social-emotional learning needs met. A staff member struggling through a divorce can also strain relationships with other staff members. Effective education relies on collaboration and teamwork. Colleagues will offer concern and support for a period of time, but their reactions will eventually swing toward frustration if the person going through a divorce creates extra work for others.

As a principal, I learned it is important to offer support when a staff member is struggling with the end of a relationship. Talk to the person directly. Start the conversation by asking, "How are you doing, and how can I help you?" However, you may need to go a step further. Adults in the midst of trauma often cannot identify what help they need or feel uncomfortable asking "too much" of someone. The following strategies can benefit staff members and students.

- Revisit the norms and accountability protocols the teacher's grade-level or content team established.

- Strategize solutions to help the teacher manage his or her workload.

- Assist with tasks (such as entering data), so the teacher is ready for a team meeting.

- Cover the teacher's class so he or she can attend legal appointments or attend to childcare duties.

- Arrange a consistent substitute teacher to create a more stable learning environment.

- Advise putting away cell phones and other personal devices during teaching hours to help separate personal events from work. In a true emergency, have others call the school office.

- Encourage the teacher to access counseling. Connect the teacher with an employee assistance program (EAP) if your school has one.

Compassionate listening is, as always, essential when supporting staff members during divorce. Be available for significant and surprising conversations. Many women especially build their self-image around marriage, family, and title, and the change of identity hurts in many unexpected ways. There may be a conversation about whether they should retain their married name or go back to using their maiden name. A highly effective veteran teacher I worked with shared that she wanted to change her name, but felt that her community life and connections were linked to her married name. Over the past twenty years, she had taught hundreds of students and interacted with the parents and grandparents connected to these students. She feared that with a name change, her identity as a respected educator and community member would be lost. This was not a decision I could make for her. As freelance writer and health and wellness expert Meagan McCrary (2020) writes:

> Sometimes when someone shares what they are going through, they aren't asking you to make it better. For whatever reason, just telling someone makes us feel a little less desolate. It's human nature to want to share, to have someone who hears us, who understands, who can sympathize with what we are going through. We want to know that we are not alone.... We don't want someone to fix our sadness.... Sometimes it's best to let someone have their space and time to feel their pain rather than attempting to solve the issues or move on. People need space to feel their emotions and it's a vital part of moving forward.

Leaders should do their best to create a balance between understanding what others are feeling and acting in ways that help staff move forward while also maintaining their job performance.

— *Reflection* —

Although the common challenges this chapter discusses may not be things you have experienced, can you think about the emotions they would likely trigger? Are they emotions you have experienced in other situations?

Conclusion

I have presented a number of common challenges as stand-alone circumstances, but of course, you may have staff who are dealing with a new baby while taking care of their parents; struggling with menopause while opening their home to a newly divorced child; or suffering the loss of a spouse while a child struggles with addiction. Life is messy! When I was a young, new principal, I did not expect to have to solve life problems for my staff. Looking back, I realize many of these problems did not require solutions from me. What my staff needed most was a leader they could trust. A leader who would listen to them without distraction or judgment. If you open your door, and listen—honestly listen—without thinking about how you will respond or the actions you need to take, you will most likely hear what staff need. And it might very well be that all they really need is someone to see them for their whole selves, the struggling humans all people are.

One of the most uncomfortable pieces of leadership is the times you are called to make the most difficult decisions. You can work with a staff member with the utmost compassion and empathy, and in the end still have to make the decision that the person cannot be in the classroom, either temporarily or permanently. Sometimes leaders hold themselves back from connecting with staff because it becomes too difficult to make the hard decisions. I think back to some advice I was given years ago: you are not doing anyone a favor by keeping someone in a position where that person is unable to be successful. *Reciprocal accountability* means you make every effort to support your staff in achieving success, but in the end, every student has the right to a teacher who is fully present.

You may have read this chapter and thought to yourself that compassion and empathy sound really nice, and if at some time in the future you have a bit more time, you'll give it a go. So, perhaps I can make one more point that will encourage you to work on using compassion and empathy right now as a part of your daily tool chest: compassion and empathy are good for *you*. They won't just make you a happier person but also will actually have demonstrable physical effects at the cellular level, and may even improve longevity because they are buffers from stress (Seppälä, 2013).

I leave you with one final piece of advice: when a struggling staff member finally opens your door and asks, "Do you have a minute?" turn off your phone, close your laptop, and listen. It is worth remembering those experiencing difficulty mostly just need someone to be there. And the wonderful thing about being compassionate and empathetic? Both are contagious.

Reflection

What systems can you put in place to monitor teachers' mental health so you can address issues while they are still just minor concerns?

How will you, as the leader, understand what staff need from you as they enter your office and ask, "Do you have a couple of minutes?"

References and Resources

American Psychological Association. (n.d.). *Marriage & divorce.* Accessed at www.apa.org /topics/divorce on October 13, 2021.

Brown, B. (2021). *Atlas of the heart: Mapping meaningful connection & the language of human experience.* New York: Random House.

Centers for Disease Control and Prevention. (2019, November). *Adverse childhood experiences (ACEs): Preventing early trauma to improve adult health.* Accessed at https://cdc.gov/vital signs/aces/index.html on December 28, 2021.

Chödrön, P. (2001). *The places that scare you: A guide to fearlessness in difficult times.* Boulder, CO: Shambhala.

Chödrön, P. (2018). *Comfortable with uncertainty: 108 teachings on cultivating fearlessness and compassion.* Boulder, CO: Shambhala.

Craig, L., & Churchill, B. (2020). Working and caring at home: Gender differences in the effects of Covid-19 on paid and unpaid labor in Australia. *Feminist Economics, 27*(1–2), 310–326. Accessed at https://tandfonline.com/doi/full/10.1080/13545701.2020.1831039 on January 23, 2022.

Craig, L., & Mullan, K. (2011). How mothers and fathers share childcare: A cross-national time-use comparison. *American Sociological Review, 76*(6), 834–861. Accessed at https://asr .sagepub.com/content/76/6/834 on January 2, 2022.

de Saint-Exupery, A. (1943). *Le petit prince.* New York: Reynal & Hitchcock.

Eaker, R., & Keating, J. (2012). *Every school, every team, every classroom: District leadership for growing Professional Learning Communities at Work.* Bloomington, IN: Solution Tree Press.

Felitti, V., Anda, R. F., Nordenberg, D., Williamson, D. F., Spitz, A. M., Edwards, V., et al. (1998). Relationship of childhood abuse and household dysfunction to many of the leading causes of death in adults: The adverse childhood experiences (ACE) study. *The American Journal of Preventive Medicine, 14*(4), 245–258. Accessed at https://ajpmonline.org/article /S0749-3797(98)00017-8/fulltext on January 2, 2022.

Feltman, C. (2021). *The thin book of trust: An essential primer for building trust at work* (2nd ed.). Bend, OR: Thin Book.

Fry, R. (2022, January 14). Some gender disparities widened in the U.S. workforce during the pandemic. *Pew Research Center.* Accessed at https://pewresearch.org/fact-tank/2022/01/14 /some-gender-disparities-widened-in-the-u-s-workforce-during-the-pandemic on February 7, 2022.

Goleman, D. (2004, January). What makes a leader? *Harvard Business Review.* Accessed at https://hbr.org/2004/01/what-makes-a-leader on September 30, 2021.

Goleman, D. (2021). Why bosses should care about work-life balance. *Korn Ferry.* Accessed www.kornferry.com/insights/articles/work-life-balance-emotional-intelligence on September 30, 2021.

Hochschild, A. (1989). *The second shift: Working families and the revolution at home.* New York: Penguin Books.

Hougaard, R., Carter, J., & Afton, M. (2021, December 23). Connect with empathy but lead with compassion. *Harvard Business Review.* Accessed at https://hbr.org/2021/12/connect-with -empathy-but-lead-with-compassion on January 10, 2022.

Kanold, T. D. (2021). *Soul! Fulfilling the promise of your professional life as a teacher and leader.* Bloomington, IN: Solution Tree Press.

Macdonald, C. (2021, October 10). World menopause day: Managing menopause in the workplace. *TrueHR.* Accessed at www.truehr.org.uk/2021/10/10/world-menopause -day-managing-menopause-in-the-workplace/ on March 1, 2022.

Makela, M. (2020). Divorce rate in Australia. *Armstrong Legal.* Accessed at: https://armstrong legal.com.au/family-law/divorce/divorce-rate-in-australia on December 28, 2021.

McCrary, M. (2020, March 1). How to respond compassionately to someone's suffering. *mbgrelationships.* Accessed https://mindbodygreen.com/0-14955/how-to-respond -compassionately-to-someones-suffering.html on September 30, 2021.

McRaney, D. (2022, January 23). The conversation lab—Misha Glouberman [Audio podcast episode]. *You Are Not So Smart.*

Moen, P. (1989). *Working parents: Transformations in gender roles and public policies in Sweden.* Madison: University of Wisconsin Press.

National Institutes of Health. (2021). *Implicit bias.* Accessed at https://diversity.nih.gov /sociocultural-factors/implicit-bias on January 20, 2022.

Organization for Economic Co-operation and Development. (2019). *Results from TALIS (Teaching and Learning International Survey) 2018.* Accessed at https://oecd.org/education /talis/TALIS2018_CN_USA.pdf on November 15, 2021.

Patterson, J. (2020, February 24). It's time to start talking about menopause at work. *Harvard Business Review.* Accessed at https://hbr.org/2020/02/its-time-to-start-talking-about -menopause-at-work on January 5, 2022.

Ryder, M. (2020). Executive presence: What it takes to get ahead, influence others, and drive results. *AASA School Administrator, 77*(3), 27–30.

Sapolsky, R. M. (2017). *Behave: The biology of humans at our best and worst.* New York: Penguin Press.

Seppälä, E. (2013, July 24). Compassionate mind, healthy body. *Greater Good Magazine.* Accessed at https://greatergood.berkeley.edu/article/item/compassionate_mind_healthy _body on February 7, 2022.

Stephen Ministries. (2000a). *Stephen Ministry training manual* (Vol. 1, Modules 1–14). St. Louis, MO: Author.

Stephen Ministries. (2000b). *Stephen Ministry training manual* (Vol. 2, Modules 15–25). St. Louis, MO: Author.

Sweet Institute. (2017, September 1). *10 tips for supporting someone through emotional pain and loss.* Accessed https://sweetinstitute.com/support-someone-through-loss on September 30, 2021.

Valdellon, L. (2018, March 12). *Compassion isn't a soft leadership skill. It's a crucial power skill.* Accessed at https://medium.com/@WriterLionel/compassion-isnt-a-soft-leadership-skill-it-s-a-crucial-power-skill-4c828e2d24af on September 30, 2021.

Winnipeg Divorce, Child Custody and Family Lawyer. (2020, May 5). *What is the divorce rate in Canada?* Accessed at https://familylawyerwinnipeg.com/divorce-rate-in-canada on January 20, 2022.

Zenger, J., & Folkman, J. (2019). Research: Women score higher than men in most leadership skills. *Harvard Business Review.* Accessed at https://hbr.org/2019/06/research-women-score-higher-than-men-in-most-leadership-skills on September 30, 2021.

Part 2

Obstacles

Julie A. Schmidt is superintendent of schools for Kildeer Countryside Community Consolidated School District 96 in Buffalo Grove, Illinois. During more than thirty years in education, Julie has been a superintendent, an associate superintendent, a high school director of student services, a school psychologist, an assistant to the superintendent, and an assistant director of special education spanning early childhood through high school. She continues to work with elementary and secondary schools across the United States as a speaker and facilitator on response to intervention (RTI), closing the gap for special education students, leadership and change, and the implementation of professional learning community (PLC) practices at all levels of an organization. She has served on the national PLC advisory board for Solution Tree. Julie received the Principals' Award of Excellence during her service at the high school level. She was recognized as the Lake County Superintendent of the Year by her colleagues for 2016 and a Superintendent of Distinction in the state of Illinois in 2017. She serves on the executive board for the Exceptional Learners Collaborative and on the board of directors for the Illinois Association of School Administrators, where she serves as the state professional development chair.

Julie earned an undergraduate degree from St. Mary's University, master's and specialist's degrees in school psychology from Southwest Texas State University, and an educational specialist's degree in educational leadership from Northern Illinois University.

To learn more about Julie's work, follow @kildeer on Twitter.

To book Julie A. Schmidt for professional development, contact pd@ SolutionTree.com.

CHAPTER 4

Looking Out the Window and In the Mirror

Julie A. Schmidt

Without reflection, we go blindly on our way, creating more
unintended consequences, and failing to achieve anything useful.
—Margaret J. Wheatley

Both my grandfather and father were lifelong educators. In fact, my dad was a teacher and a coach at the high school I attended. That is probably why I was bound and determined *not* to become an educator—I wanted to do something different and exotic with my life. I remember when my career pathway began to take shape. In tenth grade, I chose to take psychology as a social studies elective. As the semester evolved, I became fascinated with the subject and the potential of gaining insight not only into other people but also into myself. It felt a bit mystical yet empowering to realize that one could develop a deeper understanding of the reasons behind behavior and emotion. I attended class, engaged in discussion, and studied deeply. I also began to quietly and intently observe and listen. Observing behaviors and emotions unfold and, at times, being able to hypothesize how a sequence of events would occur, gave me a sense of order during times that otherwise felt chaotic or even hurtful. I also began to, at times, note differences in the behaviors, reactions, and emotions of men and women. I noted how my mom showed emotions like anger or disappointment very differently from my dad. And I wondered why life experiences (like the breakup of a relationship) seemed to have such different impacts on men versus women. As I observed and listened to those around me and those I care deeply about, I also became aware that I could have more control over outcomes by being aware of and shaping my own behaviors and emotions to meet the needs of a given situation. Interestingly, as I honed these skills, adults around me concurrently began to see leadership potential in me. While I had always been very involved in student activities, others began to appoint me to or urge me to volunteer for leadership roles. I remember feeling conflicted about whether I was authentically listening and learning, or whether I was being manipulative in this newfound awareness. This internal conflict has continued into my adulthood, as I navigate barriers and challenges in both my personal and professional life. But there is no denying these realizations pushed me to not only observe the influences around me (*to look out the window*) but also constantly consider how my own behavior and actions influence others (*to look in the mirror*).

That high school experience led me to major in psychology as an undergraduate (with a minor in vocal performance—an entirely different story!). Afterward, I moved right to graduate school. I was preparing for a career in either a mental health or correctional setting, but became disillusioned about what kind of impact I could make in those settings. I ended up in my graduate advisor's office, where he advised me to shift to educational psychology and consider becoming a school psychologist. Life comes full circle! When I called my father to inform him, he was elated, but said, "Oh honey, I am so happy. Please promise me one thing—don't ever become an administrator!"

As I write this, I have just finished my twenty-third year as a school administrator (my dad should have known I would interpret his advice as a dare). I frequently identify my background knowledge and skills as a psychologist as the most important training for leadership I ever received. It was also through my education in psychology that I learned while it is easy to identify and point to external factors for my disappointments, it is important to push myself to engage in deeper self-reflection if I am to grow as a leader. (Though to be clear, this personal realization in no way minimizes the very real external barriers that exist, particularly for women.)

I have always believed that not only in leadership but also in life people have a responsibility to both look out the window—observe and be aware of all of the external factors and facts that influence them—*and* simultaneously look in the mirror to reflect on what they control and what role they play. In this chapter, I will guide you to do both.

--- *Reflection* ---

Think about and record one celebration about
your professional journey thus far.

Reflect on and record a frustration or challenge you experienced.

*Visit **go.SolutionTree.com/leadership** to access a reproducible reflection guide for this chapter.*

Looking Out the Window

When you look out the window, you are considering external factors and facts that influence you. When it comes to the evolution of the role of women in society, understanding and studying the history can help make the path forward clearer. One of the ways to examine that history is through your own experiences in your families and communities. The experiences I share in this chapter are uniquely mine; each and every woman will tell a story unique to her family and community experiences. While my mother and I never spoke much about gender roles when I was young, I keenly observed their evolution in my own family through my great-grandmother, both of my grandmothers, and my own mother. The roles each of them played in her relationships and in the community evolved from generation to generation. My great-grandmother, whom I visited frequently as a young girl, would not have dreamed of working outside of the home except to occasionally support the various businesses my great-grandfather owned or worked for. While visiting one summer, I asked her whether she ever wanted to have a career outside the home and she smiled, patted my cheek, and responded, "Oh honey, why in the world would I do that and what would I do?"

When I was in elementary school, my maternal grandmother became the secretary at the Methodist church where she and my grandfather had been members for over thirty years. I remember my grandfather saying with pride that it was less "working" and more "serving" the church community.

And then there was my mom. She met my dad when she was working as a secretary in the campus athletic office where my dad attended college—my dad played basketball and spent a lot of time there. Once they were married and adopted me, I grew up watching my mom work as a part-time secretary in our church, then in my school. As my mom navigated some challenging times in her life, her resolve to elevate her role grew and so did her confidence. When I was in college, my mom's commitment to modernizing her role in her marriage and in our family led to her pursuing a college degree. Her success led to a new level of independence and, ultimately, to her completing a master's degree, becoming a social worker, and continuing to work long after my dad retired! Over time, my observations and experiences with the evolution of roles in my own family certainly influenced me.

My observations regarding family and professional roles prompted meaningful conversations with the most important women in my life. When I chose to go to graduate school, my maternal grandmother shared her excitement at my having access to opportunities girls only dreamed of when she was young. I began to see a sense of pride build in her as I asserted myself and ambitiously pursued my dreams. She was not shy about expressing her joy in "living through me" and eventually through my mom. Both my mom and my maternal grandmother emphasized that it was important for me to know, understand, and appreciate not only history but also how it compares to modern societal norms.

When I examine the historical data, it is apparent that women have made progress in accessing leadership roles, but there is clearly more work to be done. The challenges women have faced and continue to face when making the decision to pursue leadership positions are real. While women make up 50.8 percent of the U.S. population and hold 52 percent of all management and professional-level jobs, women continue to be underrepresented in leadership positions (Warner, Ellmann, & Boesch, 2018). According to the Canadian Women's Foundation (2017), 82 percent of Canadian women participate in the workforce but are underrepresented in leadership. In 2021, Germany enacted a second gender-quota law to increase the number of women in corporate leadership after the first such law (enacted in 2015) failed to produce the desired outcomes, with representation of women on executive boards stalled at just 7.7 percent (Gesley, 2021). And while the percentage of female school district superintendents across the United States has slowly increased (see introduction, page 1), 76 percent of superintendents continue to be men in a profession where 76 percent of the workforce are women (National Center for Education Statistics [NCES], 2021; Ramaswamy, 2020). As a female educational leader and school superintendent, this troubles me and leads me to want to understand the reasons behind this continuing trend.

Once I examine history and the evolution of roles in families, there are other factors to contend with—very real barriers that each woman experiences personally and differently at different levels. In an American Association of University Women report, some of these barriers that explain the gender gap in leadership include persistent sex discrimination, stereotypes, and bias (Hill, Miller, Benson, & Handley, 2016). While the statistical reality of the history of women in leadership and the evolution of women's roles in family and community are external factors that are outside women's control, I would contend that examining both will lead to a deeper examination of those things women *can* influence.

Looking in the Mirror

My sixteen-year-old daughter often says I take the notion of examining one's own role in situations too seriously and it's annoying. From the time she was small and would bend my ear about neighborhood drama or conflict, I have tended to first ask, "How did you react?" or "What was your role?" or even "What might you have done to contribute to what happened?" (It is the last question that angers her most.) I do not mean to suggest that external factors and others' behavior are always justified or that obstacles to advancement are your fault. However, you have more influence over internal factors, and you should not overlook this path to better outcomes.

While I was preparing to participate in my first Women in Educational Leadership conference in July 2019, I came across an article by female members of the Forbes Coaches Council (2018). The article outlines the fifteen greatest challenges women leaders face (Forbes Coaches Council, 2018).

1. **Being treated equally:** Working and interacting with others without being subject to bias or prejudice

2. **Building a sisterhood:** Generating support from other women

3. **Generating revenue:** Making a comfortable living

4. **Being confident:** Knowing what you want to achieve and speaking up to get what you want

5. **Speaking up:** Making your voice heard

6. **Building alliances with decision makers:** Building healthy relationships and creating a strong personal brand

7. **Becoming a member of the C-suite:** Knowing what you want, being relentless in your preparation, and taking the necessary risks

8. **Asking for money:** Overcoming reluctance to ask for what you are worth

9. **Standing in your success:** Speaking confidently about your accomplishments

10. **Tackling imposter syndrome:** Learning to internalize your accomplishments

11. **Overcoming perfectionism:** Setting aside perfectionistic tendencies

12. **Trusting your own voice:** Believing in your own ideas and experience

13. **Shifting your word choice:** Shifting from judgmental to neutral word choices so others respect you as a leader

14. **Dealing with negative thoughts:** Preventing negative thoughts from taking control

15. **Re-entering the paid workforce:** Combating ageism, rebuilding confidence, and adjusting to changes when returning to work after a caregiving hiatus

Though factors like being treated equally and generating revenue are fully or partially in others' hands, most of these challenges are ones each individual can significantly influence through personal reflection and modifications to behavior. As you consider these fifteen challenges, I encourage you to record your thoughts using the chart in figure 4.1. Put a check mark in the second column beside the challenges that resonate with you. Next, think of an example of a time when this challenge presented itself. Try to rate the level of impact it presented for you, with 1 indicating a minor challenge and 5 indicating a significant challenge or barrier. Finally, identify a reflection partner with whom you might dialogue about your experiences.

For the purposes of this chapter, I am going to dig into four challenges that women can make significant progress against by looking in the mirror: (1) standing in your success, (2) tackling imposter syndrome, (3) overcoming perfectionism, and (4) building a sisterhood (Forbes Coaches Council, 2018). I chose to focus on these four as they were not only the most significant for me as I grew into leadership but also the four that I most commonly observe aspiring female leaders wrestling with.

Standing in Your Success

This challenge immediately resonated with me as I read the *Forbes* article for the first time and reflected on my own journey. Women tend to shrink themselves to avoid seeming egotistical or intimidating. *Standing in your success* is the opposite: accepting that you deserve your accomplishments and drawing confidence from that knowledge (Forbes Coaches Council, 2018).

I remember preparing to interview for one of the first promotions I was passionate about. At that point, I had led numerous initiatives successfully, bringing people along by building various coalitions to accomplish the work. But I became uncomfortable as I contemplated how to describe those accomplishments. I was hypersensitive to using vocabulary that might give the interviewers the impression I was overinflating my importance in an initiative, taking credit for a team effort, or boasting. I finally sought the counsel of a mentor. When I described my struggle, he seemed confused. He asked, "Were you charged with leading this particular initiative?" When I answered that I was, he said, "Look, if you don't sell yourself by articulating your successes, you are putting yourself at a disadvantage because I guarantee you that the other candidates will do so!"

Challenge	✓	Personal Example	Impact 1–5	Reflection Partner
Being treated equally				
Building a sisterhood				
Generating revenue				
Being confident				
Speaking up				
Building alliances with decision makers				
Becoming a member of the C-suite				
Asking for money				
Standing in your success				
Tackling imposter syndrome				
Overcoming perfectionism				
Trusting your own voice				
Shifting your word choice				
Dealing with negative thoughts				
Re-entering the paid workforce				

Source: Adapted from Forbes Coaches Council, 2018.

Figure 4.1: Challenges self-reflection.

*Visit **go.SolutionTree.com/leadership** for a free reproducible version of this figure.*

What he forced me to consider was how to use one of my strengths—building a coalition of people who are willing to support an initiative—to present my case in a way I was comfortable with. Thus, I began to reimagine how I would answer the question, "What professional accomplishment are you most proud of?" It allowed me to frame accomplishments by highlighting the dedication and work of those with whom I worked. So when asked the question, I responded not by extolling the success of the initiative but rather by highlighting my success in building a coalition around it.

From my perspective, the interview went well, but I was not selected for the position. I was aware at the time that I was the only female candidate, but it was only much later I learned the interview team had concerns about the optics of promoting me—a single woman in her early thirties—to the position. For whatever reason, those making the decision were uncomfortable with that. It was fair in this case for me to look out the window, but I also got busy looking in the mirror. Why did I hesitate to stand in my success then, and why do I occasionally continue to do so now? Would standing more strongly and confidently in my success have made a difference?

It is incredibly helpful to role-play standing in your success with a trusted colleague or mentor. First, identify the traits, contributions, and successes you are most proud of and want to highlight. In my case, I was particularly proud of the success of a large initiative I had been charged to lead and my ability to build a coalition. Once you identify what you want to highlight, rehearse language that strikes the most effective tone for you.

Tackling Imposter Syndrome

Imposter syndrome refers to a mindset whereby "intelligent, capable, and successful individuals believe that their success is due to luck and fear that they will someday be exposed as imposters" (Gadsby, 2021, p. 1). While anyone could experience imposter syndrome, it was first identified and described in 1978 as a psychological phenomenon in successful professional women (Bravata, Madhusudhan, Boroff, & Cokley, 2020). When women experience success, rather than internalize it, they either consciously or subconsciously wonder when others are going to discover they are not as talented, skilled, or able as their position might suggest. This feeling can haunt women after they achieve a position or an accomplishment, and one can infer that it may also prevent them from pursuing those achievements in the first place, as I experienced myself. I had never heard the term *imposter syndrome* before reading the *Forbes* article, but I had certainly experienced it. It was difficult for me to admit to myself this was an ongoing challenge for me, but to be honest, it wasn't until I was almost fifty years old that my imposter syndrome began to dissipate. Truth be told, I spent the first five years of my superintendency wondering when someone was going to discover I wasn't qualified for my job!

As a forty-three-year-old first-year superintendent, I attended my first state superintendents' conference. When I walked into the opening session of the event with the other seven hundred attendees, I stopped in my tracks. It was early autumn and I was wearing a colorful fall dress. All I could see in the very large room were hundreds of men all dressed in black and gray suits. I immediately felt like I stuck out like a sore thumb—the opposite of my planned strategy of fading into the background, listening, and learning to navigate this new world. I spent way too much time during those few days convinced someone in the room was going to call me out for not belonging there.

For me, the most effective way to fight my imposter syndrome was to identify my role and perform it to the best of my ability, even if I felt unsure at first. I needed to establish relationships and credibility in my role not only to have my voice heard at the table but also to chip away at my internal doubt about whether my voice actually belonged at the table. Fast-forward to today, and I sit on the board of directors of the state superintendents' organization representing my region. My growth into this role has been one of the most satisfying of my career because, while I initially spent some time looking out the window and identifying the external factors that impacted my levels of comfort and confidence, once I looked in the mirror, I was able to identify a path forward. I no longer feel like an imposter.

Another lesson I learned during this part of my journey was that pretending I knew all the answers was counterproductive to battling imposter syndrome. While leaders often feel like they need to have answers to every question or solutions to every dilemma, that mindset exacerbated my imposter syndrome. If I provided an "answer" I was unsure of because I was afraid not to, it only contributed to the long list of failings others might discover about me! By contrast, when I became comfortable responding with "That's a great question! I don't know, but we'll figure it out together," the imposter syndrome began to melt away. No one has all the answers, so be comfortable in the fact you don't either.

Finally, executive coach Loren Margolis suggests a three-step approach to defeating imposter syndrome (as cited in Forbes Coaches Council, 2018).

1. Identify why you feel like an imposter.

2. Work with a coach or mentor to objectively assess your performance.

3. Seek out feedback on your strengths from other leaders.

The three elements of this process—reflecting to identify a reason, working with a trusted colleague, and seeking objective feedback—could help defeat many different challenges. This cycle of improvement, in my experience, will lead to personal and professional growth!

Reflection

Have you ever felt like you had to have all the
answers to all the questions asked of you?

Have you ever been concerned others may discover
you do not have all the skills you need to be successful?

If you answered *yes* to either of the previous questions,
how might you tackle imposter syndrome so it does not negatively
affect your personal and professional life?

Overcoming Perfectionism

Perfectionism can be paralyzing. If you feel everything must be perfect, you may be unable to move forward until it is. You get stuck. In my experience, many women who pursue leadership positions exhibit Type A personality characteristics. These characteristics can include being driven, rigidly organized, goal focused, and perhaps a workaholic (Raypole, 2021). No wonder women leaders struggle with perfectionism!

Women often feel like there is no choice other than pursuing perfectionism. For both internal and external reasons, women often need to work harder and be more skilled to be as successful as men (Risse, 2018). As a young new administrator, I committed to working more hours on more projects than many of my male counterparts. I also spent an inordinate amount of time considering every detail of a project or initiative, trying to predict issues before they happened. I often felt stuck. If there were questions unanswered or details I could not yet define, I was unwilling to move forward. I needed the plan to be *perfect*. When part of your role is to move initiatives or systems forward, feeling stuck can certainly be a barrier, as it was for me as a new school administrator. It wasn't until I embraced the concept of continuous cycles of improvement that I learned chasing perfection would distract me from the process of the work itself.

When facilitating professional learning in education I often refer to a book very influential in my work: *Learning by Doing* (DuFour, DuFour, Eaker, Many, & Mattos, 2016). There is a reason the authors chose the title *Learning by Doing* and not *Learning by Thinking About It* or *Learning by Talking About It*. People learn best by *doing*. But this means things will not be perfect in the beginning stages. In reality, perfection should not be your goal—constant improvement should be. If you get stuck in perfectionism, it becomes a barrier to improvement, resulting in worse outcomes.

Leadership coach Jill Hauwiller recommends women take a moment to reflect when they feel paralyzed by perfectionism (as cited in Forbes Coaches Council, 2018). You can even add reflective pauses to your daily schedule or the agendas of meetings you facilitate. This allows you and others time to identify what is going well and what challenges exist before contributing.

The key for me, despite all of my own perfectionist characteristics and tendencies, has been to publicly acknowledge and articulate that things will not be perfect. That we, as a school, will learn as we go. That we commit to continuous improvement. This approach feels vulnerable, but it is real, it helps me get unstuck, and it allows others to begin to get comfortable with imperfection while committing to learning together!

Building a Sisterhood

I intentionally saved this challenge for last as it focuses on personal and professional relationships with other women and, at times, is uncomfortable. The challenge of building a sisterhood is deeply rooted in the history of social norms. On one hand, women have long histories of passing important knowledge from mother to daughter, sister to sister, and friend to friend, especially when it comes to topics considered taboo in male or mixed-gender spaces, such as menstruation and pregnancy (Agarwal, 2020; Bornat & Diamond, 2007). Women in modern times continue to find value in single-sex organizations, from neighborhood groups to women's colleges (Miller-Bernal, 2011; Puri, 2016). On the other hand, women have the stark workplace reality: they must compete with one another for limited resources, often forcing a trade-off between success and relationships with other women (Marcus, 2016). For example, in her book *Tripping the Prom Queen*, nonfiction and novel writer Susan Shapiro Barash (2006) explores the idea that women find it irresistible to "trip the prom queen"—to tear one another down for personal gain. Male-dominated societies and workplaces create a scarcity of opportunity for women, and some women respond with verbal or social aggression (Marcus, 2016). Furthermore, in a patriarchal culture, men may feel pressure to demonstrate their superiority and strength, and an assertive woman can be a threat to a male ego (Grant, 2021).

Reading Barash's (2006) work prompted me to examine my own female relationships during both childhood and my professional journey. Growing up, I had long-term friendships, some of which remain today. Nevertheless, I also experienced betrayals. While I was always listening and observing to better understand the behavior and emotions of others, when it came to some of my closest friends, I was sometimes blindsided and confounded. Thankfully, when I spend time with the women whose friendships have endured, we are able to talk about those times. Interestingly, we still struggle to know why we behaved the way we did.

When it comes to female relationships in the workplace, my personal experiences have been a mixed bag. I once had a school principal who lamented being the only female principal in the district, but also seemed to wear it as a badge of honor. I looked to her as a mentor, and she frequently encouraged me to pursue a principalship, stating that my work ethic far outpaced her male counterparts'. After I unsuccessfully interviewed for the next principal opening, the superintendent shared with me that my mentor had not endorsed me wholeheartedly. I was taken aback by the incongruity between this feedback and her encouragement to pursue promotion. When I mustered the courage to have a conversation with her about the superintendent's remarks and how I wished she had helped prepare me for the position with more transparent feedback, she dismissively said he was trying to create competition between us. Unfortunately, I never gained clarity regarding the strength of her endorsement, which leaves me to wonder whether this specific circumstance actually was the superintendent creating competition between us or an instance of female rivalry rearing its head.

So clearly, when it comes to building a sisterhood there is plenty of opportunity to look out the window and identify all the disheartening obstacles. But spend some time thinking about how to empower and support one another by looking in the mirror. The first step is self-awareness. *Self-awareness* includes being aware of one's own feelings, motives, and desires. At times, just identifying the exact emotion you are feeling in any given situation, particularly a professional situation, is challenging. There are many subtle differences, like those between anger and resentment or between admiration and jealousy. I find if I force myself to name the emotion I am feeling, it supports my ability to explore my motives and desires. Even in your professional relationships, you must be self-aware and seek to develop authentic relationships.

At one point in my career, I ran a department of capable men and women. There was one woman in particular with whom I developed a close friendship. We worked side by side as each of us experienced different phases of life. Our friendship ebbed and flowed through these stages. At one point, it seemed to me as if we were drifting apart, and I knew I was contributing to the distance. She had gotten engaged, had a gorgeous wedding, and was expecting her first child. I was single at the time and working sixty-hour weeks as a school leader. Here's what I realized: I wanted to be engaged. I wanted a gorgeous wedding. I desperately wanted to be a mom. And I wanted to be able to have those things while also remaining an effective leader. I was feeling jealous, plain and simple. Since I was invested in our friendship, I needed to identify my emotions, own them, and verbalize them to her in the hope she would better understand my behavior. So I did. She cried—in part, she said, because she was flattered that I was jealous! But she also recognized my vulnerability in openly sharing my emotions and identifying my desires. Our friendship has endured for thirty-three years. We could have gone our separate ways with an excuse about being in different stages of life, but I wanted and needed her to be a part of my personal and professional sisterhood. Self-awareness was essential to maintaining that relationship.

While you cannot force others to be self-aware, you can ask questions that help you (and perhaps others as well) understand feelings, motives, and desires. Such questions include the following.

- "Why is this so important to you?"
- "I want to support you; how can I better do that?"
- "Can you describe to me an outcome you would be really happy with?"

Executive coach Nadidah Coveney implores women to empower one another, to "be humbled, show togetherness, passion, excellence and enthusiasm" (as cited in Forbes Coaches Council, 2018). Some things women can do to champion one another include specifically looking for opportunities to celebrate the accomplishments of other women, encouraging other women to pursue their goals despite self-doubt, and committing time and energy to mentoring other women (Lean In, n.d.).

Later in my career, I was blessed with a community of several supportive women. I trust them. They trust me. We can be real with one another and support one another as professionals. We are vulnerable with one another but can also celebrate one another. We, as a group, are committed to supporting female leaders and to continually improving our organizations and associations for everyone in general and for women more specifically. In fact, the state superintendents' association for which I sit on the board of directors launched a women-in-leadership strand that almost immediately benefitted current and aspiring school leaders. Building a stronger sisterhood focused on building up one another, making it safe to be vulnerable, and articulating feelings, motives, and desires with one another is how women move forward in a united and powerful way. While I always appreciate my sisterhood for cheering me on and celebrating with me when things go well, I also deeply appreciate when they reach out to acknowledge when life is hard. I need them to acknowledge I am not alone in my frustration, sadness, or anxiety. And when they do both for me and I do both for them, we all benefit.

— Reflection —

Who are the women who make up your sisterhood? How do the women in your life support you? How do you support them?

Conclusion

In this chapter, I shared my experiences not as an expert but rather as someone who believes that by authentically sharing and listening, women can continue to improve themselves and positively affect those around them. Before you move on to the next chapter of this book, return to the challenges self-reflection (see figure 4.1, page 81) and spend a few moments reflecting on how those challenges have affected your life. Add to your reflection if this chapter sparked new ideas. Then, reach out to members of your sisterhood to share your thoughts and offer to listen if they feel compelled to share.

There are countless obstacles outside the window for women who aspire to leadership roles. By looking in the mirror, you can get out of your own way and ensure that you are not a barrier to others. By looking in the mirror, women will be better prepared to embark on the journey and face those external challenges—together.

— Reflection —

What is one thing that resonated with you after reading this chapter? What surprised you?

After looking in the mirror, what is one change you want to make as a female leader?

What is one action you will take related to building a sisterhood?

References and Resources

Agarwal, S. (2020). Re-writing history: Oral history as a feminist methodology. *Stream: Interdisciplinary Journal of Communication, 12*(1), 6–30.

Barash, S. S. (2006). *Tripping the prom queen: The truth about women and rivalry.* New York: St. Martin's Griffin.

Bornat, J., & Diamond, H. (2007). Women's history and oral history: Developments and debates. *Women's History Review, 16*(1), 19–39.

Bravata, D. M., Madhusudhan, D. K., Boroff, M., & Cokley, K. O. (2020). Commentary: Prevalence, predictors, and treatment of imposter syndrome—A systematic review. *Journal of Mental Health and Clinical Psychology, 4*(3), 12–16.

Canadian Women's Foundation. (2017, August). *Fact sheet: Moving women into leadership.* Accessed at https://fw3s926r0g42i6kes3bxg4i1-wpengine.netdna-ssl.com/wp-content /uploads/2017/09/Facts-About-Women-and-Leadership.pdf on January 21, 2022.

DuFour, R., DuFour, R., Eaker, R., Many, T. W., & Mattos, M. (2016). *Learning by doing: A handbook for Professional Learning Communities at Work* (3rd ed.). Bloomington, IN: Solution Tree Press.

Forbes Coaches Council. (2018, February 26). 15 biggest challenges women leaders face and how to overcome them. *Forbes.* Accessed at https://forbes.com/sites/forbescoachescoun cil/2018/02/26/15-biggest-challenges-women-leaders-face-and-how-to-overcome-them /?sh=28ea73f64162 on November 16, 2021.

Fuller, M. (2013). *Working with bitches: Identify the eight types of office mean girls and rise above workplace nastiness.* Boston: First Da Capo Press.

Gadsby, S. (2021). Imposter syndrome and self-deception. *Australasian Journal of Philosophy.* Accessed at https://philarchive.org/archive/GADISA on November 16, 2021.

Gesley, J. (2021). Germany: Second law establishing gender quotas to increase number of women in company leadership positions enters into force. *Library of Congress.* Accessed at https://loc.gov/item/global-legal-monitor/2021-09-12/germany-second-law-establishing -gender-quotas-to-increase-number-of-women-in-company-leadership-positions-enters -into-force on January 21, 2022.

Glass, T. E., Björk, L., & Brunner, C. C. (2000). *The study of the American school superintendency, 2000: A look at the superintendent of education in the new millennium.* Arlington, VA: American Association of School Administrators.

Grant, A. (2021, February 18). Who won't shut up in meetings? Men say it's women. It's not. *The Washington Post.* Accessed at https://washingtonpost.com/outlook/2021/02/18/men -interrupt-women-tokyo-olympics on January 14, 2022.

Hill, C., Miller, K., Benson, K., & Handley, G. (2016, March). *Barriers and bias: The status of women in leadership.* Washington, DC: American Association of University Women. Accessed at https://eric.ed.gov/?id=ED585546 on January 17, 2022.

Horowitz, J. M., Igielnik, R., & Parker, K. (September 20, 2018). Women in leadership 2018: Wide gender and party gaps in views about the state of female leadership and the obstacles women face. *PEW Research Center.* Accessed at https://pewresearch.org/social-trends/2018 /09/20/women-and-leadership-2018 on October 1, 2021.

Lean In. (n.d.). *6 ways that women can champion each other at work.* Accessed at https://leanin .org/tips/workplace-ally on January 21, 2022.

Marcus, B. (2016, January 13). The dark side of female rivalry in the workplace and what to do about it. *Forbes.* Accessed at https://forbes.com/sites/bonniemarcus/2016/01/13/the -dark-side-of-female-rivalry-in-the-workplace-and-what-to-do-about-it/?sh=3ed7cccb5255 on November 16, 2021.

Miller-Bernal, L. (2011). The role of women's colleges in the twenty-first century. In L. M. Stulberg & S. L. Weinberg (Eds.), *Diversity in American higher education: Toward a more comprehensive approach* (pp. 221–231). New York: Routledge.

National Center for Education Statistics. (2021). *Characteristics of public school teachers.* Accessed at https://nces.ed.gov/programs/coe/pdf/2021/clr_508c.pdf on November 21, 2021.

Puri, L. (2016, March 14). Remarks by UN Women Deputy Executive Director Lakshmi Puri at the CSW60 parallel event "Sustainable development through women's organizations: The Norwegian and the Ethiopian experience" [Speech transcript]. *UN Women.* Accessed at https://unwomen.org/en/news/stories/2016/3/lakshmi-puri-speech-sustainable-development -through-womens-organizations on December 17, 2021.

Ramaswamy, S. V. (2020, February 20). School superintendents are overwhelmingly male. What's holding women back from the top job? *USA Today.* Accessed at www.usatoday.com /story/news/education/2020/02/20/female-school-district-superintendents-westchester -rockland/4798754002 on November 21, 2021.

Raypole, C. (2021). What it really means to have a type A personality. *Healthline.* Accessed at https://healthline.com/health/what-is-a-type-a-personality on January 16, 2022.

Risse, L. (2018, November 19). Why women have to work harder to be promoted. *CNN Health.* Accessed at www.cnn.com/2018/11/19/health/women-work-harder-gender-pay -gap-intl/index.html on November 16, 2021.

U.S. Bureau of Labor Statistics. (2021, January 22). *Labor force statistics from the current population survey: Employed persons by detailed occupation, sex, race, and Hispanic or Latino ethnicity.* Accessed at www.bls.gov/cps/cpsaat11.htm on October 1, 2021.

Warner, J., Ellmann, N., & Boesch, D. (2018). The women's leadership gap: Women's leadership by the numbers. *Center for American Progress.* Accessed at www.americanprogress .org/issues/women/reports/2018/11/20/461273/womens-leadership-gap-2 on October 1, 2021.

Suzette Lovely, EdD, spent thirty-five years serving K–12 schools in every capacity—from instructional aide to teacher to principal to central office administrator to superintendent. During her role as a superintendent in Carlsbad, California, she spearheaded several efforts to support future-ready learning, including the implementation of a career pathways grant involving eighteen school districts throughout San Diego County. Dr. Lovely was also one of a handful of superintendents invited to participate in a focus group with California's governor to discuss the state's new funding and accountability system.

Since retiring, Dr. Lovely has remained active in strategic planning work, superintendent searches, leadership coaching, and mentoring women who are rising through the ranks. She is the cofounder of the Women in Education Leadership (WEL) network and co-leads AASA's Aspiring Superintendent Academy for Female Leaders. Dr. Lovely has been recognized for her visionary leadership and educational contributions by California Senator Patricia Bates, the California PTA, Hi-Noon Rotary, the Carlsbad Chamber of Commerce, The Master Teacher company, and the San Diego County Art Education Association. Dr. Lovely is the author of four books and numerous articles on leadership development and has been a featured speaker at several local, state, and national conferences.

Following her undergraduate work at the University of California, Irvine, Dr. Lovely earned a master's degree in educational administration from National University and a doctorate from California State University, Fullerton.

To learn more about Dr. Lovely's work, follow @SuzetteLovely on Twitter.

To book Suzette Lovely for professional development, contact pd@SolutionTree.com.

CHAPTER 5

Rising Through the Ranks

Suzette Lovely

> Each time a woman stands up for herself, without knowing it
> possibly, without claiming it, she stands up for all women.
>
> —Maya Angelou

In leadership positions, men outnumber women by wide margins in every industry. Report after report reveals women are inching their way to the top at a snail's pace. For women of color, opportunities to advance to senior-level positions are particularly elusive. Despite two decades of modest gains, a 2021 study from McKinsey and Lean In notes the overall status of women in the workplace continues to hang in the balance. Moreover, the COVID-19 pandemic exacerbated gender inequities, with women reporting higher levels of stress, exhaustion, and workforce exits than their male counterparts (Burns et al., 2021). The economic side effects of COVID-19 in the form of increased unemployment, loss of childcare options, and working from home further tipped the scales in favor of men.

A common mistake is to believe one can overcome obstacles to advancement simply by working harder or gaining more experience. A pedigree of hard work or experience is not enough to elevate women leaders to where they want to be. Rather than lament all the things holding them back, women must take a strategic approach to rising up. While one's definition of *rising up* may be personal and individual, awareness of the habits and mindsets that keep women stuck should be a shared experience. Workplace structures created with men in mind can undermine best intentions. Additionally, the success markers for women look different than the success markers for men. A common example is asking for a raise. A supervisor may perceive a female employee as pushy, yet consider her male counterpart a good negotiator. A woman reluctant to draw attention to her work is often assessed in terms of her potential. Conversely, a man who is a great self-promoter is evaluated on his contributions. These implicit biases can cloud a supervisor's judgment in subtle, yet impactful ways.

There is no force more powerful than a woman determined to *RISE*. In this chapter, I introduce four levers that women can use to elevate their climb: *realistic* goal setting; *improving* effectiveness; *shaking off* insecurity; and *evaluating* performance. The following sections include pertinent anecdotes around each lever to move women beyond the most common workplace worries: "I'm not good enough, worthy enough, or smart enough to do this job." Breaking free of self-imposed barriers creates the space for better outcomes to emerge.

Realistic Goal Setting

Conventional wisdom says if people encourage children to have big dreams, these dreams will one day come true. But what if the opposite is actually the case? When people are young, their sphere of reality is fairly small. Asking first graders what they want to be when they grow up reveals pretty standard answers—teacher, police officer, firefighter, veterinarian, ballerina, professional athlete. Occupational dreams come from a child's defining experiences. Most childhood ambitions can be traced to cultural background, gender norms, media influences, and admiration for particular adults or characters in a young person's life.

Despite endless encouragement from parents and teachers to become the next Walt Disney or president of the United States, a youngster's dreams are rather miniscule. When I asked my six-year-old niece (who loves to draw flowers) if she wanted to become the next Georgia O'Keeffe, she looked at me with an exasperated glare and replied, "Aunt Sue, can you stop asking me so many questions and just hang my picture on the refrigerator?" While children may dream of going to the Olympics, they are more excited about getting to gymnastics class and doing somersaults on the floor mats.

As people get older, their dreams grow. Opportunities abound. It is next to impossible not to set grandiose goals to bring grown-up dreams to fruition. Ambitious goal setting is associated with great accomplishments, but there is a dark side to this mindset—especially for women who feel a constant need to prove themselves. Author and clinical psychologist Kelly Flanagan (2017) warns the small, ordinary dreams of childhood often become so imposing in adulthood that they eventually cave in. Dreams of doing it all or having it all can lead to shame when people fail to live up to these expectations and may lull people into stagnation as they wait to have their ideas taken seriously or hang back for that next opportunity.

For women who journey through the labyrinth of school leadership, the ability to dream small is tantamount to having an impactful professional life. Most educators would agree that setting goals—whether for themselves or their organizations—is a foundation of success. Goals help focus energy and actions. They push people to get better and inspire others. Yet all educators have witnessed how the yearly grand plans set forth in many school districts are not realistic, personal, or compelling enough to generate sustainable results. Whether they call it a goal or an improvement effort, the gap between coming up with ideas and executing those ideas is a challenging one to bridge.

Cultivating a mindset to change trajectories as women requires having smaller dreams. Although big dreams sound impressive, they are harder to accomplish. In the book *Beginner's Pluck*, entrepreneur Liz F. Bohannon (2019) shares a small-dream story that altered the course of her life. After college, Bohannon (2019) set a big, change-the-world dream to establish a philanthropic initiative that would improve the lives of millions of women across the globe. But a short video called *The girl effect* made her realize that despite having altruistic dreams, her life as a privileged White woman had not exposed her to a single girl affected by the economic or social injustices billions of women face around the globe (girleffect, 2008). Bohannon (2019) notes, "While I was busy thinking and dreaming and scheming about a million girls, the sacred importance and value of just one got lost somewhere along the way" (p. 52).

Following her epiphany, Bohannon's (2019) focus shifted from bringing a million girls out of poverty to a tiny goal—to befriend one girl who faced the horrible prospects of forced marriage or gender-based violence. Accomplishing this goal required zero degrees, zero connections, and far less money (Bohannon, 2019). At age twenty-two, Bohannon (2019) bought a one-way ticket to Uganda to embark on her new bite-sized dream. She traversed the country meeting people, visiting nonprofits, touring schools, and hosting informal focus groups to learn firsthand about the brutal realities facing women living in extreme poverty. It soon became clear that the best lever to help women escape the dreadful cycle of oppression: *education.*

Bohannon's (2019) focus was on one community with twenty-five high school girls, and she developed a new manageable goal—to generate enough revenue to sustain three students during the nine-month gap between secondary school and enrollment in university, so the girls would not have to return to their villages where they were likely to be sold or pressured into marriage due to their families' lack of financial means to provide for them. Before long, Bohannon (2019) formed relationships with three industrious women to make and sell sandals for this gap funding.

A year after arriving in Uganda, Bohannon (2019) founded Sseko Designs. The company's mission is to support training and mentor programs for college-bound students, and employ women from all walks of life as full-time staff. It has grown into a worldwide fashion brand and the largest footwear exporter in East Africa. *Shark Tank*, *Good Morning America*, *Businessweek,* and a host of other outlets have featured the Sseko story. As a rising star in the world of social entrepreneurialism, Bohannon (2019) has become a role model for thousands of women and girls around the world.

Bohannon's (2019) story reveals that small dreams matter. In fact, microscopically small dreams can catapult people to make strategic decisions that set bigger dreams in motion. For women, this approach provides much-needed momentum to move from a state of feeling overwhelmed to a state of doing, and then to a state of dreaming bigger. It also enables women to build a life of purpose and impact *now*, instead of waiting for some unforeseen time in the future.

-------------------- *Reflection* --------------------

Write down a big personal or professional dream you have right now.
How can you make this big dream smaller?

Visit **go.SolutionTree.com/leadership** *to access a reproducible reflection guide for this chapter.*

Improving Effectiveness

Effective leadership is much more than introducing fancy initiatives or conjuring up an all-inclusive strategic plan. Rather, *effective leadership* is an evolution of style and technique that fits each situation. The best leaders set direction and then use their influence to bring others along. Every woman maintains limitless potential to transform her work environment. To that end, women should apply the same advocacy they devote to student growth to their own self-improvement. The following sections introduce two areas—executive presence and sustainable velocity—to improve women's effectiveness and impact as they rise to the top.

Executive Presence

Leadership is full of intangibles. It's how leaders show up and contribute to meetings. It's the way they connect with others. It's their body language and finesse. The manner in which leaders control a room and leave others with the right impression has a name: *executive presence*. According to economist and workplace expert Sylvia A. Hewlett (2014), *executive presence* is "the amalgam of qualities that telegraphs that you are in charge or deserve to be" (p. 1).

The intangible qualities of executive presence can give female leaders a tangible advantage. Part charisma, part composure, and part *chutzpah*, experts say executive presence is often the missing link between a woman's merit and her actual success (Byrne, Kirchner, & D'Agostino, 2018). While executive presence might not earn you a promotion, a lack of it will impede your ability to get as far as you want to go. In fact, executive presence may be the only difference between a talented female leader who gets marooned in middle management and one who seems to rise effortlessly through the ranks (Byrne et al., 2018).

The good news is you can learn, practice, and refine your executive presence. Through trial and error, women can perfect their professional image and apply tactical strategies to become fearless leaders. Figure 5.1 (page 98) highlights three ingredients that create the dynamic mix of executive presence.

1. Gravitas (how you act)

2. Communication (how you speak)

3. Appearance (how you look)

Confidence accentuates gravitas, which accounts for 67 percent of how others perceive women (Hewlett, 2014). While men tend to blame missteps on external factors, women are inclined to blame themselves (Helgesen & Goldsmith, 2018). Gravitas emerges as women shed that nasty inner critic hindering their accomplishments and sabotaging future opportunities. A leader with gravitas walks into a room knowing she is an asset for whatever situation awaits. Her actions are calm, yet decisive. She accepts compliments with a polite "thank you." Although gravitas requires a sense of seriousness and dignity, a woman leader with it also deploys happiness and humor to improve the circumstances.

The second ingredient in the presence recipe is communication. The manner in which women speak and convey messages accounts for 28 percent of how others perceive them (Hewlett, 2014). Female leaders must develop a compelling and effective communication style. This means staying on point, speaking

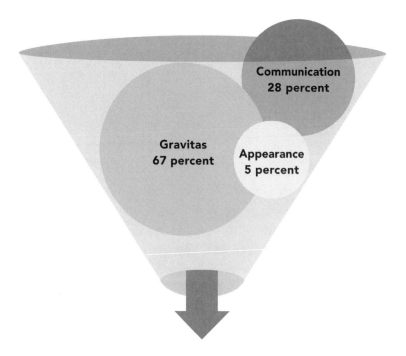

Source: Adapted from Hewlett, 2014.

Figure 5.1: Key ingredients of executive presence.

with impact, and being decisive. For example, it's common for women to say "I'm sorry" or ask for permission before interjecting (Helgesen & Goldsmith, 2018). Rather than ask, "May I say something?" using a self-assured phrase like, "I recommend this approach" packs a bigger punch. Or better yet, simply launch in and share your idea. Statements such as "I believe" and "Here is my plan," communicate surety. Scholars find when women write and speak with conviction, it increases the chance their audience will find their argument convincing (William & Mary Writing Resources Center, 2018).

To communicate with clarity and precision, write down your main points in advance of a meeting. Chunk messages into fifteen- to thirty-second segments so people remember what you want them to hear. And don't save the best for last—audiences are the most attentive at the beginning of a pitch. Furthermore, while women speak an average of twenty thousand words per day, men typically speak around seven thousand words (Helgesen & Goldsmith, 2018). "In male-centric cultures that value succinctness," coauthors Sally Helgesen and Marshall Goldsmith (2018, p. 164) point out, when women reduce the number of words they use to communicate an idea, others better receive the idea.

Pitch, tone, and pace also matter. Even an excellent message delivered in a flat or monotone way is soon forgotten. Speaking too softly may leave an impression that you may be too young or inexperienced for the job. Others perceive lower-pitched voices, regardless of gender, to be more authoritative and trustworthy. A vocal profile that exudes natural, warm tones can help you be taken seriously (Hewlett, 2014). Lastly, talking too fast may project impatience and rob an audience of the time needed to absorb the message. Speakers should insert pauses in the right places and emphasize key words with the right amount of emotion. Sometimes it is best to let silence to do the heavy lifting. If you want to work on your leadership voice, don't be shy about asking for help. Former U.K. Prime Minister Margaret Thatcher worked with a vocal coach for over a decade to sound less pitchy and to learn to speak with authority (Hewlett, 2014). Record your voice or videotape your presentations to hear how you come across. Practice speaking in the mirror. Ask for feedback from people you trust.

Like it or not, *speaking while female* is a tightrope all women walk. As business executive Sheryl Sandberg and Wharton School Professor Adam Grant (2015) write in *The New York Times*, when a woman speaks in a professional setting, "she's barely heard or she's judged as too aggressive. When a man says virtually the same thing, heads nod in appreciation for his fine idea. As a result, women often decide that saying less is more." One way to move past this double standard is to give credit to colleagues for joint ventures, while also articulating the role you played in enhancing the team's efforts. But a longer-term solution to having others value your ideas is to increase the number of women in leadership roles. As more women reach executive levels, people become accustomed to hearing what they have to say (Sandberg & Grant, 2015).

The third element of executive presence is appearance. Although rated far lower in importance than gravitas and communication, looking polished and put together still matters. Actually, 75 percent of hiring managers report that unkempt attire detracts from both men and women's executive presence (Hewlett, 2014). For women, tight or provocative clothing is the most significant deterrent. While the outfit you wear to an interview or presentation may not have any bearing on your intelligence or skills, it is a very real factor in how others perceive you. Aside from dressing the part, body language, eye contact, and posture are other physical attributes by which others judge women. The way you carry yourself and occupy space can make you appear more confident. A warm smile says you are approachable. While everyone knows crossed arms are a no-no, so too is arm waving. Hand gestures should be subdued and purposeful (Hewlett, 2014).

100 | WOMEN WHO LEAD

A healthy combination of confidence, poise, and the ability to convey thoughts with conviction can give women an edge in landing a top job in an organization. Executive presence is a real standard that helps women rise. The best combination for success is competence, warmth, and a straightforward manner that tells a roomful of people, "You're in the presence of someone who knows her stuff and is a true difference maker in the organization."

─────────────────── *Reflection* ───────────────────

Consider the three ingredients of executive presence this previous section describes: gravitas, communication, and appearance. Identify one area you would like to focus on to boost your presence in the workplace.

───

Sustainable Velocity

How many times have you neglected taking a vacation because you were afraid you would get behind at work? Do you put in fourteen-hour days to get everything done? Many women believe that more time on the ground will produce a better return. However, setting overly high personal standards can compel a leader to set similar standards for her direct staff (Helgesen & Goldsmith, 2018). This can cause resentment among staff and stifle workplace creativity. Equating hard work with favorable outcomes is likely to come back and bite you.

Let's consider the story of Cheryl (not her real name). No one in the district worked harder than Cheryl. Up at dawn and at the office into the late hours, Cheryl was the epitome of a high performer. When people wanted something done, and wanted it done well, they turned to Cheryl. As a dedicated problem solver, she rose through the ranks as a classroom teacher, a coordinator, a director, and an assistant superintendent. The school board, superintendent, and principals all relied on Cheryl to sweat the small stuff.

When the superintendent announced his retirement, Cheryl seemed like a shoo-in for the job. Although the board members loved Cheryl, they decided to do a full candidate search to leave no stone unturned. In seeking stakeholder feedback, it became clear to the board members that others highly regarded Cheryl's work ethic and dedication. However, they also found Cheryl's leadership style a bit confining. Her perfectionism turned every goal and initiative into a high-stakes endeavor. Team members who worked for Cheryl were less inclined to take risks for fear of letting her down.

When the board hired a male candidate from outside the district, Cheryl was devastated. A board member told Cheryl the new superintendent had an effervescence that made him extraordinary. Moreover, the board members had concerns about finding a sufficient replacement if they promoted Cheryl. After all, the new superintendent needed her as his "right-hand gal." Sadly, perfectionism had turned Cheryl into an unwitting hostage. Leaders who struggle with control issues make it hard for others to feel safe carrying out tasks and taking risks. Learning to set limits and let go is paramount to reaching the top and staying there.

Improving effectiveness is not about speed or quantity; it's about velocity. Speed and direction both matter. Two strategies will propel female leaders to increase their velocity at work in a sustainable way. First is a cost-benefit analysis to determine how much time and energy to spend on a given project. For most situations in life, the law of diminishing returns comes into play after a certain amount of time or effort begins to outweigh any gains. To start the analysis, list your priority projects in two columns: (1) projects worth doing extremely well and (2) projects simply worth doing. For example, if you're creating a ten-minute presentation to kick off the teacher training day, does it have to be perfect or just done well? For each task, draw a curve of diminishing returns—as figure 5.2 shows—to compare project quality with time and effort. Identify the point in the project where you reach *GETMO* or *good enough to move on* (Groeschel, 2019). Devotion to excellence at any cost robs people of precious time and energy they might better spend on tasks that yield a better return on investment.

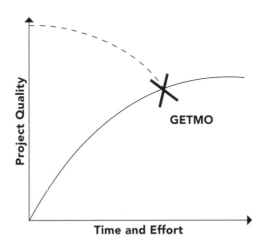

Source: Adapted from Groeschel, 2019.

Figure 5.2: The GETMO curve.

The second strategy is to master the art of delegation (Lovely, 2006). Many women are reluctant delegators. Concerns range from "Who has time to delegate?" to "If I ask for help, will people think I'm incapable of doing the job myself?" However, school leaders who dare to delegate will distribute responsibility among those with a vested interest in the outcome. Doing this says to people, "I trust you and am grateful for your contributions." Not only does effective delegation increase the quality of the end results, it also makes the leader's velocity more sustainable. Unless a task involves privileged information or is a function that only you can carry out, odds are good you can share the load. Knowing how to manage assignments and get commitments from others will keep you out of the perfection trap and enlarge your circle of doers (Lovely, 2006).

Shaking Off Insecurity

In conducting in-depth studies with countless female leaders in virtually every industry, Helgesen and Goldsmith (2018) conclude that women often undermine their success with self-sabotaging behaviors different than the behaviors that undermine men. Unconscious reasoning, analysis paralysis, and perpetual feelings of guilt all work against women. Conquering insecurity without compromising your character helps you gain perspective as you rise through the ranks. The next sections focus on two practices to break free of self-doubt: psychological jujitsu and sweat equity. The ability to move on is a precursor to the ability to move up.

Psychological Jujitsu

The Japanese martial art of *jujitsu* can teach women a lot about improving the quality of their leadership. Jujitsu moves are graceful and precise. The mental and physical aspects of the sport are equally important. While jujitsu masters might work with a coach, they view themselves as the boss. Experience, strategy, and adaptability drive technique. Jujitsu masters have no problem letting go of elements of the game that no longer serve them well. The core principle behind jujitsu is to yield to one's attacker by redirecting the attacker's energy back to them (Friedman, n.d.). Female leaders who practice psychological jujitsu tackle their "enemies" by turning defensive patterns of behavior into positive responses.

You are likely familiar with the concept of "not taking the bait" when someone tries to draw you into an argument. But how do you react when the saboteur is *you*? Many women struggle with internal barriers that hinder their rise to the top, and rumination and regret are two of the biggest (Helgesen & Goldsmith, 2018). In *How Women Rise*, Helgesen and Goldsmith (2018) note while men engage in plenty of self-defeating behaviors, they rarely get bogged down in the type of self-castigation common in women. Men are inclined to say, "Hey, I made a mistake. Everyone does. Let's move on" (Helgesen & Goldsmith, 2018, p. 171). Women, on the other hand, mull over events by convincing themselves they're trying to figure out why things went sideways. At a certain point, however, all the dwelling and disappointment can infect women with bitterness and insecurity.

Reflection

Think about a past mistake you found yourself dwelling on.
What made it hard to move on?

Recognizing and redirecting mental attacks takes vigilance. In moments of failure, it's easy to play the "coulda, woulda, shoulda" soundtrack in your head. But it is far more impactful to think about what you intend to do differently. Instead of dwelling on mistakes, replace regret with curiosity. Not only is curiosity a powerful tool for learning but also a mindset you can choose every day. Being curious pushes leaders to excel by posing provocative questions, learning from others, and expanding their worldview. Curiosity also releases dopamine and other feel-good chemicals as you encounter new ways of doing and being (Helgesen & Goldsmith, 2018). Choosing curiosity over castigation might prompt the following questions.

- "Hmm, why did he respond that way?"
- "Is there something I could have done differently?"
- "How will I learn, change, or grow from this experience?"
- "How do I plan to move on?"

Dealing with insecurity more skillfully enhances a woman's influence and effectiveness, especially when she feels attacked. Psychological jujitsu sheds the delusions that everything is your fault. Psychological jujitsu requires practice and discipline, just like other martial arts, but learning to navigate situations without rumination or regret will allow you to return to the business at hand more quickly.

Reflection

Consider the past mistake you reflected on earlier. Contemplate how you changed or grew from this experience. How did you move on? When similar situations occur, what will you do to avoid self-defeating behavior?

Sweat Equity

Leadership is both inspiration and perspiration. However, it is easy to get stuck on one end of the spectrum. All perspiration with no vision bogs people down in the daily grind of their jobs. Conversely, all cheerleader without substance leads to a slow suffocation of people's best ideas. The sweet spot on this spectrum is where you find *sweat equity*. Producing the right amount of sweat equity destines female leaders to catch others' eyes and generate collective returns for their organization.

Sweat equity is a nonmonetary benefit that comes from purposeful efforts or a special level of responsiveness that increases one's value to others (Zwilling, 2021). Although many factors determine success at work, doing something unfamiliar or unexpected can "raise your stock" with subordinates and supervisors. Rather than toil behind the scenes, women must learn to work alongside others to make noticeable contributions (Helgesen & Goldsmith, 2018). Not only does sweat equity open doors but it also ensures your persistent actions matter.

The goal of sweat equity is to boost one's reputation and visibility in a nuanced way. For example, people will say, "She does hard things well," rather than "She does a lot of things well." Or they may admiringly note, "Boy, that was a gutsy move!" Sweat equity generates returns for both you and your organization. Stories about principals demonstrating sweat equity are plentiful: for example, swapping jobs with the custodian for a day after students reach their academic testing goal, kissing a pig after students read five thousand books, or letting students turn the principal into a human sundae after the school surpasses the PTA's annual fundraising goal. Albeit silly, these stunts earn principals huge credibility with students and their community. Unfortunately, these stories are less common the higher up the leadership ladder you look. Once leaders reach the district level, it's easy to lose touch with the broader community. Pursuing sweat-equity encounters builds social capital and provides leverage for the goals you set out to achieve.

One of my most memorable sweat equity moments as superintendent surrounded the kickoff of the Great Kindness Challenge (https://thegreatkindnesschallenge .com). During the challenge, educators encourage students from kindergarten to high school to complete a checklist of kind deeds within the course of a week. Whether making a new friend, helping a neighbor, or starting a school recycling program, the goal is to create a ripple effect of kindness throughout a school and community. What started with a neighborhood group of children in

Carlsbad, California, hoping to make the world a better place, has grown into a network of 15 million schools worldwide participating in the annual challenge.

A Carlsbad parent who founded the kindness movement wanted to launch the event with a bang. Unbeknownst to me, this parent began working behind the scenes months in advance to arrange for me and two principals to skydive onto the high school football field. When she initially told me about her plan for the superintendent to "jump for kindness," I laughed and said "Sure, sure," thinking she'd never get approval from the Federal Aviation Administration (FAA) to do the stunt. After all, the town is sandwiched between Marine Corps Base Camp Pendleton and the McClellan-Palomar Airport. Moreover, the last thing I ever wanted to do was jump out of an airplane!

A week before the launch, to which the mayor, chamber of commerce leaders, other key officials, and the media had been invited, the parent called me in tears to say the FAA had put the brakes on the event. I was relieved until I heard the utter despair in her voice. I knew we had to make this thing happen somehow. So with a lot of phone calls and string pulling, we moved everything to the municipal airport in neighboring Oceanside, home of the skydiving company. With a hundred people there to watch the spectacle, the Great Kindness Challenge was set in motion with a giant leap. The local newspaper captured the fanfare with a quote that encapsulated my beliefs: "'I don't mind going into the unknown. . . . I'm adventurous and not afraid. . . . If a professional skydiver is attached [to me], they'll make sure that I'm safe. I put a lot of trust in people'" (Maio, 2016). Students, staff, parents, and constituents talked about the jump for months. Clearly, this sweat-equity moment elevated my social capital in more ways than I could have imagined.

Putting yourself out there with sweat equity shows your human side and ensures others notice your bold actions. It also enhances your ability to be mindfully present. When leaders learn to steer their thoughts away from worry, they're able to enjoy more of those fleeting work-life pleasures. Sweat equity is far more impactful to a woman's career trajectory than working quietly behind the scenes and expecting the results to speak for themselves.

--- *Reflection* ---

Consider a major project you're working on where it feels like you're producing more sweat than sweat equity. What actions might you take to be more consequential? What else could you do to raise your reputation or visibility around this work?

Evaluating Performance

Self-evaluation is a useful tool to surface the qualities that compel people to change for the better. The most successful women leaders are vigilant about their own improvement. When you identify, practice, and analyze the critical attributes of leadership I describe in this chapter, you are in a better position to escape any patterns that may be holding you back. By contrast, unrealistic goal setting, lack of presence, insecurity, or inattention to self-improvement can cause you to lose track of what it is you are trying to achieve.

When it comes to changing behavior, women actually have advantages over their male counterparts (Helgesen & Goldsmith, 2018). For example, women are often less ego driven, less defensive, and more accepting of advice from others. Scholars also find women to be more open to and diligent about altering habits that perpetuate their shortcomings. Grace and forgiveness are two of the most secure platforms women have for elevating future performance. The prompts in figure 5.3 can help you examine your current thinking and tendencies. Taking stock of the elements that prompt women to undersell or under-promote their talents allows them to become savvy self-improvers as they rise through the ranks.

Conclusion

In this chapter, I presented a vivid vision of female leadership drawn from new mindsets and habits. It is not enough to work hard, pay your dues, or wait for others to notice you. Instead, women must conquer workplace circumstances without feeling defeated, bitter, or afraid. Author Brené Brown (2017) contends that when women own their stories, they avoid being trapped as characters in the stories someone else tells. The levers of the RISE framework (that is, *realistic* goal setting; *improving* effectiveness; *shaking off* insecurity; and *evaluating* performance) will help female leaders craft their own stories as they advance their careers.

 *Reflection*

Which behaviors or experiences described in this chapter do you recognize in yourself? How have they detracted from or strengthened your ability to rise?

Which levers will you use to move closer to your career goals?

	Always (I do this consistently.)	Sometimes (I do this somewhat consistently.)	Never (I don't do this at all.)
1. I develop small dreams to make bigger dreams come true.			
2. I use tactical strategies to become a fearless competitor with men.			
3. I rely on executive presence to become a key influencer in my organization.			
4. I identify the point in projects when it's good enough to move on (GETMO).			
5. I know how and when to delegate tasks.			
6. I employ curiosity over self-castigation.			
7. I tackle "enemies" by turning defensive patterns of behavior into positive responses.			
8. I can name at least two examples where sweat equity catapulted my credibility.			
9. I create my own stories.			
10. I am vigilant about self-improvement.			
Reflection: List any insights you gleaned about yourself from this survey. What actions will you take on your leadership journey to support your ability to rise? How will you measure your success?			

Figure 5.3: Taking stock of your performance.

*Visit **go.SolutionTree.com/leadership** for a free reproducible version of this figure.*

References and Resources

Bohannon, L. F. (2019). *Beginner's pluck: Build your life of purpose and impact now.* Grand Rapids, MI: Baker Books.

Brown, B. (2017). *Rising strong: How the ability to reset transforms the way we live, love, parent, and lead.* New York: Random House.

Burns, T., Huang, J., Krivkovich, A., Rambachan, I., Trkulja, T., & Yee, L. (2021, September 27). *Women in the workplace 2021.* Accessed at https://mckinsey.com/featured-insights /diversity-and-inclusion/women-in-the-workplace on January 21, 2022.

Byrne, E. K., Kirchner, K., & D'Agostino, D. (2018, April 18). The secrets of leadership presence for every women leader. *Forbes.* Accessed at https://forbes.com/sites/ellevate /2018/04/18/the-secrets-of-leadership-presence-for-every-woman-leader/#2812d12c413d on October 1, 2021.

Flanagan, K. (2017, January 24). *Why dreaming small is way better than dreaming big (a child's wisdom).* Accessed at https://drkellyflanagan.com/why-dreaming-small-is-way-better-than -dreaming-big-a-childs-wisdom on April 15, 2020.

Friedman, W. J. (n.d.). *Psychological jujitsu/aikido/alchemy—"Conversation stoppers"* [Blog post]. Accessed at www.mentalhelp.net/blogs/psychological-jujitsu-aikido-alchemy-quot -conversation-stoppers-quot on April 25, 2020.

girleffect. (2008, May 24). *The girl effect* [Video file]. Accessed at https://youtube.com/watch ?v=WIvmE4_KMNw on November 16, 2021.

Groeschel, C. (2019, September 2). How to bend the curve [Audio podcast episode]. In *The Global Leadership Summit Podcast.* Accessed at https://globalleadership.org/podcast/leading- yourself/episode-057-craig-groeschel-how-to-bend-the-curve on May 5, 2020.

Helgesen, S., & Goldsmith, M. (2018). *How women rise: Break the 12 habits holding you back from your next raise, promotion, or job.* New York: Hachette Books.

Hewlett, S. A. (2014). *Executive presence: The missing link between merit and success.* New York: Harper Business.

Lovely, S. (2006). *Setting leadership priorities. What's necessary, what's nice, and what's got to go.* Thousand Oaks, CA: Corwin Press.

Maio, P. (2016, January 19). Carlsbad officials parachute for 'Kindness' week. *The Morning Call.* Accessed at www.mcall.com/sdut-suzette-lovely-carlsbad-parachutes-airport-2016 jan19-story.html on April 26, 2020.

Sandberg, S., & Grant, A. (2015, January 12). Speaking while female. *The New York Times.* Accessed at https://nytimes.com/2015/01/11/opinion/sunday/speaking-while-female.html on December 18, 2021.

William & Mary Writing Resources Center. (2018). *Speaking and writing with conviction.* Accessed at https://wm.edu/as/wrc/newresources/handouts/writing-with-conviction.pdf on December 19, 2021.

Zwilling, M. (2021, May 1). *8 key startup drivers bring pleasure as well as sweat* [Blog post]. Accessed at https://blog.startupprofessionals.com/2021/05/8-key-startup-drivers-bring -pleasure-as.html on December 30, 2021.

Heather Friziellie is superintendent of schools for Fox Lake School District 114 in Illinois. She previously served as a director overseeing special education as well as an elementary and middle school principal. As a leader, Heather is involved in response to intervention (RTI), closing the gap for special education–entitled students, professional learning communities, literacy curriculum development, data analysis, and staff development. With experience as a building- and district-level administrator, curriculum specialist, and classroom teacher, she has consulted with districts throughout the United States and presented at national conferences. Heather received a Those Who Excel award in Illinois in the School Administrator category. She is coauthor of *Yes We Can! General and Special Educators Collaborating in a Professional Learning Community.*

Heather earned a bachelor's degree in elementary education from Indiana University, a master's degree in curriculum and instruction from Indiana Wesleyan University, an administrative endorsement from Indiana University, and an educational specialist degree from Northern Illinois University.

To learn more about Heather's work, follow @HeatherLFriz on Twitter.

To book Heather Friziellie for professional development, contact pd@SolutionTree.com.

CHAPTER 6

Braving Difficult Conversations

Heather Friziellie

> Choosing our own comfort over hard conversations is the
> epitome of privilege, and it corrodes trust and moves us away
> from meaningful and lasting change.
>
> —Brené Brown

Be honest. How many times have you heard—or said—the following statements?

- "I can't stand conflict."
- "Confrontation makes me so uncomfortable."
- "Talking won't change anything. I'm just going to deal with it."

Here's the problem: like change, conflict is guaranteed to happen in any circumstance where people are working together. This is certainly true in schools, where a variety of individuals work together, bringing forward their perspectives, experiences, beliefs, backgrounds, and attitudes. Being a good school or district does not mean the organization has not experienced conflict; rather, a high-functioning organization can manage conflict in a way that increases its effectiveness (Larasati & Raharja, 2020).

Conflict and confrontation do not always have to end in dispute or nastiness. And once you know conflict is inevitable, you are then left with a few approaches to choose from (Patterson, Grenny, McMillan, & Switzler, 2012).

1. You act like it isn't happening and internalize your emotions about it. Nothing changes and you bear the brunt of the situation while the other person may never even know there was an issue. In most instances, when you refuse to deal with anger directly, it comes out in other ways.

2. You get angry or upset and confront the person emotionally instead of logically.

3. You deal with the situation in a strategic way that greatly increases the chances of a successful, drama-free resolution. You have a *brave conversation*.

Reflection

Which of the three preceding approaches is your go-to when it comes to conflict? How is your approach serving you? Be honest!

*Visit **go.SolutionTree.com/leadership** to access a reproducible reflection guide for this chapter.*

Let me share a real-life scenario and how it would develop using each of these three methods. Suppose a colleague continually critiques your work but isn't open to your feedback on hers. You have, from your perspective, taken the feedback and even used it to improve your outcomes. However, when you try to offer constructive input, your colleague gets defensive and makes comments like, "I think it's good enough, but thanks anyway." You are certain your suggestions are relevant and would really improve your colleague's work.

First, suppose you decide to ignore the situation. Nothing changes in your colleague's response. She continues to make suggestions to you, but refuses to take any from you. You stop offering suggestions even though they would likely improve the outcomes. You refuse to take your colleague's suggestions, even when they are good ones. Your anger bubbles out in other ways like sending passive-aggressive emails, showing up late to meetings with this person, and nonverbal communication like eye rolls, heavy sighs, or walking past without greeting the person. You may even talk about your colleague behind her back in an attempt to drum up support for your perspective. Has this made the situation better? No! In fact, the whole work environment is now more stressful for everyone, you are unhappy, and all those good ideas are going to waste because neither party is using them.

So if that didn't work, you try expressing your anger. Rather than holding it all in, you come at your colleague with a full emotional outburst. All your pent-up anger and frustration come out in a tirade that ends up sounding like a personal attack because you discharge every thought you've had about the situation and the person. In return, your colleague gets angry too and unleashes every frustration she's felt about you. Or, worse yet, she is silent, hurt, tearful, or even flees the scene. Again—was this effective? You may have let the immediate feelings out but your relationship with your colleague is now severely damaged. This short encounter may cause a long-term or permanent fissure that will be difficult, if not impossible, to repair. It can also affect the entire team or department and cause strife for everyone. The good ideas each of you has to offer are now most certainly not going to be exchanged.

So, if neither of the first two approaches worked, you dig into the third option: the brave conversation. In this chapter, I use the following questions to build understanding of this idea.

- What is a brave conversation?
- Why use brave conversations to deal with conflict?
- How do you have a brave conversation?

To answer these questions, I'll explore some research from brilliant minds and build your skill set.

What Is a Brave Conversation?

There are a few ways to define *a brave conversation*. Specifically, two definitions have impacted me and my practice, so I'll focus on them.

Author Brené Brown uses the term *rumble* to describe a difficult conversation. Brown (2018) states:

> A rumble is a discussion, conversation, or meeting defined by a commitment to lean into vulnerability, to stay curious and generous, to stick with the messy middle of problem identification and solving, to take a break and circle back when necessary, to be fearless in owning our parts and . . . to listen with the same passion with which we want to be heard. (p. 10)

In their book *Crucial Conversations: Tools for Talking When Stakes Are High*, coauthors Kerry Patterson, Joseph Grenny, Ron McMillan, and Al Switzler (2012) define a *crucial conversation* as, "A discussion between two or more people where (1) stakes are high, (2) opinions vary, and (3) emotions run strong" (p. 3).

It is easy to see the common threads in these two definitions.

- Complex context
- Critical issues
- Multiple perspectives
- Emotional stakes

Put simply, anytime people coming to a shared experience with varying perspectives and a lot of emotion invested face conflict, that merits a brave conversation.

Before moving forward, I'll revisit the scenario that opened the chapter to make sure it is a situation that merits a brave conversation.

- **Complex context:** Multiple colleagues are working to achieve shared outcomes.

- **Critical issues:** The work colleagues do together includes time for discussion, indicating this conflict concerns critical issues.

- **Multiple perspectives:** At least two people with different viewpoints are coming together to discuss and give feedback.

- **Emotional stakes:** When you are willing to take feedback but your colleague is not, emotions are elicited on both sides. Anger or defensiveness results, neither of which are helpful in working collaboratively for a shared purpose.

While ignoring or reacting likely makes the situation worse, why is having a brave conversation the most effective method to move things forward?

Reflection

Define *brave conversation*.

Why Use Brave Conversations to Deal With Conflict?

Here is the brutal truth: any response other than a brave conversation has a real and lasting negative impact. It impacts the organization in which you work and your relationship with the person on the other side of the dispute. Simply put, when leaders do not manage conflict well, it has a negative impact on the organization as a whole. Conversely, when leaders do manage conflict properly with an appropriate, effective, and strategic approach, it can have positive impacts and results—for example, increased creativity and innovation (Larasati & Raharja, 2020).

In addition to avoiding negative repercussions, brave conversations also have far-reaching positive implications. Patterson and colleagues (2012) identify research-based outcomes beyond the impact on the immediate situation.

1. The ability to have a brave conversation can kick-start your career. Simply put, the most influential individuals are those who master having difficult conversations. People who hold these difficult

conversations are able to express controversial or difficult content in a productive way. They are both honest and effective.

2. The entire organization's performance can improve. When people do not speak up—when crucial conversations do not happen—productivity and positivity decline. If people are willing to speak up when they see things going wrong, projects are far less likely to fail. In the worst companies, ineffective performers are transferred—effectively ignoring the problem. In the highest-performing organizations, everyone holds one another accountable, regardless of level or position.

3. Your relationships can improve when you are willing to have difficult conversations. People who consistently choose to have productive conversations rather than holding in emotions or attacking the other person have a better chance for their relationships to flourish as a result. When you avoid disagreements, you compromise your true feelings and store up frustration. Avoiding conflict can also negatively impact your relationships because you cut off honest communication with other people in your life. Conversely, disagreeing productively can provide deeper understanding and make it easier to connect with friends, partners, and coworkers (Scott, 2020).

4. Having brave conversations can improve your own health! Research shows your immune system improves and your susceptibility to life-threatening diseases decreases when you hold brave conversations. Holding in negative emotions and engaging in toxic conversations damages your health. A 2013 study finds that bottling up your emotions can increase the risk of premature death, including death from cancer (Chapman, Fiscella, Kawachi, Duberstein, & Muennig, 2013). Additional negative health-related consequences that may result from avoiding conflict include "mental health challenges, such as depression, anxiety, and increased stress," which talking about the disagreement can mitigate (Sreenivasan & Weinberger, 2018).

It's important to note that, typically, men and women have different approaches to conflict, especially workplace conflict. For example, women are more likely to avoid conflict because they do not want others to perceive them as aggressive (Parker, 2021). However, when women do have brave conversations, they benefit themselves, their colleagues, and their organizations (Parker, 2021).

- Women who take on the role of mediator are better able to facilitate an outcome acceptable to all parties and meet organizational interests than their male counterparts.

- Women in leadership roles show a greater ability to adjust behavior to situations rather than relying on power-based or autonomous behaviors.

- When women negotiate, they are better able to show empathy and respect to help facilitate the resolution of conflicts.

So now you know. Ignoring the situation won't help. Reacting with emotion does damage. Having a brave conversation can have a positive impact on the situation with even broader positive implications. The next step, then, is to strategically build your skills to have more brave conversations.

Reflection

Why should you have brave conversations?

How Do You Have a Brave Conversation?

Brave conversations are difficult. If they weren't, you wouldn't have to be brave to have them. While there is no linear approach to the process, reviewing the research and reflecting on my own experience, there are a few essential strategies I want to share that will help you along the way. In my work, I regularly refer to *Crucial Conversations: Tools for Talking When Stakes Are High* (Patterson et al., 2012) and *Learning by Doing: A Handbook for Professional Learning Communities at Work* (DuFour, DuFour, Eaker, Many, & Mattos, 2016). Following, you will find strategies from these two texts along with insights from my own key learnings.

1. **Make a plan:** A surefire way to make the mess even bigger is to react in the moment or jump into the conversation without thinking it through.

    - Develop a clear idea of what you hope results from the discussion, including what you want for yourself, for and from the other person, and for your relationship moving forward.

    - Play out the situation in your head and even practice the words you plan to say. You may even want to role play the conversation with a trusted friend to build your comfort and confidence.

    - Make a bulleted list of your key points—not necessarily to use as while talking, but because writing things down aids processing and memory (Goodwin, 2018).

2. **Reflect:** Remember, you have a part in this situation too.

   - Consider and own the ways you may have contributed to the conflict.

   - Decide what you are willing to do or commit to in order to improve things.

3. **Make the conversation as safe as possible:** Blindsiding people with a difficult conversation when they aren't expecting it or in locations where they do not feel comfortable is likely to lead to more conflict. This is an opportunity to give a little to put the other person in a more comfortable position where, hopefully, the person is more likely to engage and not become defensive or feel attacked.

   - Schedule a time to talk with the person and convey the topic in advance. Meet at a time that works for the other person's schedule.

   - Meet in the other person's office or use a virtual meeting if the other person prefers.

4. **Launch the dialogue strategically:** Easing into the conversation, rather than jumping into the deep end, helps get things started on the right foot.

   - Express appreciation for the other person's time.

   - Acknowledge that the conversation may be a little awkward, but it's important.

   - Consider starting a brave conversation by saying, "I'd really appreciate it if you would allow me to share my perspective fully without interrupting." If the other person tries to interrupt while you are talking, simply state, "Please let me finish. I promise I'll be quiet and hear your perspective when I've shared mine."

5. **Be concise:** If you have a plan and clear intentions, you should then be able to concisely articulate your perspective and your desired outcomes.

   - Avoid rambling. It makes you seem less confident and can leave the other person unsure of your desired outcome.

   - State your perspective briefly and neutrally. In doing so, you create a space to acknowledge the lens through which you are considering the situation and convey that you are coming at the situation from a fact-seeking perspective. In my experience, an effective strategy for doing this is to begin with a statement like, "I am coming at this situation from my own lens, where I am seeing [preplanned statement of your perspective]. I know you are coming at this from your own lens, and that may be different than mine."

- Use I-statements when discussing emotions. Sentence frames like "I feel _____ because _____" or "I understand why you feel _____" reduce hostility in contentious discussions (Rogers, Howieson, & Neame, 2018).

- Conclude by expressing your desired outcomes—What do you hope will be the result of the conversation?

6. **Listen:** This can be a hard part, because by stopping to listen and really understand the other person's perspective, you give up control of the conversation. You must be willing to hear that person's view on the situation, and it may contain information that you may not be thrilled to hear. However, remember that a conversation is two-directional.

- Offer the floor and be quiet while the other person responds. Resist interrupting.

- Be willing to push pause on the discussion, as the other person may need or want time to process what you have said before responding. This is part of the process, though it can certainly feel excruciating if you were hoping for a quick resolution.

- Remain calm and manage your nonverbal reactions. This is no time for eye rolls, big sighs, or other dismissive body language.

- Apply active listening strategies. Key elements of *active listening* include maintaining eye contact, waiting for the speaker to pause before asking clarifying questions, asking questions to ensure understanding, giving verbal and nonverbal signals to show you are listening, and summarizing to ensure accuracy and show understanding (Schilling, 2012).

7. **Attempt to find mutual purpose or shared perspectives:** After sharing your perspective and hearing from the other person, there will almost certainly be common ground. With the other person's perspective, you will have a more complete view of the situation and be more informed on how to move forward.

- Use techniques like paraphrasing to restate what you heard and affirm that you were listening. I like to use the phrasing, "What I think I heard you say was _____."

- If you are unsure about any points, ask questions to understand. As with paraphrasing, this helps you see through the other person's lens and signals you care about understanding the other person's perspective and creating an improved reality.

- Seek out and state points or aspects of the discussion where you agree and build on those.

8. **Dig in on disagreements:** Perhaps your colleague is unable to meet all the expectations you hoped for, and maybe you are unable to meet the ones the person has presented to you. Where can you meet in the middle to start moving forward?

- When there are points where you continue to disagree or have differing perspectives, talk together to try to find compromise points.

- Find similarities in perspectives or priorities and come to consensus so you can both move forward with certain understandings or commitments in place. It is important to clarify these agreements to avoid confusion or underlying continued disagreement. In practice, this sounds like, "Based on our conversation, it seems like we can agree that [common understandings]. Can we both agree that these are points where more focus is needed?"

9. **Conclude with clarity:** After both sides share their perspectives, identify points of agreement and compromises on disagreements to ensure you both walk away from the conversation with the same understanding. This dramatically increases the likelihood that what you just discussed will actually come to fruition.

- Summarize each person's accountability points. Make a short list of what each person will do or change going forward.

- Consider sending a follow-up email to reiterate how much you appreciate your colleague's time and to restate your shared agreements. Not only does this clarify the conversation but it also creates a history of the conversation should you ever need it.

Think back to the scenario that opened this chapter (page 112). How would a brave conversation look in that scenario? What might the result be? While I certainly cannot guarantee that all issues will be resolved and the colleague will now be magically open to receiving and acting on feedback, I am confident the outcomes will be dramatically improved over doing nothing or having an emotional reaction. Figure 6.1 displays a guide you can use when planning and conducting a brave conversation.

─────────────── *Reflection* ───────────────

How will you have brave conversations?

Conclusion

Brave conversations are not easy. They are uncomfortable and anxiety provoking. However, these are signs they are also *important*. If they didn't matter, they would be as easy as a discussion over a recent movie, a topic on which there's already shared agreement, or any other pleasant conversation. The fact that they are hard, that they push you out of your comfort zone, and that they require planning and strategy indicate they are essential work. Brown (2018) writes, "I always bring my core values to feedback conversations. I specifically bring courage, which means that I don't choose comfort over being respectful and honest—choosing politeness over respect is not respectful" (p. 202). Only by being brave and honest can you navigate the tough conversations and take charge of working to find a better resolution. As a woman leader, regardless of your role, learning to navigate difficult conversations is an essential skill for your own development, professional growth and progress, and even your own mental health. As with any skill, you must practice, but perfection is not the target. Rather, making progress, developing your confidence, and applying skills to adapt to different situations are invaluable to your success.

─────────────── *Reflection* ───────────────

Imagine that, in your current role, you learn a colleague has taken credit for a plan you developed. Apply the strategies in this chapter to brainstorm how you would handle the situation.

Think of a situation where you should have had a difficult conversation— professionally or personally—but didn't. Why did you avoid the conversation? What were the outcomes?

Think of a situation where you engaged in a difficult conversation— professionally or personally—and it didn't end as well as you would have liked. What would you do again? What would you do differently if you had the chance to do it all over?

Think of a situation where you engaged in a difficult conversation—
professionally or personally—and successfully navigated it. How did you
prepare? How do you know it was successful? How did you feel afterward?

Planning questions:

- What's the conflict?

- Who do you need to talk with to try to improve the situation?

- What does "better" look like?

Key Steps	Your Notes
Make a plan. • What are you hoping results from the conversation? • Practice the conversation. Consider role-playing it with a trusted friend or colleague. • Make a bulleted list of key points.	
Reflect. • What's your role in the conflict? Be honest! • What are your boundaries related to moving forward?	
Make the conversation as safe as possible. • Schedule the time with the other person in advance. • Meet in the other person's space or use a virtual platform if that's preferred.	

Figure 6.1: Planning guide for brave conversations.   continued ▶

Key Steps	Your Notes
Launch the dialogue strategically. • Express appreciation for the other person's time. • Acknowledge that the conversation may be awkward, but is important. • Use a starter stem like, "It would be great if I could share my thinking without being interrupted, then I'll do the same for you."	
Be concise. • Get to the point and don't ramble. Practicing ahead helps! • State your perspective briefly and in a neutral tone. • Use I-statements. • End by expressing your desired outcomes.	
Listen. • Be quiet when the other person responds. • Be willing to pause the conversation to allow the other person space to process the information and his or her emotions. • Remain calm and monitor your nonverbal reactions. • Apply active listening strategies.	
Attempt to find mutual purpose or shared perspectives. • Use paraphrasing. • Ask questions to understand. • Seek out and state points where you agree or have common ground.	
Dig in on disagreements. • Try to find compromise points. • Find a place where you can both agree to move forward.	

Conclude with clarity.	
• Summarize each person's accountability points or next steps. • Consider sending a follow-up email to show gratitude for the time and to clearly restate your shared agreements for moving forward.	

*Visit **go.SolutionTree.com/leadership** for a free reproducible version of this figure.*

References and Resources

Brown, B. (2018). *Dare to lead: Brave work, tough conversations, whole hearts.* New York: Random House.

Chapman, B. P., Fiscella, K., Kawachi, I., Duberstein, P., & Muennig, P. (2013). Emotion suppression and mortality risk over a 12-year follow-up. *Journal of Psychosomatic Research*, 75(4), 381–385.

DuFour, R., DuFour, R., Eaker, R., Many, T. W., & Mattos, M. (2016). *Learning by doing: A handbook for Professional Learning Communities at Work* (3rd ed.). Bloomington, IN: Solution Tree Press.

Goodwin, B. (2018, April 1). Research matters: the magic of writing stuff down. Alexandria, VA: Association for Supervision and Curriculum Development. Accessed at https://www.ascd.org/el/articles/the-magic-of-writing-stuff-down on January 11, 2022.

Larasati, R., & Raharja, S. (2020). *Conflict management in improving schools effectiveness.* Accessed at https://atlantis-press.com/article/125933565.pdf on January 11, 2022.

Parker, S. (2021). Managing conflict. *Women in Research.* Accessed at https://womeninresearch.org.au/managing-conflict on January 11, 2022.

Patterson, K., Grenny, J., McMillan, R., & Switzler, A. (2012). *Crucial conversations: Tools for talking when stakes are high* (2nd ed.). New York: McGraw-Hill.

Rogers, S. L., Howieson, J., & Neame, C. (2018). I understand you feel that way, but I feel this way: The benefits of I-language and communicating perspective during conflict. *PeerJ* 6:e4831. Accessed at https://peerj.com/articles/4831 on November 17, 2021.

Schilling, D. (2012, November 9). Ten steps to effective listening. *Forbes.* Accessed at https://forbes.com/sites/womensmedia/2012/11/09/10-steps-to-effective-listening/?sh=1c955c443891 on January 11, 2022.

Scott, E. (2020, September 20). Effects of conflict and stress on relationships. *Verywell Mind.* Accessed at https://verywellmind.com/the-toll-of-conflict-in-relationships-3144952 on January 11, 2022.

Sreenivasan, S., & Weinberger, L. E. (2018, March 15). *Conflicts in relationships* [Blog post]. Accessed at https://psychologytoday.com/us/blog/emotional-nourishment/201803/conflict-in-relationships on January 11, 2022.

Part 3

Self-Growth

Jessica Kanold-McIntyre is an educational consultant and author committed to supporting teacher implementation of rigorous mathematics curriculum and assessment practices blended with research-informed instructional practices. She works with teachers to meet the needs of students. Specifically, Jessica specializes in building and supporting the collaborative teacher culture through the curriculum, assessment, and instruction cycle. She has served as a middle school principal, assistant principal, and mathematics teacher and leader. As principal of Aptakisic Junior High School in Buffalo Grove, Illinois, Jessica supported her teachers in implementing initiatives, such as the Illinois Learning Standards; the Next Generation Science Standards; and the College, Career, and Civic Life Framework for Social Studies State Standards, while also supporting a one-to-one iPad environment for all students. She focused on teacher instruction through the professional learning community (PLC) process, creating learning opportunities on formative assessment practices, data analysis, and student engagement. She previously served as assistant principal at Aptakisic, where she led and supported special education, response to intervention (RTI), and English learner staff through the PLC process. As a mathematics teacher and leader, Jessica strived to create equitable and rigorous learning opportunities for all students while also providing them with cutting-edge 21st century experiences that engage and challenge them. As a mathematics leader, she developed and implemented a districtwide process for the Common Core State Standards in Illinois and led a collaborative process to create mathematics curriculum guides for K–8 mathematics, algebra 1, and algebra 2. She has also served as a board member for the National Council of Supervisors of Mathematics.

Jessica earned a bachelor's degree in elementary education from Wheaton College and a master's degree in educational administration from Northern Illinois University.

To learn more about Jessica's work, follow @jkanold on Twitter.

To book Jessica Kanold-McIntyre for professional development, contact pd@SolutionTree.com.

CHAPTER 7

Seeking Mentorship and Sharing Your Expertise

Jessica Kanold-McIntyre

Everyone who achieves excellence gets support and coaching
along the way.

—James M. Kouzes and Barry Z. Posner

As a little girl, I was always playing school, practicing and preparing to become a teacher. I wanted to be a teacher just like my dad! When I was hired to my first teaching job, I was so excited about getting my very own classroom and starting my career. Little did I know that first teaching job would connect me with one of my great mentors and role models of my career, Theresa Dunkin.

Theresa is a retired superintendent of a K–8 district in the suburbs of northwestern Illinois. She was the epitome of a "daring leader"—someone who leads with courage and cares for and connects to the people they lead (Brown, 2018, p. 12). Theresa's genuine care and compassion for others inspired collaboration and trust. She encouraged a culture that valued teachers as learners and leaders and endorsed risk taking as a necessity in moving the vision forward. Her leadership was a living model of leading with heart: "Leadership is about love. . . . You must fall in love with leading, with the purpose you serve, and the people with whom you work in fulfilling that purpose" (DuFour & Marzano, 2011, p. 197).

Theresa had a passion for leading and serving others, and she encouraged me in many different ways. Sometimes her nudges were actual words of encouragement, but more often they were intertwined in our conversations and the opportunities she often guided my way. She pushed the limits I had unknowingly set for myself—the myths I had told myself about my potential—by providing opportunities for me to step out of my comfort zone and into courage. Her actions were whispers of advocation and trust. She believed I could do the job. And that was the push I needed to believe in myself as a leader.

In part thanks to Theresa, my leadership journey started much earlier than I had envisioned. At the age of twenty-seven, I was hired to be a junior high assistant principal. By twenty-nine, I was serving as the principal of the building. When I think back to the beginning of my leadership story, I am humbled and reminded that I did not arrive at these positions of leadership due to my own innate ability or skill. I was able to begin acquiring the "observable, learnable set of skills and abilities" that constitute leadership because of key mentoring relationships early in my career (Kouzes & Posner, 2016, p. 5).

The term *mentor* refers to "someone who teaches or gives help and advice to a less experienced and often younger person," ("Mentor," n.d.a) or a "trusted counselor or guide" ("Mentor," n.d.b). It is interesting to note the word *trusted* here. A mentor is not simply someone who has positional authority or who has been assigned to you. A mentor in your leadership journey is someone you trust and intentionally seek out for support, guidance, and feedback. It is someone you personally connect with or look up to as a leader you hope to become.

Reflection

Who are the mentors who have been a part of your story? What was it about their mentorship that had an impact on your leadership-skill development?

---

*Visit **go.SolutionTree.com/leadership** to access a reproducible reflection guide for this chapter.*

Having a mentor increases your drive to achieve goals and effect change. According to organizational psychologist Adam Grant (2016) in his book *Originals: How Non-Conformists Move the World*:

> Role models have a foundational impact on how children grow up to express their originality. When hundreds of women who graduated from Radcliffe College were asked in their early thirties to name the people who had the greatest influence on their lives, the vast majority mentioned parents and mentors. Seventeen years later, psychologists Bill Peterson and Abigail Stewart measured the women's commitments to changing things for the better for future generations. Naming a parent as a major influence accounted for less than one percent of the women's motivations to drive meaningful change. The women who were pursuing originality had been influenced a decade and a half earlier not by their parents, but by their mentors: Mentioning a mentor accounted for 14 percent of differences in women's desires to improve the world. (p. 171)

Furthermore, in a 2013 research study examining strategies to increase the proportion of female superintendents, female superintendent participants suggest mentoring as a beneficial support in navigating the superintendency and encourage all women interested in a superintendent position to seek out a mentor (Wallace, 2015). Chief executive officer in the Office of Educational Services for Los Angeles Unified School District Thelma Meléndez de Santa Ana (2008) reports the same finding in her article "Opening Up the Superintendency," and recommends that any woman who aspires to lead at any level in an organization would benefit from a mentor along the way. A mentor has the ability to change the trajectory of your career by adding value to your growth and development toward your goals while also helping build your self-confidence as a leader and connecting you with a broader leadership network.

Mentoring is also a mutually beneficial relationship. For mentors, the relationship offers an opportunity to leave a legacy of their work for the next generation of leaders. For mentees, the relationship is a way for them to learn from the wisdom and experiences of another leader to grow and become better leaders themselves. Mentoring relationships are beneficial at all stages of your leadership journey and can serve different purposes. Mentors are not just for first-year teachers or first-year administrators. Moreover, you may have more than one mentor at a time. If you "seek multiple mentors with diverse expertise and experience, you'll get more access to better guidance" (Grant, 2019). Every leader or aspiring leader has a responsibility to seek out and engage with trusted mentors as well as mentor others. In this chapter, I discuss both of these responsibilities and strategies for each.

Responsibility to Seek Out Trusted Mentors

If you research famous athletes, actors, leaders, or artists, you will usually discover they had mentors who guided, challenged, and encouraged them. These people often supported them, helped them master their fields, and pushed them in areas where they needed it. To become your best self personally and professionally, you can't do it alone. To serve your school and school community well, you have a responsibility to become the best version of yourself as a leader. A mentor can help challenge fixed beliefs you may have set for yourself, and challenge you to try to new things outside your comfort zone—pushing you to think differently in areas where you need to grow.

To become the best version of yourself as a leader, "you have to seek new experiences, test yourself, make some mistakes and keep climbing back up that learning curve" (Kouzes & Posner, 2016, p. 97). You must be willing to take risks, reflect on feedback, and take new steps going forward. Trusted mentors play a role in this learning process and your growth as a leader. They can help you reach your goals. With this in mind, you should consider certain key qualities and characteristics to look for in a mentor while also being strategic about how to set up a successful relationship.

───────── *Reflection* ─────────

What qualities do you value in a mentor? Describe your ideal mentor.

The key to identifying and connecting with the right mentor is to first identify your goals in your areas of desired growth. These goals can be related to both personal and professional growth, which often overlap. For example, you might have a goal to become a more compassionate leader at work, which starts with your own personal growth and reflection. Alternatively, maybe you struggle with self-care due to the high demands of your job and want to take better care of yourself while maintaining performance in your role.

Once you set your growth goals, the next step is to brainstorm about leaders you know who could support you and your goals or areas of desired growth. A trusted mentor could be a friend, a parent, a coworker, a supervisor, a college professor, a colleague in another district, someone you met at a conference, a connection from a state or national organization—the list goes on. Match potential mentors' areas of experience and expertise with your goals.

A mentor for personal growth might help you wrestle with questions that build a deeper understanding of yourself and how you work. Self-knowledge and awareness of your strengths are prerequisites for reaching your potential (Drucker, 2004). Your mentor may ask questions to help you more clearly identify your strengths, weaknesses, fears, and feelings within your leadership story. As author Brené Brown (2018) writes in *Dare to Lead*, we, as leaders, must "invest time attending to our own fears, feelings, and history or we'll find ourselves managing our own unproductive behaviors" (p. 113).

A mentor for professional growth can provide guidance and support as you navigate a new position or aspire for a new position. This mentor could be someone who already has the job you seek or is in a position beyond that job. For example, if you are an assistant principal seeking to advance to a principal position, you might look to your principal, a principal from a neighboring district, or even a former or retired principal. Whoever you intentionally identify, it should be someone you respect and believe will help you achieve your goals and actions for areas of development. Your mentor does not have to be a direct supervisor.

As you think through your list of potential trusted mentors, consider the personal and professional characteristics and qualities important to you in a mentor. Here are some qualities and characteristics to consider.

- **Curiosity:** Find mentors who will listen and ask questions, share parts of their own stories to show vulnerability, and treat guidance and feedback as a two-way street.

- **Generosity:** Great mentors have no agenda except to invest in you. They are there to add value to your leadership story: "Enabling the development of others' leadership requires moving away from a focus on one's personal power so that others may be recognized for their achievements" (Valerio & Sawyer, 2016). A mentor may introduce you to other leaders, connect you with professional organizations, and bring you into leadership experiences that push you beyond your own perceived capacity.

- **Integrity:** Mentors should demonstrate integrity in their work and act as role models. A mentor who demonstrates integrity "chooses courage over comfort; what's right over what is fun, fast or easy; and practices their values rather than just professing them" (Brown, 2018, p. 226).

- **Growth mindset:** To learn from the best, you need to look for mentors who continue to learn and grow themselves. Whether you are an emerging leader or have been in a leadership position for many years, to become the best leader you can be, think of learning itself as the "master skill of leadership" (Kouzes & Posner, 2016, p. 49).

Finally, consider whether your goals are best suited to a mentor who shares your demographics or background. Often, a mentor's race, gender, and other personal characteristics are not as relevant as finding a mentor who believes in inclusive leadership. Someone who is very different from you in terms of race, gender, and other personal characteristics might offer unique insights. However, certain goals or growth areas may call for mentors with whom you share experiences or characteristics. For example, Kenneth R. Magdaleno (2006), a professor at California State University, Fresno, finds that same-gender mentors can provide support for personal experiences with gender barriers. This does not mean women should *only* seek female mentors. In some cases, "receiving mentorship from senior males can increase compensation and career progress satisfaction for women, particularly for those working in male-dominated industries" (Valerio & Sawyer, 2016). As you reflect on possible mentors, there may be different points in your career where you find a female mentor could support and provide guidance in areas where a male mentor may not have experience and vice versa. The key is finding a mentor who exhibits curiosity, generosity, integrity, and a growth mindset.

Once you reflect on a potential mentor for you in your leadership journey, there are specific strategies to consider as you connect and build the relationship.

Reflection

What personal or professional goals are you currently working on?

Who is someone you could seek out for support and mentoring?

Strategies for Success With a Mentor

As a mentee, the mentoring relationship is about developing your skills as a leader. But that does not mean you are a passive recipient of information from your mentor. There are actions you should take to ensure success. The following sections describe four strategies for success with a mentor.

Connect With Your Mentor

It is important to formally ask your chosen person to be your mentor so the person knows your interest and intent. It is best if you can ask in person, but email is also acceptable. You could start by asking your potential mentor if he or she has time to meet for coffee or a few minutes to connect on a virtual call. Either way, when you ask someone to be your mentor, remember to explain why you are interested in that person as a mentor and what your goals are for the mentorship. This allows the potential mentor to make an informed decision about fully committing to the mentorship. The following script exemplifies how you might begin the conversation.

> *Thank you for meeting with me today. I was wondering if you would be interested in mentoring me for this school year. I am hoping to continue to build my leadership skills in the area of [your goal], and I would value your insight and guidance as I continue to grow. I have always admired how you are able to lead with [your potential mentor's strength] and I want to make that a focus of my work this year. Please feel free to take time to answer; maybe we can circle back later this week.*

Set Clear Expectations

Once you officially have a mentor, then you can work out the details of meeting frequency, time frame, and location. This gives you both an opportunity to discuss what is realistic, given your schedules. Depending on your goals and your time line, these meetings could occur monthly or even once per quarter. There may be other times you meet weekly because you are working toward a goal that needs more frequent communication. These meetings can occur virtually, in person, or on the phone.

To guide your time together, be sure to create an agenda for each meeting. It is beneficial to both parties to build the agenda together; unless you know there are specific topics you want to discuss, your mentor may have great insight into topics that would be helpful to discuss. At the end of each meeting, collaboratively list topics you hope to address at the next meeting.

During your first meeting, it is also important to discuss boundaries for your mentoring relationship. As Brown (2018) explains, "setting boundaries is making clear what is okay and what's not okay, and why" (p. 39). For example, is it OK for you to call your mentor on the phone when you need advice and perspective, or would your mentor prefer you email your question? What are your agreements on confidentiality? What type of accountability are you looking for from your mentor?

Stay Open to Feedback and Accountability

Mentors are meant to push and challenge you to become a better version of yourself. This means they are there to provide feedback and keep you accountable to your goals. Therefore, you must be willing to receive feedback. At the root of this mindset is your belief in your ability to learn: "If you believe that you can learn, it's significantly more likely that you will" (Kouzes & Posner, 2016, p. 51). It is important to enter the mentorship with an open mind for growth and curiosity to learn. As you communicate your goals (see page 130) to your mentor, be sure to discuss how your mentor can help keep you accountable to your goals. For example, would you benefit from regular check-ins via text on how you are progressing? Would you rather bring artifacts to share at one of your meetings?

Believe in Your Ability to Become a Better Leader

In *Learning Leadership: The Five Fundamentals of Becoming an Exemplary Leader*, coauthors James M. Kouzes and Barry Z. Posner (2016) find that to become a better leader than you are right now, "the first fundamental thing you have to do is to *believe you can* make a difference and *believe you can* be a better leader" (p. 6). This is critical. There is always room for growth and improvement; it may not be easy, but the first step is believing you can be better. Everyone can be better!

Throughout your leadership story, there will be many moments when a mentor will encourage and help you grow into the leader you have the potential to become. Are you open to listening? Are you seeking to continually grow and become the best version of yourself?

------- *Reflection* -------

What experiences have helped to build your belief in yourself as a leader?

Another way you can continue to learn and grow as a leader is by sharing your knowledge and mentoring other women in their journeys.

Responsibility to Mentor and Serve Others

Female leaders—*all* leaders—in education have a responsibility to continue to develop and show compassion for the next generation of leaders. The most successful and capable leaders want to see their organizations become even more successful in the next generation. They channel their ego needs away from themselves and into the larger goal of the organization (Collins, 2001). Not only are there benefits to the community of education and your organization but also to you personally. In her book *The Happiness Track: How to Apply the Science of Happiness to Accelerate Your Success*, Emma Seppälä (2016), science director of Stanford University's Center for Compassion and Altruism Research, finds that an other-focus mindset, especially in the form of compassion, leads to greater levels of trust, engagement, and health for the individual exhibiting compassion:

> Through compassion, you get in touch with your full potential for strength, power and vitality. Through compassion, you find purpose. When our brains move from a modality of self-focus and stress to a new modality of caring, nurturing and connecting, our heart rate decelerates and our ability to relax is strengthened, and we release hormones that are a key for connection and bonding. . . . Acting with compassion is as pleasurable, if not more than, receiving something. (p. 151)

Mentoring is an act of compassion toward another person. However, there is an art to mentoring others with compassion. Mentoring is not just imparting knowledge in the hope that your mentee will absorb some of it. Mentoring is about guiding and sharing wisdom through a connected partnership while also allowing mentees to find their own way and make their own decisions. My experience has been the more I demonstrate compassion toward others, the more they are willing to be vulnerable and ask for help, which in turn builds deeper trust. Trust is a crucial aspect of life because it makes people feel safe (Seppälä, 2016). Creating a trusting mentor-mentee relationship is the foundation for success.

Reflection

Have you been a mentor to others in your personal or professional life?
How did that relationship benefit you and your mentee?

If you are considering becoming a mentor, there are specific actions you can take to help ensure a successful mentorship that builds trust and supports growth.

Mentor Actions for a Successful Mentorship

Think about the best coaches or mentors you ever had—what made them great? When you brought issues to their attention, how did they respond? In my experience, the best mentors empower you to make your own decisions and ask questions to help you process your own thoughts rather than giving you solutions or advice immediately. Mentorship is about guiding, not directing. There are three overarching mentor actions for a successful mentorship: (1) build trust, (2) share guidance and advice, and (3) offer feedback and encouragement.

Build Trust

To develop a trusting relationship with a mentee, it is important to understand how trust is built: "in the smallest of moments . . . not through heroic deeds, or even highly visible actions, but through paying attention, listening, and gestures of genuine care and connection" (Brown, 2018, p. 32). You show support to your mentee by listening and connecting on both a personal and professional level.

In a *Harvard Business Review* article, Rick Woolworth (2019), cofounder and president of Telemachus, a nonprofit with a mission of mentoring emerging leaders, suggests getting to know your mentees by asking them to share their stories. Woolworth's (2019) approach is to say:

> Start at the beginning and take your time—20 or 30 minutes. I may ask a few questions, and everything you say will be confidential between us. Then, when you're finished, I'll tell you my story if you want me to.

Woolworth (2019) goes on to say this type of opening activity allows you both to get to know each other personally and professionally. He is intentional about sharing a challenge or two he had to overcome personally or professionally in an effort to show he is also human (Woolworth, 2019). The key component to establishing a trusting mentorship is connection.

Additionally, it is smart to have a list of questions to engage in conversation with a mentee. The questions can help you learn more about your mentee, and may also help your mentee learn more about him- or herself. Here are a few to consider.

- What are you most proud of in your work?
- How do you disconnect from the busyness of life? How do you find stillness in your day?
- How would you define *long-term success*? What are your long-term career goals?
- How do you practice self-care?
- What hobbies or activities interest you?
- What's on your mind?

As your mentoring relationship continues over time, you will continue to build trust by remaining curious about your mentee's goals and values, being generous with your time and guidance, modeling integrity within your own leadership decisions, and showing a growth mindset for your own work and your work together.

Share Guidance and Advice

As Grant (2018) shares in his *Work in 0:60* video, "Good mentors help you follow their path, but great mentors help you navigate your own path." When a mentee brings a challenge or issue to you, avoid the urge to solve all problems for your mentee. In his book *The Coaching Habit*, Michael Bungay Stanier (2016), best-selling author and founder of Box of Crayons, provides clear guidance for how to say less and ask more. The goal is to figure out how you can "call the mentee forward to learn, improve and grow, rather than to just get something sorted out" (p. 40). He suggests starting with the question, "What's on your mind?" to get the conversation started and to help mentees begin to share (Stanier, 2016). Then, ask follow-up questions. Be patient in the process, asking only one question at a time (Stanier, 2016).

Stanier (2016), like Grant (2018), argues that the best mentors coach for development rather than performance. By coaching for *development*, you help build your mentee's skills and knowledge for the long term rather than just helping solve an immediate issue. If you have a tendency to provide solutions too quickly, you can use Stanier's (2016) *3P model*.

1. **Projects:** Consider if the challenge focuses on the content of the situation.

2. **People:** Consider the person or group you are working with; is there a relational issue you need to address?

3. **Patterns:** Consider patterns of behavior that may be contributing to the situation.

Usually, a question tied to one of these topics is the trigger for the real issue, or the issue that would benefit from your counsel and guidance. Dig into each of the three Ps (projects, people, and patterns) until you find the one at the heart of the matter. Once you determine the area of concern, then your guidance and questions can focus in on that specific area. Your goal is to help your mentee come up with a "course of action on their own" (Woolworth, 2019).

Offer Feedback and Encouragement

Your feedback and encouragement as a mentor have the potential to deeply impact your mentee's growth and development as a leader. *Feedback* is the process of providing information and data about progress toward specific goals. Of course, to provide effective feedback, you must be aware of your mentee's specific goals. Feedback must include actionable steps a mentee can take to improve, and then the mentee must follow through for new learning and growth to take place. As you look to provide feedback, consider phrasing it as questions rather than direct comments or lectures. Stay curious and dig deeper into understanding. Brown (2018) provides some examples of phrases you can use to get started.

- I'm curious about . . .
- Tell me more.
- I'm wondering . . .
- Help me understand . . .
- Tell me why this doesn't work for you.

Encouragement—positive feedback—is effective for building your relationship with your mentee (Kouzes & Posner, 2003). Providing encouragement shows that you see moments worth celebrating with your mentee. Don't pass up opportunities to celebrate your mentee for a job well done or a goal achieved. A note or word of encouragement can give someone a boost to keep working toward challenging goals. It was a word of encouragement from one of my mentors that launched my journey into a leadership position. I was teaching my third-period eighth-grade mathematics class when my assistant principal, a mentor of mine, walked through the door to tell me about an assistant principal opening in a nearby district. I clearly remember thinking, "Wow, does he *really* think I am ready? He must *actually* believe in me to go out of his way and tell me in person!" I had never imagined or planned on applying for an administrative job so soon. I was fresh from completing my master's in educational leadership and I was still in my twenties. "Am I really qualified?" I thought. "Do I have enough experience? Am I ready? What about my family?" There were so many questions running through my mind, but the most prominent thought was, "If Mr. Michels is encouraging me to apply, then he must think I am ready to start pursuing a career in an administrative position." Mr. Michels knew my career goals and my current level of performance in my role as a teacher and teacher leader. His encouragement and belief in me were just what I needed to take a step out of my comfort zone and into a role that would require courage.

Throughout my career, my mentors (family members, colleagues, and supervisors) encouraged me in my journey to become a teacher leader, assistant principal, principal, and even a district-level administrator. They saw in me a potential I was still discovering. Serving as a mentor to others not only contributes to the growth of another through sharing your knowledge and skills but also functions as a way to continue your legacy as a leader. Your compassion and commitment to focus on others also feeds into your own success and happiness as a leader.

Conclusion

Early in my teaching life, I did not aspire to be a building or district leader. Great leaders surrounded me in my personal and professional life, but I didn't believe I was near their quality of leadership, nor did I believe I ever could be. I was always very confident in my passion for teaching, but I waivered in my belief in my ability to be a leader. It was the encouragement and coaching of my mentors and leaders that helped me see myself differently and take a risk to start applying. I am a living example of how mentorship can build into and lift up the next generation of female leaders. When I think back to that little girl who knew she wanted to be a teacher, I will always be grateful to the many mentors who helped me to grow in my belief in myself and develop my skill set as an educator and leader. Every leader at every phase of leadership benefits from trusted guides along the way. If women want to have equal gender representation in leadership positions, it is critical for female leaders to surround themselves with great leaders and offer support to the next generation.

Reflection

As a woman in leadership, how are you mentoring and encouraging other potential leaders around you? Name one or two teachers or emerging leaders you could encourage and steward this school year.

References and Resources

Brown, B. (2018). *Dare to lead: Brave work, tough conversations, whole hearts.* New York: Random House.

Collins, J. (2001). *Good to great: Why some companies make the leap . . . and others don't.* New York: Harper Business.

Drucker, P. F. (2004, June). What makes an effective executive. *Harvard Business Review.* Accessed at https://hbr.org/2004/06/what-makes-an-effective-executive on February 18, 2022.

DuFour, R., & Marzano, R. J. (2011). *Leaders of learning: How district, school and classroom leaders improve student achievement.* Bloomington, IN: Solution Tree Press.

Gallagher, L., & Roberts, D. (2015, September 24). 40 under 40: The best advice I ever got. *Fortune.* Accessed at https://fortune.com/2015/09/24/40-under-40-best-advice-2015 on June 24, 2020.

Grant, A. (2016). *Originals: How non-conformists move the world.* New York: Viking.

Grant, A. (2018). *Work in 0:60* [Video file]. Accessed at https://facebook.com/AdamMGrant /posts/good-mentors-help-you-follow-their-path-great-mentors-help-you-navigate-your-own /2052255024825245 on June 25, 2020.

Grant, A. [@AdamMGrant]. (2019, October 14). You don't need a mentor. You need a group of mentors. The people who have the most sage advice for [Tweet]. *Twitter.* Accessed at https://twitter.com/adammgrant/status/1183738660124012548?lang=en on June 25, 2020.

Kouzes, J. M., & Posner, B. Z. (2003). *Encouraging the heart: A leader's guide to rewarding and recognizing others.* San Francisco. Jossey Bass.

Kouzes, J. M., & Posner, B. Z. (2016). *Learning leadership: The five fundamentals of becoming an exemplary leader.* Hoboken, NJ: Wiley.

Magdaleno, K. R. (2006). Mentoring Latina and Latino educational leaders. *Educación y Ciencia, 10*(34), 65–69.

Meléndez de Santa Ana, T. (2008). Opening up the superintendency. *Leadership*, *38*(S/O), 24–27.

Mentor. (n.d.a). In *The Britannica Dictionary online*. Accessed at https://britannica.com /dictionary/mentor on February 18, 2022.

Mentor. (n.d.b) In *Merriam-Webster online dictionary*. Accessed at https://merriam-webster.com /dictionary/mentor on June 22, 2020.

Peterson, B. E., & Stewart., A. J. (1996). Antecedents and contexts of generativity motivation at midlife. *Psychology and Aging*, *11*(1), 21–23.

Seppälä, E. (2016). *The happiness track: How to apply the science of happiness to accelerate your success*. New York: HarperCollins.

Stanier, M. B. (2016). *The coaching habit: Say less, ask more & change the way you lead forever*. Toronto, Ontario, Canada: Box of Crayons Press.

Valerio, A. M., & Sawyer, K. B. (2016, December 7). The men who mentor women. *Harvard Business Review*. Accessed at https://hbr.org/2016/12/the-men-who-mentor-women on January 17, 2022.

Wallace, T. (2015) Increasing the proportion of female superintendents in the 21st century. *Advancing Women in Leadership Journal*, *35*, 42–47.

Woolworth, R. (2019, August 9). Great mentors focus on the whole person, not just their career. *Harvard Business Review*. Accessed at https://hbr.org/2019/08/great-mentors-focus -on-the-whole-person-not-just-their-career?referral=03759&cm_vc=rr_item_page.bottom on March 5, 2020.

CHAPTER 8

Preparing for Promotion

Jasmine K. Kullar

> I always did something I was a little not ready to do. I think that's
> how you grow. When there's that moment of "Wow, I'm not really
> sure I can do this," and you push through those moments, that's
> when you have a breakthrough.
>
> —Marissa Mayer

To close the gender gap in education and have more female leaders join the
principal and superintendent ranks, women must begin thinking about
promotions and career advancement. Whether you are a teacher, an assistant
principal, a principal, or a central office administrator, think about the next step
in your career. Challenge yourself to move up in your career so you can make a
bigger impact on the students you serve. There are many obstacles and reasons
women in education are not promoted, but there are also many opportunities—
if you are prepared to take them. This chapter explores the mental preparation
and skills you can acquire to be ready to move up the career ladder.

--------- *Reflection* ---------

What are some reasons you have not moved up your career ladder yet? If you
are already at the top, what struggles did you go through to get there?

---

*Visit **go.SolutionTree.com/leadership** to access a reproducible reflection guide for this chapter.*

Why Do You Want a Promotion?

First and foremost, you have a decision to make. Do you want that promotion? It is a simple question, yet one some women hesitate to answer. You might

overthink it or dismiss it—but you must make a decision. Do you want to take that next step in your career? Where do you see yourself in five years? Doing what you're doing or in the next position doing more? Only you can decide whether you want to seek promotions or next-level job opportunities.

As part of that decision, you should analyze your reasons. Before going for any promotion or career change, make sure you know why you are going for it. Sometimes, people seek promotions for the wrong reasons, like the following.

- **Burnout:** Burnout is incredibly common among educators. Education professor and Fulbright Specialist Jenny Grant Rankin (2016) argues that teacher burnout is an international epidemic, and RAND Corporation surveys find that stress is the top reason teachers quit (Diliberti, Schwartz, & Grant, 2021). So, if your current position is wearing you out, you might think a promotion is the solution. If you are a teacher exhausted from being in the classroom, maybe you think getting out of the classroom and becoming an administrator will give you a break. Or if you're an assistant principal, tired of doing all the tasks related to bus duties, discipline, schedules, and so on, you look toward a principalship as potential relief. Or as a principal, you want to get out of the school and into the central office. Being tired of your current position is *not* a good reason for seeking that promotion. Higher-level jobs hardly ever involve fewer tasks or stressors—just different ones. Educational leaders field near-constant requests from stakeholders (Drake, 2021) and, as in most professions, "the reward for getting promoted is more work" (Crawford, 2018). The days become longer and longer as you have so many more responsibilities.

- **"I can do it better" mentality:** Most people have probably been in a situation where they thought, "If I had that job, I would do it better." Whether it's decisions, communication, or some practical task, people think they are better suited than the person who is currently doing the job. These people dream up their own ideas and plans that would be so much more effective if only they had that job. But thinking you can do it better than the current person is *not* a good reason for seeking that promotion. Until you are in that position, you cannot have the full perspective or knowledge. For instance, I've worked with some assistant principals who think they would be much better principals if they had the job. When they do become principals, they realize how much they didn't know and how many obstacles they could not see from the assistant principal seat.

- **Entitlement:** Sometimes people seek a promotion because they feel like it's their right—"I've been with the district a long time; I've been loyal, so now it's my turn." Some think seniority entitles them to be next in line for a promotion. They feel they deserve it—just because they have put in so many years in their current position. However, a certain number of months or years in a role does not qualify you to move up. As *Business Insider* editor Jacquelyn Smith (2013) writes, "Your contributions need to create value, and you should be perceived as the most logical choice for the new role." Feeling entitled to the promotion is *not* a good reason for seeking that promotion—focus on your accomplishments rather than the length of your tenure.

If these are some of the reasons you are seeking a promotion, you may want to rethink things. You want to ensure that once you have decided to pursue a promotion, it is for the right reasons. Instead of seeking that promotion because you're burned out, ask, "Why am I feeling that way in my current position? Are more work and more responsibility really going to fix that?" Instead of comparing yourself to the current person in the job, ask, "What unique skill set will I bring to the table that will enhance what is already being done?" Instead of developing a sense of entitlement based on the years you've put in, ask, "What value have I brought during my tenure, and more importantly, what value will I continue to bring to the table if I get that promotion?" Working with aspiring leaders, I find that the right reasons for seeking promotion include things like being ready to make an even bigger impact based on accomplishments in your current position, or wanting an opportunity to follow through on a vision for improving the school or district. Successful candidates demonstrate a passion for improvement and a commitment to personal and professional growth.

In other words, when thinking about why you want the promotion, think about how you can bring something to the position that makes your school or district better. Then think about what you get in return: Is it the contentment of knowing you can make a bigger impact on students? Knowing you will have the ability to change more student lives for the better? Challenging yourself so you grow professionally? Your promotion should benefit both you and the organization.

Once you've decided to go for that promotion, you can start preparing for the increased work and responsibility that will come with it.

Reflection

Why did you or why do you want to move up the career ladder?

How Can You Prepare for the Challenges That Come With Promotion?

It is important not to be naïve when thinking about that next position in your career. There is no doubt the higher up you go, the harder the job is going to be. You have to truly understand the challenges it will entail—but embrace those challenges instead of letting them intimidate you. The following sections outline common challenges that come with leadership roles, along with strategies for dealing with them. If you prepare for the challenge with these tools and skills, you may feel more confident applying for a new role, and you can overcome difficulties much more quickly and be more successful in that promotion.

Longer Hours

Most likely, you will work longer hours. Whether you go from teacher to assistant principal, assistant principal to principal, principal to central office administrator, or central office administrator to superintendent, you will probably be putting more hours in your new position. For instance, principals work an average of sixty hours a week (Sparks, 2016) while superintendents' workweeks may exceed eighty hours (Kim-Phelps, 2018; Marulli, 2021). With the ubiquity of cell phones and laptops, people are always reachable by call, text, or email—which makes it harder to clock out at 5:00 p.m. Don't shy away from these longer hours, but prepare for them with the following strategies.

- Establish a support system now with family and friends to help you.
- Start a self-care routine you can maintain in a more demanding role.
- Lean on others to help you—and don't be afraid to ask for help.
- Practice delegating, trusting others, and letting go of your need to be in control of everything.

Increased Responsibility

By definition, you will have more responsibility in your new role. For instance, as an assistant principal, you may just be responsible for a couple of departments or grade levels, but as a principal, you are responsible for the entire school. As a superintendent, you are responsible for the entire district. Don't shy away from increased responsibilities, but prepare for them with the following strategies.

- Begin seeking more responsibility now to get used to it. If you are a teacher looking to become an assistant principal, what higher-level responsibilities could you volunteer for? I once worked with a teacher who would spend her planning periods in the administrative office helping with student discipline investigations or parent phone calls. She was seeking more responsibilities specific to the job to which she was aspiring.

- Take on more in your current position. If higher-level responsibilities are not available, try taking on additional tasks in your current position. Anytime there is an opportunity to do more, do more. Don't wait passively for someone to ask for volunteers; actively step up. For example, if you are an assistant principal who wants to be a principal one day, volunteer to solve a problem you see in your school.

- Research and learn to become an expert in something. Make a point to learn new things that will help you in the job you aspire to. For instance, if you want to be a superintendent, you might learn about finances and work on becoming an expert on budgets. If the school or district you hope to work for has a specific focus or initiative, learn as much as you can about it and become an expert in that area.

Conflict and Negativity

As you move up in your career, you will likely deal with much more conflict and negativity. One reason for this is that people bring conflicts to leaders to solve. This is true at every level. Teachers may solve disputes between students, but superintendents deal with conflicts that arise between any and all stakeholders, including parents, teachers, principals, board members, business leaders, students, and so on. Using the COVID-19 pandemic as an example, superintendents faced heated debates and pressure from stakeholders regarding mask policies. As you become responsible for more people, the number of potential conflicts also increase and those conflicts become a source of negativity.

Another source of negativity is reactions to your decisions. As a leader, you must make decisions and, in most cases, you will not have 100 percent support or agreement. Some people will always be upset with you. A principal who changes the field trip policy, an assistant principal who decides to expel a student for participating in a fight, and a superintendent who hires a principal from outside the district will all face some upset constituents, even if they have majority support. Workforce development and human capital consulting firm chairman Glenn Llopis (2015) states, "Leadership requires mental toughness. If you are not being criticized, you are not leading and guiding the organization to grow, innovate, and explore endless possibilities." Again, you can handle it, but preparing with the following strategies will help you navigate through these situations more efficiently and effectively.

- Develop thick skin—you will never please everyone.
- Control how you respond, rather than reacting carelessly.
- Create a comprehensive decision-making process and own your decisions.

Accountability

The higher up you go, the more accountable you will be to your stakeholders. This means you will even be held accountable for other people's failures. No matter who is actually at fault, at the end of the day, it will fall on your shoulders because you are the leader. However, accountability does not just mean accepting blame; it also involves creating a positive culture around innovation, mistakes, and problem solving, as table 8.1 shows.

Table 8.1: Blame Versus Accountability

	Culture of Blame	Culture of Accountability
Believes	People are the problem. Admitting weaknesses makes you look weak.	People are problem solvers. We are all still learning.
Focuses On	Who is wrong The individual The past	What is wrong The process The future
Results In	Hiding problems Distrust Turf wars Waiting until told	Acknowledging problems and solutions Trust Interdepartmental cooperation and collaboration Taking initiative

Source: Adapted from Timms, 2017.

Accountability means focusing on fixing problems and being solution oriented (instead of blaming others), admitting when mistakes are made, being open minded to changing processes when they do not work, and so on (Timms, 2017). Don't shy away from being accountable, but prepare for it with the following strategies.

- Assume responsibility, even when you may not have directly done something wrong.
- Focus on solutions and fixing problems.
- Look at your school or district's procedures and processes with a critical eye to identify what can you change so this failure does not happen again.

Politics

Politics play a bigger role the higher up you go. Knowing how to navigate the political arena becomes critical. First, be aware that "organizational politics emerge when an individual has her own agenda or interest at heart without regard for how her actions affect the organization as a whole" (Ferguson, n.d.). Staff members might take the easier route (avoiding that person or not getting involved), but as a leader, you must learn to work through these situations—no matter how difficult they may seem. Don't shy away from politics, but prepare for it with the following strategies.

- Begin learning the politics in your school and district.
- Start listening and learning who stands for what—your board members, your parent leaders, and so on.
- Research who knows one another and who is connected to whom.

Loneliness

It is pretty common for leaders to feel lonely. As you move up, there are fewer and fewer people in the same position as you. For example, when you move from teacher to assistant principal, you go from having many teacher colleagues to very few assistant principal colleagues. As a principal or superintendent, you are likely only one in that position. With fewer similarly positioned colleagues, it becomes difficult to create a network of people you can confide in or talk to. While you must face the other challenges I have discussed, this one is preventable with the following strategies.

- Start networking now!
- Begin making friends and socializing with people who are in similar positions every time you move up.
- Look to neighboring schools and districts to expand the pool of colleagues at your level.

—————————————— *Reflection* ——————————————

Which of these challenges is the most concerning to you? Why?

What Obstacles Will You Face?

Even if you are seeking a promotion for the right reasons and prepare yourself for the added challenges, you will, without a doubt, run into some obstacles. Despite significant progress in terms of workplace gender equality, advancement is still more difficult for women than for men. Here, I will discuss a few of the barriers that women in particular face.

Unconscious Gender Bias in the Workplace

All people have biases, many of them unconscious. Unfortunately, unconscious gender bias in how others perceive women at work remains an obstacle. The International Labour Organization (2017) cites the "Heidi Versus Howard" study, in which participants were given descriptions of two candidates for a job. Both candidates had the exact same experiences: cofounding a technology company, becoming an executive in a huge business, and then moving into venture capital. The only difference was the name: one candidate's name was Heidi, while the other candidate's name was Howard. The participants rated each candidate's competency level as well as likeability. Participants rated Howard as competent as well as likeable. On the other hand, participants rated Heidi as competent but unlikeable. So while career accomplishments and the personality traits others assume go along with them are celebrated in men, they can be seen negatively for women.

Catalyst (2007), a research group with a focus on women at work, describes this concept as a *double-bind dilemma* for women in the workplace. A qualitative study analyzed data from interviews of twelve hundred leaders about gender stereotypes (Catalyst, 2007). The study finds that male stereotypes include men taking charge—they are strong, decisive, and assertive. Stereotypes of women center on women taking care—they are nurturing, emotional, and communicative. The study concludes that the *double bind* occurs when women take charge, and others see them as competent leaders but typically disliked; when women take care, others like them, but view them as less-competent leaders. In other words, "women leaders are seen as competent or likeable, but rarely both" (Catalyst, 2007, p. 7).

Assumptions

Along with unconscious gender bias, there are certain assumptions people make more often about women than men. In effect, people in positions of power make decisions for women about what they want or can handle, even when those women never articulate or express a preference (King, 2020; Ogden, 2019). Assumptions can include the following.

- "She's too nice as a teacher; she wouldn't want to be an assistant principal."
- "She has young children; the stress of the principalship would be too much."
- "She wouldn't want a central office job; it would be too far to drive, and she has to get home for her family."

People may not verbalize these assumptions *to* women, but they may express them in conversations with others. Perhaps a school administrator team is talking through potential future leaders in the teaching staff, or the human resources team at the district office is talking about which principals could make good central office administrators. Such presumptions pose a barrier: the teams may never even consider a women for a promotion because of what someone else has decided is true about her (Tabassum & Nayak, 2021). And the woman may never even know about it.

Competition Among Women

There is a perception in some of the literature on leadership and modern workplaces that women act as obstacles to other women—that they engage in backstabbing and gossip, tearing one another down to get themselves ahead. The most common term for this phenomenon is *queen bee syndrome*, which dates from the 1970s and refers to women who have achieved high ranks in male-dominated organizations and criticize lower-ranking female colleagues (Derks, Ellemers, van Laar, & de Groot, 2011; Groskop, 2015). Unfortunately, this concept is not without truth. Some women in senior roles do seek to dissociate from other women and even denigrate junior women (Andrews, 2020; Derks, van Laar, Ellemers, & de Groot, 2011; Faniko, Ellemers, & Derks, 2020; Marcus, 2016). But this self-serving behavior at the expense of others is not inherent to or typical of women; rather, "the queen bee phenomenon is itself a consequence of the gender discrimination that women experience at work" (Derks, van Laar, & Ellemers,

2016, p. 456). It arises when women perceive a bias against them and feel their career goals could be jeopardized because of their gender—so they begin to distance themselves from other women to show they are not like typical women.

In male-dominated organizations and cultures accustomed to traditionally male styles of leadership, women are pressured to separate themselves from their gender and take on traditionally masculine characteristics to achieve individual success (Cooper, 2016; Derks, Ellemers, et al., 2011; Derks, van Laar, et al., 2011). While downplaying one's femininity in this way can be effective, it often comes with labels like *cutthroat, catty*, and *queen bee*, which notably people do not apply to men who are competitive at work. Sociologist and researcher on gender, women's leadership, diversity and inclusion, the future of work, financial insecurity, and economic inequality, Marianne Cooper (2016) exposes this double standard by describing another archetype of women in the workplace: the *righteous woman*, who is a foil to the queen bee. The former is the woman who believes that, as a woman, you have a moral obligation to support other women. The latter is the woman who believes there is just something in the female sex that causes them to undermine one another at work. Neither archetype is very realistic—"one a model, the other a cautionary tale" (Cooper, 2016)—but together they demonstrate how women are between a rock and a hard place due to persistent gender bias in the workplace.

Executive coach, author, speaker, and podcast host Bonnie Marcus (2016) notes this manufactured competition for the scarce resource of leadership positions amplifies other psychological and social causes of female rivalry. For example, a woman who is insecure may not believe she will get promoted based on her own skills. As a result, she is wary of other women as "potential threats" (Marcus, 2016). Girls and women are also inundated throughout their lives with messages telling them to expect spiteful attacks from other women, from popular moves like *Mean Girls* and *The Devil Wears Prada* all the way back to, as Marcus (2016) points out, fairy tales such as *Snow White* and *Cinderella*. No wonder some women accept the idea other women are out to get them, "especially if you are ambitious, certainly if you are beautiful and talented. You always have to guard your back" (Marcus, 2016).

Women who internalize the mindset of female rivalry or distance themselves from other women in response to sexism may present as "mean girls" at work. Psychotherapist Katherine Crowley and management consultant and executive coach Kathi Elster (2013) associate this term (*mean girls*) with subtle, indirect displays of aggression. While some behaviors are so bluntly mean they are hard to miss, other behaviors commonly associated with feminine competition are harder to recognize, but mean nonetheless. Crowley and Elster (2013) give examples such as a woman who rolls her eyes at you, a woman who looks you up and down in silent judgment, or a woman who gossips about you behind your back. These behaviors exist and can become obstacles at work. Gender stereotypes normalize overt competition between men and often reward them for it, while "women often compete more covertly and behind the scenes. This covert competition and indirect aggression is [*sic*] at the heart of mean behavior among women at work" (Crowley & Elster, 2013, p. 3).

While these are behaviors to watch out for in others, they are also ones to avoid in yourself. Awareness of the queen bee phenomenon and mean girl behaviors, along with the knowledge that women adopt these roles in reaction to sexism, allows you to break the cycle. Future female leaders do not have to perpetuate behaviors that make them obstacles to other women. Fortunately, several studies in the 2010s indicate rivalry and sabotage among women are already on a downward trend, which is accelerating as younger generations of women join the workforce (Andrews, 2020; Arvate, Galilea, & Todescat, 2018; Gomstyn, 2016; Groskop, 2015). Women are starting to work against the systems that pit them against one another. For example, investment manager and executive Anne Welsh McNulty (2018) describes how she opened communication with junior women, shared advice, and guided them to stand up for themselves at work to prevent those women from having the negative experiences she had early in her career. Women are stronger when they support one another.

Fewer Opportunities

Another obstacle women encounter is fewer opportunities to move up. Women in education are concentrated at the elementary level, where a large majority of teachers *and* principals are women. In contrast, 81 percent of superintendents were previously middle school or high school principals or already worked in the district office (Ramaswamy, 2020). In other words, most superintendents have a secondary background, but the majority of women have an elementary background, and that makes it difficult for women to ascend the career ladder (Glass, n.d.; Ramaswamy, 2020). Journalist Swapna Venugopal Ramaswamy (2020) states, "It's those roles as principal, particularly in the middle and high schools, that most often lead to a superintendency, and that's where women are most lacking." Furthermore, "high school and middle school teachers have many more entry points for a move into administration and the first step toward the superintendency," such as department chairs, coordinator positions, and coaching roles, which often do not exist in elementary schools (Glass, n.d.).

Additionally, women interact less with people who could help them get promoted, such as principals, superintendents, or board members. *Society for Human Resource Management* (*SHRM*) editor and writer Kathy Gurchiek (2018) cites a report showing that "women receive less day-to-day support and less access to senior leaders than men, impeding their career growth." Women are on their own to figure out if they want a promotion, and if so, how to get it. In many fields, including education, a great deal of networking and mentoring occurs at social events rather than during the workday. For example, when there is a charity golf tournament, senior leadership in the district (usually men) attend these tournaments. When a high school sports team is playing in a championship game, typically, men from senior leadership are invited and attend. Women can be left out of these social events, putting them at a disadvantage when looking at access to senior leaders.

Another lack of opportunity for women is in the area of mentorship, which aids in career advancement (Carter & Silva, 2010). Gender is a barrier here as well. A Lean In (n.d.) survey shows 60 percent of male leaders are uncomfortable mentoring women. Since most existing senior leaders are men, it is more difficult for women to get that support than it is for their male colleagues. Whether it's formal or informal, "women get less of the mentorship and sponsorship that opens doors. Whether this is driven by sexism or because men (perhaps unconsciously) gravitate toward helping other men, the result is that women miss out" (Lean In, n.d.).

Reflection

Have you experienced any of the barriers the previous section discusses? How have they affected your career?

How can you break the competitive cycle and collaborate with other women to help one another grow and climb the career ladder?

So How Do Women Get Promoted?

There is no doubt women face numerous obstacles that hinder their ascent up the career ladder—if that were *not* the case, there would not be such a big gender gap in leadership positions in education. The remainder of this chapter highlights several strategies to help women land that promotion despite all the challenges in their path.

Standing Out

Think about everyone who wants to move ahead in their career and apply for those next-level jobs. They are your competition. If you are a teacher, think about all the applications principals receive for assistant principal openings. If you're an assistant principal, think about all the applications central office staff receive for principal vacancies. Applications usually vastly outnumber vacant positions. So how do you stand out from all the other applicants?

Your mindset needs to shift from what you have *done* to what you have *accomplished*. Too many prospective candidates focus on the things they have done—typically a regurgitation of the job description. If you're an assistant principal, coming to work on time every day, conducting teacher evaluations, and creating duty schedules are all things you've done as part of your job. But your competitors vying for that same principalship have done those exact things too. Fulfilling the duties and responsibilities of your job description does not make you stand out; it's "your unique skills and accomplishments" that make you more visible (Buj, n.d.).

The answer lies in emphasizing what you accomplished. What did you accomplish *as a result* of being an assistant principal (or teacher or principal)? What kinds of things did you achieve? What problems did you solve? Identify those innovative, creative, outside-the-box initiatives you led that resulted in something positive (such as increased student achievement or decreased student discipline referrals). For example, an assistant principal who was looking to become a principal one day decided to help build business and community partnerships for her school. She put together a comprehensive plan that included a series of events and activities to bring local businesses and community members into the school. Her initiative led to a significant increase in partnerships, which led to the school receiving more resources to fund programs that benefitted students. This is certainly an accomplishment the assistant principal should highlight in her future job interviews!

Writing Résumés and Cover Letters

Writing résumés and cover letters may seem basic, but they are the first step in determining whether you get the job—so make a good first impression! The first challenge of writing a résumé is remembering all the things you have accomplished, especially when it has been a while since you wrote a résumé. Therefore, my first advice is to *always* have a résumé ready. Every summer, take the time to update your résumé, adding whatever accomplishments you achieved in that particular year. In other words, keep an active, updated résumé ready to go at all times for any opportunity that may come your way.

Another hard thing about writing résumés and cover letters is how to structure them. There is a glut of opinions on résumé organization; no matter where you look, you will have different and sometimes even opposing views (Chin, Chan, Li, & Ng, 2017). Ultimately, the choice is yours. My suggestion is to begin your résumé with a synopsis of your accomplishments. This section will set you apart from other applicants. It could be titled "Highlights of Qualifications" or "Summary of Accomplishments," and should list those few big accomplishments or qualifications others may not have. Examples include the following.

- Bilingual; fluent in English and Spanish

- Led positive behavioral interventions and supports (PBIS) implementation, which resulted in a 23 percent decrease in student referrals

- Created a comprehensive school safety plan later featured as a model in national media

- Developed a robust inclusive teaching plan and was selected to train other schools on the program

The sections after this appear in order of importance, beginning with work experiences and then ending with education. Organize work experiences to reflect each job you have had over the last ten years if they are different jobs with different experiences. If you have been in the same role for the last ten years (even in several different schools or districts), then summarize the job experiences by topical headings so you're not repeating yourself. For example, if you've been a principal for ten years, instead of listing your three principal jobs separately, you might have headings such as "Human Resources" (list all the things you've done related to human resources as a principal) and "Organizational Management" (list the things you've done related to financial management, schedules, and so on). The headings could reflect your state's leadership evaluation standards.

After work experience, briefly list any specialized training you have, as well as your employment history in chronological order. Alternatively, organize your experiences by levels (school level, district level, state level) or your job titles (principal experiences, assistant principal experiences, teaching experiences). The last section is education. Here, list all your educational experiences, including each degree or program and where you completed it. Overall, your résumé should never exceed two pages. Keep in mind that page one should stand out the most—begin with the section that separates you from others and then get right into your work experiences. Figure 8.1 (page 158) shows an example of a résumé template.

Cover letters are sometimes even more important than résumés because they give a quick introduction to you. It is in your best interest to ensure your cover letter does exactly that. It can seem intimidating to write a letter, especially when there's pressure to make an impression. It helps to have a template to follow when writing your cover letter.

Your first paragraph can be pretty short—it's your declaration of the position for which you are applying. It's a quick way for you to let the person reading your letter know the position in which you are interested. After announcing your interest, follow up with a short sentence stating *why* you are the perfect person for this job. It's almost like writing an essay: give two or three reasons in the introduction as to why you should be hired for the position and then the rest of the letter will expand on each of those reasons. The following is an example of what the first paragraph could look like.

> *I am interested in the director of accountability and research position with XYZ School District. My qualifications and experiences from ten years as a principal, in addition to my strong knowledge of accountability systems, make me a strong candidate for this position.*

Your introduction sets up the rest of the letter; the content of your letter is a more detailed explanation of the experiences or strengths that set you apart from others. Your content (the body of your letter) should be two or three paragraphs. Using the preceding example, the second paragraph would briefly describe the candidate's experiences as a principal that helped prepare her for the accountability and research position. The paragraph after that describes how she has applied her knowledge of accountability systems to produce results for the schools she led. The last paragraph then is a summary, reiterating interest in the position and perhaps including a phone number and email address so the reader can set up an interview. In total, a cover letter is four or five paragraphs long and never exceeds one page.

YOUR NAME HERE

Summary of Accomplishments

This section is all about highlighting your qualifications. What specific qualifications set you apart from others? What special skill set or unique experiences do you have that others may not? Examples include the following.

- Fluent in English and Punjabi

- Elementary, middle, and high school experience

- Increased state mathematics assessment scores from 56 percent proficient to 75 percent proficient over a two-year period

- Named educator of the year by local business association

- Authored the following articles (then list the articles)

Experience

By the time you are looking for an educational leadership position, you probably have a lot of experience, so organize this section with your diverse experiences without just repeating job descriptions. One suggestion is to organize your experience by levels: school-level experiences, district-level experiences, and state-level experiences. Alternatively, organize your experiences by your job titles: principal experiences, assistant principal experiences, teaching experiences.

Specialized Training or Areas of Expertise

List any specific trainings helpful for the position you are applying for, or any specific areas of expertise beneficial for where you want to work. This list should be no more than three to five bullets.

Employment History

This section is a chronological list of your employment history. Just list your position, where you worked, and the dates employed.

Education

This section is a chronological list of your educational history. List what degree you earned, from where, and the date.

In these examples, you can see speaking another language is definitely a skill that sets you apart from others, as is having multiple school-level experiences. Finally, sharing concrete results of your leadership or highlighting specific awards is also great to start your résumé that captures attention.

Figure 8.1: Résumé layout example.

*Visit **go.SolutionTree.com/leadership** for a free reproducible version of this figure.*

Interviewing

If you have a promotion in mind, you should be practicing for that interview today. It goes along with always having an updated résumé ready—always be ready for an interview.

The best way to prepare for an interview for a school- or district-level leadership role is to examine your state's evaluation system for school or district leaders. One example is the Marzano Focused School Leadership Evaluation Model, which has six domains (Carbaugh & Marzano, 2020).

1. A data-driven focus on school improvement
2. Instruction of a viable and guaranteed curriculum
3. Continuous development of teachers and staff
4. Community of care and collaboration
5. Core values
6. Resource management

Another model is the one presented in *Principal Evaluation: Standards, Rubrics, and Tools for Effective Performance*, which describes six standards for school leaders (Stronge, 2013).

1. Instructional leadership
2. School climate
3. Human resources leadership
4. Organizational management
5. Communication and community relations
6. Professionalism

The following list is an example of evaluative domains for superintendents (DiPaola, 2010).

- Policy and governance
- Planning and assessment
- Instructional leadership
- Organizational management
- Communication and community relations
- Professionalism

The purpose of looking at the evaluative domains or standards for the position you are applying for is to understand what your role will entail. And chances are, your interview questions will relate to them, so the standards or domains become a guide for your interview preparation.

Next, use the standards or domains to create a portfolio for yourself. Write each standard or domain on a tab and begin collecting any artifacts that demonstrate your experience in each area. Using the *Principal Evaluation* (Stronge, 2013) model as an example, let's say you created a robust school-business partnership program for your school. Put that program under the communication and community relations tab of your portfolio. Or, if you created a series of professional development workshops for your teachers on engaging instructional strategies, put that behind the instructional leadership tab in your portfolio. If you led an initiative to decrease student discipline incidents, that would fall under the school climate section. Building this portfolio gives you a clear road map for your interview. You now have experiences to talk about that support the standards, plus stories and exemplars that show evidence for your answers.

Another benefit to building a portfolio is that you will see which standards you lack experience in. For example, you may realize you have many artifacts for instructional leadership because that is clearly your strength area, but you have few examples to show for organizational management. Once you identify your weak areas, begin seeking experiences to bolster those categories.

My last suggestion for interview planning is to always prepare for the *Why you?* question. Why should we select you for this job over the other six candidates we're interviewing? What makes you so special? Even if the interviewers do not ask this question directly, it is the perfect way to end your interview. Conclude by telling the interviewers why they should pick *you* for the vacancy. This two-minute "elevator pitch" lets people in positions of power know why you should be the next principal or superintendent. To craft your answer, think about what you have on your résumé under that first highlights section—what makes you stand out. What special skills and experiences do you bring to the table that your competitors do not?

Networking

Networking is an area where many women can do more. As daunting as it sounds, women should look outside classrooms and schools and connect with people in other areas or other districts. Over the course of your career, you need to stay connected with people you meet. You never know who will end up helping you with your promotion—or whom you may be able to help. Marcus (2018) provides six suggestions for effective networking.

1. **Change your mindset:** Your mindset for networking should not be "What will I get out of this?" Instead of viewing networking

as self-serving, consider it in terms of creating mutually beneficial relationships with people. Approach networking for the purpose of developing a relationship where both sides gain value.

2. **Expand your network:** People tend to create networks with people they like, people who look like them, or people with similar experiences and opinions. This *closed network* "limits our exposure to people who can offer new connections and ideas" (Marcus, 2018). Think of all the valuable insight you could gain by networking with people outside your comfort zone.

3. **Network strategically:** Networking does not mean randomly sending emails to people you've crossed paths with or suddenly reaching out to people when you need something from them. *Being strategic* means having a system for creating your network—even by keeping a diary of some sort. Then, strategically reach out to people to build those relationships. Find out more about the people in your network— from basic things like their birthdays to their professional interests. A birthday message or a resource on someone's area of interest gives you a genuine reason to open or reopen the lines of communication.

4. **Network proactively:** You should never wait to start networking until you hear about a job posting or when you need something. Build connections with people before any positions open up. If you only reach out to people once there is a job available, they may perceive that you are using them and feel disinclined to help you as a result. Proactively keeping in touch with your network develops authentic relationships and is what makes networking successful.

5. **Schedule time for networking:** The best way to be proactive with networking is to schedule time for networking. Put it on your calendar—maybe every three months. Set aside time to make phone calls to say "hello." Routinely send out birthday wishes or good luck messages at the start of the school year. In addition, when you go to events (like professional learning workshops or conferences), schedule time to meet people you can include in your network. Then put a reminder on your calendar to follow up with new connections. Too often, people meet really great contacts at these events, but fail to keep in touch with them (until they need something and feel awkward reaching out because they never kept in touch with them).

6. **Leverage relationships:** As mentioned previously, the goal of networking is mutually beneficial relationships—not just collecting

business cards or adding contacts to your phone. Over time, you can and should leverage those relationships. Get to know people—what are their career goals and interests? What are they currently working on, or what challenges do they have? Offer help and connect them with relevant opportunities. They will do the same for you.

Handling Rejections

Finally, you must acknowledge that no matter how hard you try or how prepared you are for that interview, sometimes you will get rejected. Rejection is a part of life; everyone has been there. How you handle rejection could potentially make or break your career. Rejections can be an obstacle for women; research shows "women who are rejected for positions are less likely than men to apply for future opportunities" (Bapna, Benson, & Funk, 2021, p. 2). One reason for this is the way the message is delivered impacts women differently than men. A rejection citing a poor fit between the candidate and the position is much less discouraging than a rejection based on the candidate's personal characteristics (Bapna et al., 2021). Of course, you cannot control how the rejection message is given, but you can control your reaction to it.

After you hear you were not selected for the job, everyone will be watching to see how you react and how you behave moving forward. Showing bitterness or anger can decrease your chances of ever being promoted. Handling rejection with grace and continuing to learn and grow as a leader are ways to set yourself up for the next opportunity (Bitte, n.d.). When rejection happens, take a couple of days to be upset privately, but then get over it and move on. Don't live in that space or it will consume you. And remember—maybe it wasn't the position for you to begin with. You will be even better and more prepared for the right position you do end up getting in the future.

Conclusion

In this chapter, I reviewed the importance of first making a decision—know you want that next step in your career, and know why you want it. I examined the challenges and obstacles that come with getting promoted but then also discussed ways to prepare for those challenges so you can be successful in your new position. Then, I explored practical strategies for how women can help themselves get promoted, from how to stand out, to résumé- and cover-letter-writing skills, to preparing for the interview and networking. These are strategies women can benefit from no matter what position they are currently in to help advance in their careers.

—————————— *Reflection* ——————————

Which of the strategies for getting promoted do you need to work on the most? Why?

Think of a successful female leader in your school or district. What makes her successful? What have you learned from her to help you grow in your career?

References and Resources

Andrews, S. (2020, January 21). Why women don't always support other women. *Forbes.* Accessed at https://forbes.com/sites/forbescoachescouncil/2020/01/21/why-women-dont -always-support-other-women/?sh=bbb179c3b05b on November 18, 2021.

Arvate, P. R., Galilea, G. W., & Todescat, I. (2018). The queen bee: A myth? The effect of top-level female leadership on subordinate females. *The Leadership Quarterly, 29*(5), 533–548.

Bapna, S., Benson, A., & Funk R. (2021, October 22). Rejection communication and women's job-search persistence. *SSRN (Social Science Research Network).* Accessed at https://papers.ssrn.com/sol3/papers.cfm?abstract_id=3953695 on January 25, 2022.

Bitte, R. (n.d.). The realistic way to bounce back when you're passed over for a promotion. *The Muse.* Accessed at https://themuse.com/advice/the-realistic-way-to-bounce-back-when-youre -passed-over-for-a-promotion on January 31, 2022.

Buj, M. (n.d.). Powerful career strategies for women: 11 top tips for advancement. *Live Career.* Accessed at https://livecareer.com/resources/jobs/search/women-career-strategies on January 25, 2022.

Carbaugh, B. G., & Marzano, R. J. (2020). *2018 update: The Marzano Focused School Leader Evaluation Model—Reframing the right balance for instructional and operational leadership* [White paper.] Accessed at https://marzanocenter.com/wp-content/uploads/sites/4/2020 /01/MC07-02-Focused-School-Leader-Evaluation-Model.pdf on October 13, 2021.

Carter, N. M., & Silva, C. (2010). *Mentoring: Necessary but insufficient for advancement.* Accessed at www.catalyst.org/wp-content/uploads/2019/01/Mentoring_Necessary _But_Insufficient_for_Advancement_Final_120610.pdf on March 3, 2022.

Catalyst. (2007). *The double-bind dilemma for women in leadership: Damned if you do, doomed if you don't.* Accessed at https://catalyst.org/wp-content/uploads/2019/01/The_Double _Bind_Dilemma_for_Women_in_Leadership_Damned_if_You_Do_Doomed_if_You _Dont.pdf on January 25, 2022.

Chin, S.-F., Chan, S. K., Li, S. Y., & Ng, A. (2017). Teaching resume writing: Comparing two perspectives to enhance classroom practice. *The English Teacher, 38,* 95–110.

Cooper, M. (2016, June 23). Why women (sometimes) don't help other women. *The Atlantic.* Accessed at https://theatlantic.com/business/archive/2016/06/queen-bee/488144 on October 8, 2021.

Crawford, M. G. (2018, February 2). The harsh truth of being promoted you probably didn't think about. *Fast Company*. Accessed at https://fastcompany.com/40525032/the-harsh-truth -of-being-promoted-you-probably-didnt-think-about on January 25, 2022.

Crowley, K., & Elster, K. (2013). *Mean girls at work: How to stay professional when things get personal.* New York: McGraw-Hill.

Derks, B., Ellemers, N., van Laar, C., & de Groot, K. (2011). Do sexist organizational cultures create the queen bee? *British Journal of Social Psychology, 50*(3), 519–535.

Derks, B., van Laar, C., & Ellemers, N. (2016). The queen bee phenomenon: Why women leaders distance themselves from junior women. *The Leadership Quarterly, 27*(3), 456–469.

Derks, B., van Laar, C., Ellemers, N., & de Groot, K. (2011). Gender-bias primes elicit queen-bee responses among senior policewomen. *Psychological Science, 22*(10), 1243–1249.

Diliberti, M. K., Schwartz, H. L., & Grant, D. (2021). *Stress topped the reasons why public school teachers quit, even before COVID-19* [Research report]. Santa Monica, CA: RAND Corporation. Accessed at https://rand.org/pubs/research_reports/RRA1121-2.html on January 25, 2022.

DiPaola, M. (2010). *Evaluating the superintendent* [White paper]. Arlington, VA: American Association of School Administrators.

Drake, L. (2021). *Crisis management: Effective school leadership to avoid early burnout.* Lanham, MD: Rowman & Littlefield.

Elsesser, K. (2020, August 31). Queen bees still exist, but it's not the women we need to fix. *Forbes*. Accessed at https://forbes.com/sites/kimelsesser/2020/08/31/queen-bees-still-exist -but-its-not-the-women-we-need-to-fix/?sh=15aa93026ffd on November 18, 2021.

Faniko, K., Ellemers, N., & Derks, B. (2020). The queen bee phenomenon in academia 15 years after: Does it still exist, and if so, why? *British Journal of Social Psychology, 60*(2), 383–399.

Ferguson, G. (n.d.). The relationships of leadership to the politics of the organization. *Chron.* Accessed at https://smallbusiness.chron.com/relationship-leadership-politics-organization -34221.html on October 8, 2021.

Glass, T. E. (n.d.). Where are all the women superintendents? *AASA.* Accessed at https://aasa .org/schooladministratorarticle.aspx?id=14492 on October 8, 2021.

Gomstyn, A. (2016, October 11). Queen bee syndrome, dethroned. *Credit Suisse.* Accessed at https://credit-suisse.com/about-us-news/en/articles/news-and-expertise/queen-bee-syndrome -dethroned-201611.html on November 18, 2021.

Groskop, V. (2015, June 8). *"Queen bee syndrome": The myth that keeps working women in their little box* [Blog post]. Accessed at https://theguardian.com/lifeandstyle/womens-blog/2015 /jun/08/queen-bee-syndrome-myth-working-women on November 18, 2021.

Gurchiek, K. (2019, May 21). More men say they are uncomfortable interacting with women at work. *SHRM.* Accessed at https://shrm.org/resourcesandtools/hr-topics/organizational -and-employee-development/pages/more-men-say-they-are-uncomfortable-mentoring -women.aspx on October 8, 2021.

International Labour Organization. (2017, August). *ACT/EMP Research note: Breaking barriers—Unconscious gender bias in the workplace.* Accessed at https://ilo.org/wcmsp5 /groups/public/---ed_dialogue/---act_emp/documents/publication/wcms_601276.pdf on October 8, 2021.

Kim-Phelps, M. (2018, April 12). A day in the life of a school superintendent. *San Diego Union Tribune.* Accessed at https://sandiegouniontribune.com/pomerado-news/our -columns/sd-cm-pow-column-back-to-school-0412-htmlstory.html on January 31, 2022.

King, E. (2020). *Can work-life inclusion reshape gender and ideal workers norms?* Accessed at https://docs.lib.purdue.edu/cgi/viewcontent.cgi?article=1000&context=worklifeinclusion on January 31, 2022.

Lean In. (n.d.). *Men, commit to mentor women.* Accessed at https://leanin.org/mentor-her on October 8, 2021.

Llopis, G. (2015, August 11). 4 constructive ways leaders can handle criticism. *Forbes.* Accessed at https://forbes.com/sites/glennllopis/2015/08/11/4-constructive-ways-leaders -can-handle-criticism/#636a53505615 on October 8, 2021.

Marcus, B. (2016, January 13). The dark side of female rivalry in the workplace and what to do about it. *Forbes.* Accessed at https://forbes.com/sites/bonniemarcus/2016/01/13/the -dark-side-of-female-rivalry-in-the-workplace-and-what-to-do-about-it/#4a0e820f5255 on October 8, 2021.

Marcus, B. (2018, May 22). The networking advice no one tells you. *Forbes.* Accessed at https://forbes.com/sites/bonniemarcus/2018/05/22/the-networking-advice-no-one-tells -you/?sh=639aeccf7772 on October 8, 2021.

Marulli, L. (2021, June 21). School superintendents working 15 hours Sunday to Sunday. *Moms.* Accessed at https://moms.com/school-superintendents-working-15-hours on January 31, 2022.

McNulty, A. W. (2018, September 3). Don't underestimate the power of women supporting each other at work. *Harvard Business Review.* Accessed at https://hbr.org/2018/09/dont -underestimate-the-power-of-women-supporting-each-other-at-work on December 15, 2021.

Muguku, D. (n.d.) *25 practical tips on how to get promoted at work* [Blog post]. Accessed at https://thriveyard.com/25-practical-tips-on-how-to-get-promoted-at-work/#14 on October 8, 2021.

Ogden, L. E. (2019, April 10). Working mothers face a "wall" of bias—but there are ways to push back. *Science.* Accessed at https://science.org/content/article/working-mothers-face -wall-bias-there-are-ways-push-back on January 31, 2022.

Ramaswamy, S. V. (2020, February 20). School superintendents are overwhelmingly male. What's holding women back from the top job? *USA Today* Accessed at https://usatoday.com /story/news/education/2020/02/20/female-school-district-superintendents-westchester -rockland/4798754002 on January 25, 2022.

Rankin, J. G. (2016, November 22). *The teacher burnout epidemic, part 1 of 2* [Blog post]. Accessed at https://psychologytoday.com/us/blog/much-more-common-core/201611/the -teacher-burnout-epidemic-part-1-2 on January 25, 2022.

Smith, J. (2013, October 24). 16 mistakes employees make when trying to get a promotion. *Forbes*. Accessed at https://forbes.com/sites/jacquelynsmith/2013/10/24/16-mistakes -employees-make-when-trying-to-get-a-promotion/?sh=130b61ed35f1 on January 25, 2022.

Sparks, S. D. (2016, November 1). Principals work 60-hour weeks, study finds. *Education Week*. Accessed at https://edweek.org/leadership/principals-work-60-hour-weeks-study -finds/2016/11 on January 25, 2022.

Stronge, J. H. (2013). *Principal evaluation: Standards, rubrics, and tools for effective performance*. Alexandria, VA: Association for Supervision and Curriculum Development.

Tabassum, N., & Nayak, B. S. (2021). Gender stereotypes and their impact on women's career progressions from a managerial perspective. *IIM Kozhikode Society and Management Review*, *10*(2), 192–208.

Timms, M. (2017). Creating a culture of accountability, not blame. *Avail Leadership*. Accessed at https://availleadership.com/culture-of-accountability on October 8, 2021.

Tina H. Boogren, PhD, is a fierce advocate for educators and an award-winning educator, best-selling author, and highly sought-after speaker. She has proudly served as a classroom teacher, a mentor, an instructional coach, and a building-level leader and has presented for audiences all over the world.

Dr. Boogren is deeply committed to supporting educators so they can support their students. She conducts highly requested and inspiring keynotes, workshops, and virtual webinars that focus on quality instruction, coaching, mentoring, and educator wellness, and she hosts a weekly podcast, *Self-Care for Educators With Dr. Tina H. Boogren*. Additionally, she is codirector of Solution Tree's Wellness Solutions for Educators™ with Timothy D. Kanold.

Dr. Boogren was a 2007 finalist for Colorado Teacher of the Year and a recipient of her school district's Outstanding Teacher Award eight years in a row, from 2002 to 2009. She is the author of numerous books, including *In the First Few Years: Reflections of a Beginning Teacher*; *Supporting Beginning Teachers*; *The Beginning Teacher's Field Guide: Embarking on Your First Years*; *180 Days of Self-Care for Busy Educators*; *Take Time for You: Self-Care Action Plans for Educators*, which was the Independent Publisher Book Awards' gold winner in the Education category; and *Coaching for Educator Wellness: A Guide to Supporting New and Experienced Teachers*. She is a coauthor of *Educator Wellness: A Guide for Sustaining Physical, Mental, Emotional, and Social Well-Being* with Timothy D. Kanold and *Motivating and Inspiring Students: Strategies to Awaken the Learner* with Robert J. Marzano, Darrell Scott, and Ming Lee Newcomb, and is a contributor to Richard Kellough and Noreen Kellough's *Middle School Teaching: A Guide to Methods and Resources* and Robert J. Marzano's *Becoming a Reflective Teacher*.

Dr. Boogren holds a bachelor's degree from the University of Iowa, a master's degree with an administrative endorsement from the University of Colorado Denver, and a doctorate from the University of Denver in educational administration and policy studies.

To book Tina H. Boogren for professional development, contact pd@SolutionTree.com.

CHAPTER 9

Taking Care of Yourself

Tina H. Boogren

True self-care is not salt baths and chocolate cake, it is making
the choice to build a life you don't need to regularly escape from.
—Brianna Wiest

The year is 2015, and I am living the good life in Denver, Colorado, where
residents have the gift of over three hundred days of sunshine and more
than eighty miles of bike trails within the city limits. I have a husband who
makes me laugh and loves me relentlessly, I have a puppy with floppy ears and
an affectionate demeanor, and I enjoy leisurely brunches on outdoor patios with
my girlfriends, where we sip mimosas and talk about books. To top it all off, I
have my dream career: I get to conduct workshops, give keynote presentations,
deliver professional development sessions to educators of all levels and backgrounds all over the United States, and rack up airline miles and hotel awards.
It's all just *so* fantastic.

What I should say is, it's all just so fantastic *according to my social media posts*.

Truth be told, while none of what I was posting was a lie, it also wasn't the full
picture. Sure, I lived in an amazing city, but I was hardly ever home to enjoy it.
Yes, my husband made me laugh and loved me relentlessly, but I was also feeling disconnected and isolated from him due to my travel schedule. Our sweet
puppy required constant attention and couldn't be trusted to not destroy power
cords and favorite blankets. I loved time with my girlfriends, but I was also totally
fried and resentful of their long weekends enjoying the mountains when I was
landing at the airport after midnight on Friday and gearing up to fly out again
on Sunday. My job *was* amazing, but it was also really hard. There were unkind
participants, unreasonable requests, and so many missed flights and crappy hotel
rooms, I could hardly keep up. I rarely posted pictures of my face or my body

on my social media accounts because I was ashamed I was twenty-five pounds overweight, hated the adult acne that had suddenly shown up on my face, and was totally embarrassed that the bags under my eyes had turned into buckets.

What showed up on my social media accounts was the life I *wanted* to be living. In *real* life, though, I was filled with loneliness, anxiety, stress, and an emptiness I attempted to fill by secretly binging on pizza and cheese fries in my hotel rooms, abusing Amazon's 1-Click Ordering button, and making excuses for why I didn't have room for my workout clothes in my suitcase. I stayed cheerful and energetic during my workshops but when I arrived back home, I was snappish and irritable toward my husband and far too exhausted to accept his kind invitations to date night.

I was completely burned out.

I was barely hanging on.

And I didn't share any of this with *anyone*.

Instead, I continued posting pictures of my adorable puppy on Instagram and tagging myself in all the amazing locations I got to visit as part of my job. I was the life of the party at book club brunch. I continued to say "yes" to every opportunity that came my way—even if that meant three flights in one day, a two-hour drive from the airport to the hotel, and three hours of sleep *if* everything was on time (and trust me, flights are *rarely* on time). But the reality was the thought of prepping for a two-day workshop on brand-new material, scheduling my complicated travel, completing expense reports, submitting receipts, and finding time for phone calls with busy superintendents and principals was taking a dramatic toll on me both mentally and physically.

As fate would have it, I was also digging into the initial research and starting to write the first draft of the book *Motivating and Inspiring Students: Strategies to Awaken the Learner*, which I was coauthoring with Robert J. Marzano, Darrell Scott, and Ming Lee Newcomb (2017). We utilized psychologist Abraham Maslow's (1943) famous hierarchy of needs as a framework for the book and attached specific classroom strategies to each level of the hierarchy to help teachers take care of all students' social-emotional needs. Like a lightning bolt, it hit me: *How can I ask teachers to do this for their students when* I'm *not doing this for* myself? As I researched the importance of sleep, nutrition, exercise, safety, self-esteem, and a sense of belonging, I had the awful realization that I was ignoring so many of my own *basic human needs*.

Thus, I decided to change my life.

Or at least take back my life and make it something more like what I was portraying online. I started with the basics—level one of Maslow's (1943) hierarchy, which concerns physiological needs. I implemented the research on how to get more quality sleep by replacing my phone alarm with an old-school alarm clock, wearing a sleep mask, and setting the thermostat to 68 degrees. I pushed out my afternoon diet soda habit by slowly increasing my water intake to sixty-four ounces each day. I met with nutritionists, got tested for food allergies, kept a meticulous wellness journal, and overhauled my diet by eliminating the foods that didn't work for my body. I started going to the grocery store rather than out to a restaurant when I was on the road. I carried apples and protein powder in my carry-on bag and politely refused the complimentary food that comes with travel status. I saved wine for special occasions only and instead sipped sparkling water with lime in the evening. None of this happened overnight. To be clear, these changes occurred over a span of three years and I am *still* tweaking my diet, sleep, and exercise habits as I continually fight the urge to numb my challenging emotions with food.

I also had a long, honest talk with my husband and asked him for help. I shared that I desperately needed to come home from travel to a clean house and fresh groceries. I requested date night at home (rather than out) because my introverted self couldn't stand the thought of going to a crowded restaurant for at least twenty-four hours after returning from a work trip. And I promised him if he could help me with these requests, I would be an extraordinary wife in return. He had no idea I was struggling, but the minute I asked for help, he said "yes" without hesitation and asked what else he could do. He immediately took over the cleaning, stocked the fridge with healthy food, started doing my expense reports, and made sure the sheets were always clean when I got home.

I learned how to focus on the workshop participants who were open to my message and let unwarranted, unkind comments roll off my back rather than lodge in my head. I committed to always packing my tennis shoes and workout clothes in my carry-on, even if that meant ironing the same pair of work pants three days in a row. I set an alarm to *go* to bed. I allowed myself two full hours of unfrenzied time in the morning and developed mindful habits like meditation and writing down five unique things I was grateful for each day to be centered each workday. I stopped watching Netflix and TV and began voraciously reading novels again. I set daily intentions to stay true to the healthy boundaries I established for myself.

And guess what? It worked!

My skin cleared up, I was sleeping for the recommended seven or eight hours a night (most nights), my weight dropped, and I was a kinder, gentler, more patient presenter, passenger, friend, and wife. I felt *so* good. This is not to say I am perfect, or that it's easy, or that I don't fall back into old patterns sometimes. The difference is in the deliberate desire to make different *choices*. And I want the same for you, my fellow women in education. Because here's what I know for sure: if you're disregarding your own needs and you find yourself numbing and isolating more often than you'd like, you *will* burn out, just like I did.

This chapter will dive into the research on educator burnout, how to engage in self-care by making better choices, and the role of habits to automate those choices. Once you prioritize your own needs and make small changes that support those needs, you'll be able to live your best life and step fully into your role as the leader you desire to be.

Reflection

As you read my story, could you relate to any part of it? In what ways?
Take a moment to reflect on what my story brought up for you.

Visit **go.SolutionTree.com/leadership** to access a reproducible reflection guide for this chapter.

Educator Burnout

I don't have to remind you how difficult your job is. But I will anyway because you need to remember *all* you do on a daily basis. No matter what your formal title is, I'm willing to bet your life is some combination of the following: you get up before dawn, stay up too late, and grade papers, plan lessons, or answer emails on the weekends and during your child's soccer games. You meet with parents who sometimes aren't on your side and deal with students who look you in the eye and say cruel things when you're trying to help them. You create lessons or professional development workshops from scratch—which sometimes flop in spite of your very best intentions. You sit in or lead team meetings with colleagues, some of whom have burned through all their passion and don't seem committed to doing what is best for students. You chaperone, coach, lead, and hustle. You give up your lunch period, planning time, happy hour, and book club because your to-do list is too long, and the days are too short. You worry, fret, hug, and love beyond what any non-educator can even fathom, and you do it every single day. You might work in a broken-down building or a classroom where things are literally falling apart. You use your paycheck to buy pencils, notebooks, snacks, and socks for students who have none. You feel guilty for all the time away from your family when you're at school, and you feel guilty for the time away from your students when you're at home. You make decisions that will have a lasting impact on students, families, and entire communities.

And sometimes you lose it. You cry in your car, in the bathroom, or under your desk. You say things you wish you hadn't said. You get resentful, irritated, mad, and anxious. You cave to your sugar cravings, pour yourself another glass of wine, or buy something else online; whatever your numbing vices, you indulge. Then you feel bad and guilty, and make promises to do better. And you do—for a while. But then your best intentions start to slip away, little by little, and once again, you find yourself at the bottom of your own to-do list and you barely recognize yourself anymore.

As a female educator, you spend so much time, energy, and mental brainpower attempting to meet the staggeringly diverse needs of your students, communities, and families that you often find yourself overwhelmed, exhausted, and stressed. Those challenging emotions can lead to burnout if you're not careful. According to coauthors Melinda Smith, Jeanne Segal, and Lawrence Robinson (2021), "Burnout is a state of emotional, physical, and mental exhaustion caused by excessive and prolonged stress." If you need any more proof that teaching is a stressful job, consider this example sentence from *Merriam-Webster's* dictionary entry for the word *burnout*: "Teaching can be very stressful, and many teachers eventually suffer *burnout*" ("Burnout," n.d.). Burnout is so common for teachers and other educators they've become the example.

According to an American Federation of Teachers (2017) survey, 61 percent of educators say their work is always or often stressful. That's a staggering percentage related to such a negative state of mind. As a point of comparison, educators in the United States experience much more stress and mental health problems than other workers (American Federation of Teachers, 2017; Krame, 2021). Additionally, the educators in the American Federation of Teachers (2017) study recognized they were sleep deprived and reported experiencing poor health. These outcomes are no surprise when you consider that stress has a negative impact on physical and mental well-being, including headaches, chest pain, fatigue, and upset stomach (Mayo Clinic Staff, 2021).

Stress and burnout are not exclusive to educators in the United States. Burnout is also increasing among educators in Canada. Over 80 percent of teachers in British Columbia report their mental health is slightly or significantly worse compared to before the COVID-19 pandemic (Wilson, 2021). Additionally, in Australia, 58 percent of educators report feeling quite a bit or a lot of stress in their jobs (Thomson, 2020).

Burnout is the *number one* reason educators leave their jobs (Russell et al., 2020). The World Health Organization (2019) classifies burnout as a workplace phenomenon, typically characterized by exhaustion, cynicism, and reduced efficacy. I have yet to meet an educator, particularly a female educator, who doesn't immediately recognize the term *burnout* and its common symptoms: emotional exhaustion, depersonalization, and a decreased sense of accomplishment (Freudenberger, 1975). Instead, I typically receive a knowing nod and a reaction of, "Yes, this" when the term enters the conversation.

Women, particularly those who are mothers, are more likely than men to "manage a more complex set of responsibilities on a daily basis—an often-unpredictable combination of unpaid domestic chores and paid professional work," (Cox, 2021). In a LinkedIn study, 74 percent of women said they were very or somewhat stressed for reasons related to their profession versus 61 percent of the men surveyed (Anders, 2021). Additionally, in the largest-ever study of working parents, Great Place to Work (2020) reports working mothers are 23 percent more likely to experience burnout than working fathers. A 2018 University of Montreal study shows women are more vulnerable to burnout than men (Beauregard et al., 2018). During the COVID-19 pandemic, women, particularly mothers, spent significantly more time on both childcare and household chores than they did before the pandemic, which resulted in a decreased sense of well-being (Giurge, Whillans, & Yemiscigil, 2021). Clearly, educators and women are suffering.

It doesn't have to be this way. It *can't* continue to be this way. Because if this continues, the field of education will lose countless more educators; it may lose *you*. I know you're not going to leave education because of the pay, working conditions, parents, or overcrowded classrooms. No, if you're going to go, it's going to be because you are completely, totally, and undeniably burned out. And students cannot afford to lose you.

Reflection

What is your personal relationship to burnout? Take a moment to reflect on your career and when you've felt close to burnout and why.

The Self-Care Solution

If you have ever been on an airplane, you've heard the safety announcement that reminds you to secure your own oxygen mask before assisting others. This is a lesson for educators to live by: you can't help others if you don't take care of yourself first.

Here's how you start: reconsider your choices. As you move through your day, be conscious of what you are doing in each moment and ask yourself if you can (or should) make a different choice. Then make that choice and see what happens. Maybe instead of hitting the snooze button, you choose to get up the first time your alarm goes off. Maybe you choose to sit down and eat lunch rather than stuffing a handful of crackers into your mouth when you realize you haven't eaten all day. Maybe you conduct your afternoon meeting on a walk rather than sitting in the conference room. Maybe you choose to have warm tea out of your favorite mug rather than reaching for that glass of wine when you get home from work. Maybe you choose to set some limits on your social media consumption. Maybe you decide to go to bed early instead of zoning out in front of Netflix. Making those different choices is *the self-care solution*.

Self-care is not a bubble bath, beach vacation, or facial. While I'm all for those things, they are not what's actually going to help you on a daily basis. Individual moments of bliss will not sustain you when you are working fourteen-hour days and providing a supportive environment for traumatized students. As Fred Luskin, director of the Stanford University Forgiveness Projects, explains:

> If you take a bath just to get away from the kids, the minute you open the
> door, it's like you didn't even take a bath. . . . Or how many people take a
> vacation, and on the plane coming back they're just as stressed? It's atti-
> tude and where your mind is, not just what your body is doing. (as cited in
> Laird, 2018)

What *is* going to sustain you and allow you to shift from surviving to thriving are all those choices you make *within* your fourteen-hour day and *after* you've done your best to support your struggling students. The choice to drink water and pause for lunch, the choice to shut your door and do a five-minute meditation, the choice to have an apple rather than the leftover cake in the staff lounge—*that's actual self-care*. That's how you care for your own self.

Fundamentally, *self-care* is "the practice of taking action to preserve or improve one's own health" and "the practice of taking an active role in protecting one's own well-being and happiness, in particular during periods of stress" ("Self-care," n.d.).

It is how you can cope with your daily stressors (Lawler, 2021). Research finds that self-care promotes positive physical health outcomes, reduces stress and anxiety, boosts your self-esteem, protects your mental health, leads to better relationships, and fosters resiliency (Circle Health Group, n.d.; Lawler, 2021). You can even take Socrates's famous directive to "Know thyself" as a self-care motto. In other words, when you know yourself and your needs, you are caring for yourself in the most fundamental sense (Laird, 2018).

To give you a few examples, here are the self-care choices I'm currently working on.

- Choosing to work out instead of scrolling through social media
- Embracing JOMO (*joy* of missing out) over FOMO (*fear* of missing out)
- Reading a novel rather than another educational research book (and not feeling guilty about it)
- Drinking eight ounces of water before coffee ever passes over my lips in the morning
- Cooking at home rather than eating out
- Unfollowing social media accounts that cause negative comparisons to spiral out of control
- Eating vegetables and drinking water even when I don't want to

Self-care is in the choice. As an educator, you make choices—both personal and professional—all day long. Research claims teachers make fifteen hundred educational decisions per day (Goldberg & Houser, 2017). Unfortunately, there's a heavy price to pay for making all those decisions: with each choice you make during the day, your willpower depletes and making good, thoughtful choices becomes nearly impossible (American Psychological Association, 2019; Pignatiello, Martin, & Hickman, 2020). When you deplete your willpower, your brain looks for shortcuts. One shortcut is to act recklessly, making quick decisions without thinking through the consequences. Another is to do nothing (Oppong, 2018). When decisions exhaust your brain, you may often find yourself choosing what feels good in the moment but doesn't serve you in the long term. This explains why it is so hard to get to the gym after a long workday or why you may find yourself cruising through the drive-through on the way home even though you told yourself you would make dinner tonight. You're not thinking of the consequences of your choices, you're taking the easy way out because you are exhausted. To prevent decision fatigue and make healthy choices even when you are fatigued, you should automate laborious decisions so they become habitual.

——————————————— *Reflection* ———————————————

Pause to consider when you act recklessly and when you do nothing because you've reached decision fatigue. Are there any patterns that emerge for you? (For example, Is Monday a particularly tough day for you?)

Habits and Rituals

If self-care consists of choices but choices can deplete your willpower and good intentions, one of the best things you can do for yourself is create daily habits and rituals that reduce the number of decisions you must make. Choices such as whether to hit the snooze button, what to wear to work, what route to take to school, when to respond to email, what to eat for dinner, who is picking up the kids after school, and so on can all become good habits if you commit to regulating or automating them. According to Neil Pasricha (2017), author of *The Happiness Equation*, if you can automate and regulate at least some of your choices, you will be able to more thoughtfully consider the decisions that *really* matter—like those around students and learning.

In *The Power of Habit*, author and journalist Charles Duhigg (2014) outlines the three-step process that forms a *habit loop*: (1) cue, (2) routine, and (3) reward. The *cue* is the trigger that nudges you to do something, the behavior is the *routine*, and that awesome feeling you get as a result of engaging in the behavior is the *reward*. Knowing this, you can identify and improve your habit loops. Consider the following tips to help with this identification (Parker-Pope, 2020).

- Pair or link your habits by attaching a new habit to an existing habit (the cue). For example, pair taking your daily vitamins and supplements with brushing your teeth.

- Start small. For example, take a short walk around the block to jump-start an exercise routine or commit to eating an apple as a snack to help jump-start changes in your eating habits.

- Do it every day (the routine). Because it can take eighteen to 254 days for a task to become automatic, depending on the person and the task, it's important to repeat your habit often (Lally, van Jaarsveld, Potts,

& Wardle, 2010). In other words, it's better to take that walk around the block every day than try to commit to an hour at the gym three days a week.

- Make it easy. Clear the obstacles that stand in your way of good habits. For example, put your tennis shoes in your work bag so you can easily go for that walk at any given moment.

- Reward yourself (the reward). Build in immediate rewards that reinforce your new habit. For example, download a new audiobook to listen to on your walk.

Every time you make a certain choice, you deepen that pathway in your brain—if you do it over and over again, you've created a new habit that no longer requires a conscious choice (Rodriguez, 2018); it's just what you do, it's who you are. If the habit centers on something that supports your overall health and well-being, you'll also start to feel better, have more energy, feel (re)inspired, and have more to offer to your students, colleagues, family, and friends—which will encourage you to keep up your good habits. *This* is how you change your life for the better.

In addition to forming good habits, another way to reduce decision fatigue is to automate certain choices. The following are some examples of ways to eliminate certain minor decisions in your day.

- Choose one day a week to do paperwork rather than bringing that stack of papers home and dragging them back to school (often untouched) every morning.

- Make double the amount of dinner and then immediately pack leftovers for lunch tomorrow.

- Utilize a navigation app to outsource decisions about the best route to take to work or a meeting.

- Lay out tomorrow's clothes the night before.

- Buy an alarm clock *without* a snooze button.

You get the idea here. Start small and see how it feels to have some willpower left over at the *end* of your day rather than feeling totally wiped out by lunchtime. Ask yourself how this changes your mood, your interactions with others, your relationships with your colleagues and family, and your entire outlook on your job and your life. I'm willing to bet it changes *everything*, in a good way, just like it did for me.

Conclusion

Burnout and stress are big, real problems for women educators. But true self-care—regular healthy choices, not momentary escapes—can help. Once you recognize you're teetering on the edge of burnout, it's essential that you engage in self-care by making better choices and establishing habits and routines that help you automate those choices. What I hope more than anything is that you find ways to thrive, in both your personal and professional life. You can do this! It all starts with *one* choice. Just one. Choose *you* and see what happens. I'm willing to bet you can change your entire life—*for the better*—when you take care of yourself.

Reflection

After reading this chapter, what is one different choice you will make in the name of self-care?

How will you hold yourself accountable to your commitment, and how will you celebrate your success?

References and Resources

American Federation of Teachers. (2017, October 30). *Survey shows educators are feeling stressed out*. Accessed at https://aft.org/news/survey-shows-educators-are-feeling-stressed-out on April 5, 2020.

American Psychological Association. (2019, December 9). *Harnessing willpower to meet your goals*. Accessed at https://apa.org/topics/personality/willpower-goals on February 7, 2022.

Anders, G. (2021, August 25). So stressed! Women report bigger burdens but see a lot more escapes. *LinkedIn*. Accessed at https://linkedin.com/pulse/so-stressed-women-report-bigger-burdens-see-lot-more-escapes-anders on January 8, 2022.

Beauregard, N., Marchand, A., Bilodeau, J., Durand, P., Demers, A., & Haines, V. Y., III. (2018). Gendered pathways to burnout: Results from the SALVEO study. *Annals of Work Exposures and Health, 62*(4), 426–437. Accessed at https://academic.oup.com/annweh/article/62/4/426/4870017?login=true on January 8, 2022.

Burnout. (n.d.). In *Merriam-Webster online dictionary*. Accessed at https://merriam-webster.com/dictionary/burnout#examples on October 11, 2021.

BusyTeacher. (n.d.). *Teachers: The real masters of multitasking* [Infographic]. Accessed at https://busyteacher.org/16670-teachers-masters-of-multitasking-infographic.html on February 26, 2018.

Circle Health Group. (n.d.). *What is self care and why is it important?* Accessed at https://circle healthgroup.co.uk/health-matters/health-and-wellbeing/what-is-self-care-and-why-is-it -important on February 7, 2022.

Cox, J. (2021, October 3). Why women are more burned out than men. *BBC Worklife.* Accessed at https://bbc.com/worklife/article/20210928-why-women-are-more-burned-out -than-men on January 8, 2022.

Duhigg, C. (2014). *The power of habit: Why we do what we do in life and business.* New York: Random House.

Freudenberger, H. J. (1975, January). The staff burn-out syndrome in alternative institutions. *Psychotherapy: Theory Research and Practice, 12*(1), 73–82.

Giurge, L. M., Whillans, A. V., & Yemiscigil, A. (2021). A multicountry perspective on gender differences in time use during COVID-19. *Proceedings of the National Academy of Sciences of the United States of America, 118*(12). Accessed at www.pnas.org/content/pnas /118/12/e2018494118.full.pdf on February 7, 2022.

Goldberg, G., & Houser, R. (2017, July 19). *Battling decision fatigue* [Blog post]. Accessed at https://edutopia.org/blog/battling-decision-fatigue-gravity-goldberg-renee-houser on November 19, 2021.

Great Place to Work. (2020). *Parents at the Best Workplaces™: The largest-ever study of working parents.* Accessed at https://info.mavenclinic.com/pdf/parents-at-the-best-workplaces ?submissionGuid=5ac95855-8079-46ac-9ba5-f8b11c2ae5c5 on February 7, 2022.

Krame, K. (2021, February 19–21). *The efficacy of mindfulness-based interventions on occupational stress and burnout among K–12 educators: A review of the literature.* Paper presented at 2nd World Conference on Teaching and Education, Vienna, Austria. Accessed at https://dpublication.com/wp-content/uploads/2021/01/39-303.pdf on February 7, 2022.

Laird, A. K. (2018, July 20). Why your self-care methods aren't working—and how to fix that. *SELF.* Accessed at https://self.com/story/why-your-self-care-methods-arent-working on January 8, 2022.

Lally, P., van Jaarsveld, C. H. M., Potts, H. W. W., & Wardle, J. (2010). How are habits formed: Modelling habit formation in the real world. *European Journal of Social Psychology, 40*(6), 998–1009.

Lawler, M. (2021, May 19). What is self-care and why is it so important for your health? *Everyday Health.* Accessed at https://everydayhealth.com/self-care on January 8, 2022.

Marzano, R. J., Scott, D., Boogren, T. H., & Newcomb, M. L. (2017). *Motivating and inspiring students: Strategies to awaken the learner.* Bloomington, IN: Marzano Resources.

Maslow, A. H. (1943). A theory of human motivation. *Psychological Review, 50*(4), 370–396.

Mayo Clinic Staff. (2021, March 24) Stress symptoms: Effects on your body and behavior. *Mayo Clinic.* Accessed at https://mayoclinic.org/healthy-lifestyle/stress-management/in -depth/stress-symptoms/art-20050987 on October 11, 2021.

Oppong, T. (2018, June 8). Depleted by decisions (how your brain makes choices that sabotage you and what to do about it). *Ladders.* Accessed at https://theladders.com/career-advice/how-your-brain-makes-choices-that-sabotage-you-and-what-to-do-about-it on October 11, 2021.

Parker-Pope, T. (2020, February 18). How to build healthy habits. *The New York Times.* Accessed at https://nytimes.com/2020/02/18/well/mind/how-to-build-healthy-habits.html on January 8, 2022.

Pasricha, N. (2017). *The happiness equation: Want nothing + do anything = have everything.* London: Vermilion.

Pignatiello, G. A., Martin, R. J., & Hickman, R. L., Jr. (2020). Decision fatigue: A conceptual analysis. *Journal of Health Psychology*, *25*(1), 123–135.

Rodriguez, D. G. (2018, February 7). How habits help you make decisions. *Medium.* Accessed at https://medium.com/thrive-global/how-habits-help-you-make-decisions-e39e7c1468a7 on February 7, 2022.

Russell, M. B., Attoh, P. A., Chase, T., Gong, T., Kim, J., & Liggans, G. L. (2020). Examining burnout and the relationships between job characteristics, engagement, and turnover intention among U.S. educators. *Sage Open*, *10*(4), 1–15.

Self-care. (n.d.). In *Lexico.* Accessed at https://lexico.com/en/definition/self-care on February 7, 2022.

Smith, M., Segal, J., & Robinson, L. (2021, November). Burnout prevention and treatment. *HelpGuide.* Accessed at https://helpguide.org/articles/stress/burnout-prevention-and-recovery.htm on January 8, 2022.

Thomson, S. (2020, August 18). TALIS: Stress levels among Australian teachers. *Teacher Magazine.* Accessed at https://teachermagazine.com/au_en/articles/talis-stress-levels-among-australian-teachers on January 8, 2022.

Wilson, J. (2021, November 3). Record number of teachers experiencing burnout. *Canadian Occupational Safety.* Accessed at https://thesafetymag.com/ca/topics/psychological-safety/record-number-of-teachers-experiencing-burnout/315415 on January 8, 2022.

World Health Organization. (2019, May 28). *Burn-out an "occupational phenomenon": International Classification of Diseases.* Accessed at https://who.int/news/item/28-05-2019-burn-out-an-occupational-phenomenon-international-classification-of-diseases on February 7, 2022.

Bob Sonju is an award-winning educational leader, author, and consultant recognized for his energetic commitment to coaching educational leaders, building effective teams, developing response to intervention (RTI) structures that support teachers and students, and creating effective school cultures committed to learning for all students. Bob was formerly the principal of nationally recognized Fossil Ridge Intermediate School and has also served as a district leader, high school and middle school administrator, and special education teacher. Previously, Bob was the executive director of teaching and learning for the Washington County School District. After six years as a district-level administrator, Bob's deep desire to work together with teachers and students again led him back to school as principal of Washington Fields Intermediate.

While leading Fossil Ridge, Bob and his staff developed a true learning community that continues to produce extraordinary results. In 2013 and 2016, Fossil Ridge received the prestigious National Breakthrough School Award from the National Association of Secondary School Principals. Fossil Ridge continues to be listed as a national model professional learning community (PLC) school, and the school has been featured on AllThingsPLC (www.allthingsplc.info) and in *Principal Leadership* magazine.

As a district leader, Bob led the implementation of the PLC process in a district of fifty schools. The Utah Association of Secondary School Principals named Bob 2011 Principal of the Year for middle-level schools, and the National Association of Secondary School Principals selected him as one of three finalists for National Principal of the Year. His work has been published in *Principal Leadership* magazine and in the Solution Tree publications *Help Your Team*; *Best Practices at Tier 2: Supplemental Interventions for Additional Student Support, Elementary*; *Best Practices at Tier 2: Supplemental Interventions for Additional Student Support, Secondary*; and *It's About Time*.

Bob earned a bachelor's degree, a master's degree, and an endorsement in school administration from Southern Utah University.

Jason Andrews, EdD, is superintendent of Windsor Central School District and was named the 2019 New York State Superintendent of the Year. Previously, he served as a high school teacher, coach, cocurricular adviser, and middle school principal.

As superintendent, Dr. Andrews focuses on systemic implementation of professional learning communities (PLCs) as the vehicle to ensure student learning and a culture of continuous improvement. He is also an adjunct professor at the State University of New York (SUNY) Oswego, where he is codirector of the New York State Superintendents Development Program and serves on the SUNY Broome Community College Board of Trustees.

Dr. Andrews is a leader among superintendents and serves as an officer in the New York State (NYS) Council of School Superintendents, NYS Education Commissioner's Advisory Council, and National Center for Educational Research and Technology National Board. He is also a charter member of the Institute for Innovation. In addition, Dr. Andrews facilitates board of education strategic planning sessions and retreats across New York State for the NYS School Boards Association. He has served on the board of directors for the NYS Council on Leadership and Student Activities, National Association of Student Councils, and School Administrators Association of NYS. Dr. Andrews served on the board of education for the Harpursville Central School District from 1993 to 2000. He also serves on numerous community boards and committees, with a particular emphasis on issues related to workforce development and poverty.

Dr. Andrews received a bachelor's degree in political science and secondary social studies from SUNY Cortland, a master's degree in education from the University of New England, a certificate of advanced studies in educational administration from SUNY Cortland, and a doctorate in educational leadership at Sage Graduate School in Albany, New York.

To book Bob Sonju or Jason Andrews for professional development, contact pd@SolutionTree.com.

CHAPTER 10

Learning From Women Leaders

Bob Sonju and Jason Andrews

No country can ever truly flourish if it stifles the potential of its women and deprives itself of the contributions of half of its citizens.

—Michelle Obama

Decisions to enter the educational profession are sometimes simple ones. Bob became a teacher because of a chance meeting with a university counselor:

My junior year saw numerous changes to my major field of study—business to communications, then English—but nothing seemed to feel just right for a career. The gravity of graduation and a lifelong profession was at the forefront of my thoughts, and I knew it was time to officially get serious about a career. I had just decided that my most recent major was not a good fit and looked to the university guidance counselor for advice. After a short conversation about my interests, we narrowed down the things I enjoy: people, relationships, helping others, and baseball. My beloved Chicago Cubs were certainly not knocking on my door, so we focused our efforts on my other interests: people, relationships, and helping others. Continually resonating in my head was my dad's wise advice playing like a broken record, "Find something you love to do because you're going to do it the rest of your life!" Suddenly, it was right there in front of me: I was going to be a teacher!

For Jason, growing up the youngest in a family filled with only brothers on a dairy farm in upstate New York, education was not a natural field to enter:

No one in my immediate family had ever been an educator except for my Great-Aunt Mabel, who had been the teacher in the one-room schoolhouse where my paternal grandparents met and went to school through eighth grade (which was the highest grade offered). My grandmother would then ride a milk train to a neighboring town to finish high school, while my grandfather began to work on the railroad. With their own family, they always emphasized the critical importance of education. Perhaps it was my grandparents' value in education that drove my early interest to become deeply involved in school and eventually even elected to the board of education while still a senior in high school. I then decided to remain in the field I was so connected to. I have been drawn to education since first visiting that one-room schoolhouse so critical to my heritage, which sits just seven miles from my office today.

Like most educators, a deep desire to help others and, somewhat idealistically, to make the world a better place through preparing the next generation motivated us both to enter the profession. During our initial years in the classroom, a few things became apparent: (1) there are some deeply embedded unwritten norms and practices in the educational landscape; (2) teaching is way tougher than our undergraduate work; (3) there is a need to advance quickly to make a living; and (4) the majority of our colleagues were women.

Despite the unwritten norms and hard work, we soldiered on, knowing we would need to move up the ranks and become leaders in our schools and districts to achieve financial comfort and more importantly, to make a significant difference in the lives of the teachers and students we served. As we each considered the possibilities of advancement, it seemed the sky was the limit! We were both secondary educators, where the preparatory path to leadership opportunities was direct. Most secondary schools have assistant principal positions, which generally lead to principal positions, which provide a strong platform for the jump to district administrator and superintendent. Bob saw a clear path to leadership for himself:

After nine years in the classroom, I came to realize the profound influence that a teacher can have on the lives of students. I wanted to have a greater influence beyond the students in my classroom; I wanted to help students and teachers in an entire school community.

For Jason, climbing the ladder seemed straightforward as well:

After five years in the classroom, I became a principal and then, almost by accident, became the superintendent of schools at just thirty years old. I have remained in that position in the same district for the past seventeen years and have seen the power of transforming an entire community through the systematic commitment to the professional learning community (PLC) process.

Along the way, when we were not sure exactly what to do, we leaned on others to provide guidance and support. But as we followed this logical progression to leadership, we noticed a serious inequity: no longer were the majority of our peers women. Education reporter Nick Morrison (2018) reaffirms this observation: "Although teaching has long been a female-dominated profession, men are more likely to occupy leadership roles."

As mentioned in the introduction (page 1), three-quarters of U.S. teachers are women, but only just over half of principals are women. In secondary schools (where we have spent most of our careers), nearly 70 percent of principals are men (National Center for Education Statistics, 2020, 2021). Only 24 percent of superintendents are women (Ramaswamy, 2020). Denisa R. Superville (2016), assistant editor at *Education Week*, describes the state of U.S. educational leadership this way: "Even though K–12 education is largely a female enterprise, men dominate the chief executive's office in the nation's nearly 14,000 districts, numbers that look especially bleak given that the pool of talent is deep with women." Considering these statistics, the "United States Census Bureau has characterized the superintendency as the most male-dominated executive position of any profession in the United States" (Glass, Björk, & Brunner, 2000, p. 17).

The inequity of women in leadership is not limited to education or the United States. According to UN Women (2021), the United Nations entity dedicated to gender equity, "Data from 133 countries shows that women constitute 2.18 million (36 per cent) of elected members in local deliberative bodies. Only two countries have reached 50 per cent." As of September 2021, only twenty-six women were serving as heads of state. They predict, "At the current rate, gender equality in the highest positions of power will not be reached for another 130 years" (UN Women, 2021). As educational leaders, we find these sobering statistics startling and upsetting to say the least.

The underrepresentation of women in educational leadership is even more shocking when we consider the talent and dedication of women educators with whom we have worked over the years. As we entered the field of educational leadership, we recognized the many challenges that come with leading a team, school, or district, and the skills needed were quite extensive. The daily managerial tasks, combined with discovering solutions to complex problems, resolving conflict, and providing a compelling vision while functioning as the leader of learning oftentimes seem complex and overwhelming. Along with this, it also became painfully apparent that the margin of error for our female colleagues was much narrower than for their male counterparts. For example, we observed if a male leader was firm in his decisions, others viewed him as strong and decisive. Yet, if a female leader demonstrated these same strong, decisive characteristics, others viewed her as overbearing and intimidating. Likewise, if a male leader was compassionate regarding a decision, others saw him as empathetic and understanding. Yet, others viewed the female leader who exhibited this same compassionate approach as weak and soft. It just didn't seem equitable.

We know women reading this chapter are aware of or have experienced these inequities firsthand. Rather than belabor the obvious inequalities of gender in educational leadership, we want to share five lessons we've learned from outstanding women educational leaders.

1. Work hard at the right work.
2. Be a solution-oriented learner.
3. Get in the room.
4. Seek constructive feedback.
5. Believe in your talents.

Regardless of job title—teacher, paraprofessional, principal, administrator, or superintendent—women at all levels of the educational profession demonstrate leadership qualities everyone can seek to emulate.

Work Hard at the Right Work

In education, and perhaps in any profession, a strong work ethic is fundamental to the success of any leader. It seems most successful leaders we have worked with possess a characteristic that seems to separate them from others: *they are the hardest working people in the room.* However, it is not uncommon for the number of initiatives and demands ever present in today's educational landscape to quickly overwhelm an educational leader. This educational "noise" can easily consume a leader's time and effort and divert attention from the work of ensuring *every* student learns at high levels. Although not intended, this diversion can cause confusion among staff and a lack of clear direction for the school or district. With the myriad of demands constantly pulling at leaders, we suggest leaders work hard at maintaining a focus on two critical elements of leadership often sacrificed in the hustle and bustle of daily leadership responsibilities: (1) building, nurturing, and sustaining relationships and (2) staying true to the purpose of the organization.

Oftentimes, as leaders plan and design the work of their school or district, the work of colleagues can go unseen or unnoticed. As leaders, we recognize planning and attention to detail can make the difference in whether an organization realizes success. We also acknowledge the need to frequently recognize and validate the work of colleagues. One of the reasons senior leaders are still mostly men is that "women's contributions are systematically overlooked at work" (Fielding-Singh, Magliozzi, & Ballakrishnen, 2018), even when these women invest time and energy in tasks outside their official responsibilities (Burns et al., 2021). The *right work* begins by taking time to observe and recognize colleagues' contributions, no matter how large or small. Observing, recognizing, and validating the work of others are essential to developing relationships that create a culture of respect and appreciation, elements schools and districts need to thrive. Acknowledging the work of others can have a significant impact on the motivation and morale of staff, and can also support the development of a positive school climate. Jason learned this firsthand from a principal while he was a classroom teacher:

> My principal systematically and deliberately acknowledged and celebrated the contributions and efforts of everyone on the staff. We would regularly receive handwritten notes and cards of appreciation and recognition for going above and beyond to support students and accomplish goals. I have always remembered how much I appreciated that the principal took the time to simply acknowledge my time and work. I wasn't alone in my gratitude, as I would regularly see her notes hanging in my colleagues' classrooms, offices, and even the kitchen. This simple gesture of appreciation made a big difference as to how we felt about the work we were doing. I learned of the value of the acknowledgments of efforts I received as a teacher, and I followed the example set by my principal and her thoughtfulness. As a leader, I have always tried to replicate the model I experienced. Now, it is my cards, notes, and certificates that are seen hanging across the district.

Although recognition and validation of work are important first steps, these actions are only a precursor to what prospective women leaders truly need: a mentor or sponsor. As Jessica Kanold-McIntyre discussed in chapter 7 (page 127), women leaders and prospective leaders need advocates—influential people who will promote their work and provide opportunities for them to grow. Susan R. Madsen (2019), founder of the Utah Women & Leadership Project (https://usu.edu/uwlp), reaffirms this through her research: "Our data revealed that what women really want is 'sponsorship.' Sponsors go beyond advice and praise. Sponsors act." Sponsors and mentors are important figures throughout a woman's career, from childhood to retirement. When influential leaders inspire, whether male or female, they frequently recognize the contributions of women and utilize their influence to position women for success.

As First Lady of the state of New York from 1983–1994, Matilda Raffa Cuomo made mentoring a priority and has continued that work in the decades since. In 2016, Cuomo invited Jason and a small group of superintendents to discuss establishing mentoring programs in schools:

> Since that time, my staff (at Windsor Central School District) and I have been able to establish dozens of mentoring relationships between professionals in our community and elementary and middle school students. One particularly powerful mentoring partnership was between a woman engineer and a fourth-grade student. This student lived in significant poverty and had experienced a great deal of trauma in her life. The bond they formed has had a dramatic impact on both the mentee and mentor. The student is now in our engineering program in our high school, and her mentor continues to support, challenge, and impact the student. My staff and I simply could not have replicated the power of this relationship in our school.

As critical as working hard and sponsorship are for leaders and prospective leaders, the ability to create a clear focus for the organization is equally important. Effective leaders work together with their staff to build a school or district's purpose that defines the culture and practices of the organization. As Yvette Jackson and Carmen Jiménez explained in chapter 1 (page 13), a leader's personal purpose will drive the work of defining the organization's purpose. A concise, action-oriented purpose all stakeholders live by is foundational to the right work of a school or district.

We were both fortunate enough to learn directly from Richard DuFour and Rebecca DuFour. We listened to their presentations and participated in their workshops dozens of times. Becky was absolutely masterful when speaking about clarity of purpose. In simple, direct terms, she would compel her audiences to examine everything through the lens of learning, to assess every policy, procedure, and practice through the litmus test of whether it would lead to higher levels of learning for students. Becky's clarity and uncompromising precision of purpose serves as a powerful model for us both in our leadership, so we share these strategic questions as prompts for deep discussions regarding the school or district's purpose (DuFour, DuFour, Eaker, Many, & Mattos, 2016, p. 39).

1. Why do we exist?

2. What must our school become to accomplish our purpose?

3. How must we behave to achieve our vision?

A clear purpose for the school or district provides an essential touchstone for leaders and teachers. It drives the beliefs, decisions, and actions of the personnel in the organization and provides an opportunity to measure the organization's success. The development of and daily attention to its compelling purpose is essential for a school or district and at the foundation of the right work for leaders.

—————————————— *Reflection* ——————————————

Who are your mentors?

What is the focus for your work?

—————————————————————————————————————

*Visit **go.SolutionTree.com/leadership** to access a reproducible reflection guide for this chapter.*

Be a Solution-Oriented Learner

As educational leaders, we are quite literally in the business of learning. Yet, as educators take on increasing responsibilities, their colleagues start to seek them out for answers to complex questions and solutions to difficult problems. As Julie A. Schmidt related in chapter 4 (page 75), new leaders frequently make the mistake of trying to answer every question others pose to them; these new leaders feel they must somehow be the expert on everything in the school or district. During our careers, we learned a valuable lesson when it comes to solving problems as a leader: see problems as opportunities for growth and *do not* try to solve every problem. The leader who immediately solves every challenge effectively reinforces two undesirable habits. First, if a leader immediately provides a solution for every problem, that leader unintentionally sends the message, "Bring me your problems and I will solve them for you." Single-handedly fixing every problem limits the solution to one perspective, which leads to the second negative habit: stunting the growth of those with whom the leader works. Instead of wielding authority in every scenario, great leaders use these opportunities to seek out varying opinions, perspectives, and possible solutions. They want to hear the challenges perplexing their colleagues, but they work *with* them to identify workable paths forward instead of dictating their own view. This approach leads to growth for leaders and staff alike. True leadership blossoms when you surround yourself with people who have varying perspectives and are solution oriented. Biographer and political commentator Doris Kearns Goodwin (2008) reaffirms this: "Good leadership requires you to surround yourself with people of diverse perspectives who can disagree with you without fear of retaliation" (p. 4).

These differing perspectives and insights allow for creative problem solving and expand the leader's professional skill set.

Cheri Stevenson, a highly effective educational leader, has spent a career committed to education. Having worked at various levels of school and district administration, Cheri successfully refined the skill of problem solving with colleagues, and offers four critical steps as leaders assist and model the skills needed to problem solve (C. Stevenson, personal communication, January 2, 2022).

1. **Listen:** Slow down, withhold judgment and hear what the person is saying. Ask questions to help gain greater clarity on the problem.

2. **Honor:** Honor the person's expertise and unique perspective.

3. **Identify:** Identify how the problem started. What's the backstory? What led up to this problem? What are the intricacies of the problem?

4. **Consider:** Consider other perspectives and points of view.

Each problem is an opportunity to learn, consider unique perspectives, and develop relationships on the pathway to a solution. The strong connections built through brainstorming and solving problems are indispensable to leaders and those they work with.

Bob learned a great deal on this topic from Jennifer Throndsen, director of teaching and learning for the Utah State Board of Education. As any leader, Jennifer deals with myriad challenges on a daily basis. Her optimistic, innovative approach to educational leadership is inspiring. She describes her strategies for working with colleagues as they collectively solve problems this way:

> In general, I use three main processes to solve problems. First, I evaluate the research evidence or literature in the arena under inspection to see what the evidence base would indicate as appropriate solutions. In the world of education, it is important that we rely on the evidence so that the strategies we employ have a high likelihood of success and positive impact on students. Second, I engage with experts and other stakeholders in the space to get their insights, perspectives, and recommendations, considering those that may have more knowledge than me as well as those on the ground working in districts or schools who have different lenses on a particular problem than I may have. By seeking their insights, I can more fully consider the issue, the complexities and realities of the problem, and generate more effective solutions. Finally, I consider past experiences and what worked and what didn't work to inform what may work given the current situation and context. By integrating these three approaches, I can triangulate the findings

across strategies to develop potential solutions to complex problems. (J. Throndsen, personal communication, January 11, 2022)

What a great approach to solving problems! Evaluate, gather insights and varied perspectives, and learn from past experiences.

Another strategy for helping build a leader's skill set and colleagues' capacity for solving problems is a technique we refer to as the *1:2 strategy*. Simply put, leaders create the expectation that every challenge or problem should have two possible solutions. If you are bringing a problem to your supervisor or team, present two possible solutions to the problem. If you are a leader people turn to for guidance in challenging times, set the expectation that staff members bring two potential solutions to present along with the problem. For example, a teacher might approach her principal with a concern about students being tardy to class. As she describes the problem, she also suggests a first option: to better support students in being on time by possibly tracking student tardies and providing an immediate intervention for those who reach a certain number of tardies. A second option may be to establish the expectation that teachers stand outside their doorways during each passing period and encourage students to get to class on time. The teacher and the principal would then discuss and explore these options, along with additional solutions that may arise during their discussion, before settling on a potential solution.

The 1:2 strategy shifts the focus from simply bringing a problem to the leader to solve to solutions, allowing all parties to learn from others' unique perspectives. This strategy develops two critical characteristics that contribute to a school or district's culture while also creating the conditions for a solution-oriented organization. First, you develop your capacity and that of your colleagues to not only identify problems but also (and more importantly) to think through a variety of possible solutions. Second, with the expectation of two potential resolutions, the 1:2 strategy challenges you and your colleagues to go beyond the initial solution and think deeply about alternatives, shifting the focus from describing problems to identifying a variety of viable solutions. Current and aspiring leaders can use this approach to adopt a flexible, problem-solving mindset, which is beneficial to any school or district.

Reflection

How comfortable are you seeking out and listening to input from colleagues?

What is your strategy for solving problems and facing challenges?

Get In the Room

Education is also a people business. Your days are filled with students, parents, and colleagues. To achieve a leadership position and find success there, you must continuously develop mutually beneficial relationships with others and make the human element of your work a priority. As Jasmine K. Kullar explained in chapter 8 (page 143), these can be obstacles for women if male leaders exclude them. One of Bob's colleagues, Kim Monkres, a distinguished secondary school principal and president of the Utah Association of Secondary School Principals, shares that oftentimes, women are not part of the unofficial meetings where important decisions are made or relationships are being established, stating, "There are many times when decisions are made on the golf course or at informal lunches where women are not included. This puts women at a disadvantage" (personal communication, December 27, 2021). When working toward leadership positions, she advises women to:

> Get in the room. Look for opportunities to be involved. What I mean by this is to get involved in everything you can. Volunteer for those frequent committees that come along and while there, be genuinely interested and curious as you develop relationships with people you're serving with. Get your voice in the room. (K. Monkres, personal communication, December 27, 2021)

Once established in key roles, leaders can use their influence to develop mutually beneficial relationships and help get other women into the room. A key consideration for developing mutually beneficial relationships is to ensure both people are committed to making those around them better. Relationships should be symbiotic in nature. According to *Merriam-Webster* the concept of symbiotic relationships is derived from the Greek words *syn-* and *bios*, which translated mean *with* and *life*, or *life together* ("Symbiosis," n.d.). Mutual benefits and accountability to one another should exist in professional networks. Renowned educators Richard DuFour and Michael Fullan (2013) explain, "This obligation to provide others with the resources and assistance they need to meet expectations is commonly referred to as *reciprocal accountability*" (p. 52). Establishing an effective and diverse network of professionals committed to one another is a powerful leadership asset to embrace. Mutually beneficial relationships are essential to develop colleagues and to ensure the betterment of the organization. Jason shares what he has learned on this topic from attorney Jacinda Conboy:

Jacinda "Jazz" Conboy, Esq., is the general counsel for the New York State Council of School Superintendents. In her position, she is the primary person responsible for negotiating contracts and representing the school superintendents in New York State. She quite literally is responsible for protecting the livelihood of the overwhelmingly male district leaders. As an officer on the council, I have worked closely with Jazz and observed how she got in the room and quietly, but strategically, began to own it. She has built both credibility and trust among the membership. Jazz is the first call superintendents make when they are in trouble or need help. Even though her role provides plenty of work and challenge already, Jazz was not satisfied with the inequities among the number of women leading school districts. In New York State, the teacher workforce is about three-quarters women, yet in the superintendency, that number is about one third (New York State Council of School Superintendents, 2015; New York State Education Department, 2019). So, she initiated the Women's Initiative to support women leaders, identify women in education who have leadership potential, and help those who aspire to leadership roles. Jazz hosts conferences and events, speaks, and encourages men to support women in leadership. In 2020, the American Association of School Administrators recognized her efforts; she was named a recipient of the Friend of AASA Award. Jazz got into the room, learned the layout, and started working to make some renovations and improvements. She is a strong leader working to support others to have a lasting impact.

Once you assume a building or district administrator role, it is easy to get caught up in tedious managerial tasks that can easily consume an entire day and diminish the opportunities to develop relationships. It is important for leaders to prioritize and dedicate time each day to developing relationships that support people and drive the work of a school or district. This can be done in a variety of ways, including the following.

- **Take a sincere interest in people and their work:** Have frequent conversations with people and find out about their interests, successes, challenges, and so on (C. Stevenson, personal communication, January 2, 2022). Whether a student is learning a new skill, or a colleague is attempting a new teaching strategy, a sincere interest says, "I value you."

- **Allow for discussion of opinions and ideas:** More than anything, students and educators want the leader to recognize and value their ideas and work. Healthy discussions and the respectful exchange of opinions not only helps develop these essential relationships but also allows the effective leader to model what productive discussion looks like. Come to the table with ideas but constantly learn and seek input from others, and if you make a mistake, be the first to admit it (C. Stevenson, personal communication, January 2, 2022).

- **Make yourself available:** As necessary as managerial tasks are to a leader, being available to colleagues, parents, and staff is more important. Being available is more than just declaring an open door policy. To truly be available as a leader, you must make time with team members a priority when devoting time to be present for both scheduled and unscheduled conversations. Collaborate with stakeholders on projects and committees with a dedication to support and honor the commitments (C. Stevenson, personal communication, January 2, 2022). Getting out of the office and walking the halls to deliberately seek out contact with team members will increase your availability and build supportive relationships. Providing availability should be an active rather than passive pursuit.

No matter what room you are in, a leader needs to cultivate relationships that provide a foundation of trust with colleagues. Cheri offers this simple advice: "You don't need to be the smartest person in the room. Instead, be viewed as the one who is constantly learning" (C. Stevenson, personal communication, January 2, 2022).

───────────── *Reflection* ─────────────

What is your strategy for getting in the room?

How do you find time to develop mutually beneficial relationships?

Seek Constructive Feedback

Constructive feedback is essential to growth. Feedback from a respected colleague, or a *critical friend*, allows leaders or prospective leaders to learn about their strengths and areas for professional and personal growth. Critical friends differ from critics, who will be plentiful for leaders. In your leadership, you will have many who will second-guess every decision you make. A *critical friend* will honestly and supportively provide constructive feedback with your best interests in mind. Oftentimes, this may be a trusted mentor or advocate (see page 189). Honest and supportive feedback can assist in the growth of the leader by discussing decisions, learning from mistakes, and generating a variety of solutions to challenges. Kim Scott (2019), cofounder of an executive educational firm and workplace comedy series *The Feedback Loop* (https://radicalcandor.com/the-feedback-loop), asserts:

> Challenging others and encouraging them to challenge you helps build trusting relationships because it shows 1) you care enough to point out both the things that aren't going well and those that are and 2) you are willing to admit when you're wrong and that you are committed to fixing mistakes you and others have made. But because challenging often involves disagreeing or saying no, this approach embraces conflict rather than avoiding it. (p. 14)

Jason learned the importance of critical friends from a member of his district's board of education:

> *After a board meeting one night, one of the women on the board approached me. She shared that every time I spoke or presented, I would spend most of my time looking at the two male board members, rarely presenting directly to the five women on the board. At first, I reacted to this feedback with defensiveness and denial. I thought there was no way this was possible; I felt that I treated all of the board members equally and with respect. On reflection, however, and after paying closer attention at the next board meeting, it became evident that she was right. I was unintentionally nonverbally communicating a message I did not intend. Consequently, both the governance and leadership teams in the district began to carefully monitor body language and other nonverbal communications in an attempt to ensure that messages were clear and intentional. Members of both teams actively and systematically offered and received critical feedback after every meeting. We adopted the phrase "fix your face" to give one another feedback when facial expressions were sending messages perhaps inconsistent with the communication intended. This honest, direct, feedback takes vulnerability and trust, but it has improved communication and the culture in the district. Were it not for the honesty and willingness to offer critical feedback from this strong female community leader, my colleagues and I would have missed an opportunity and the consequences could have been significant. Her action as a critical friend turned a problem into an opportunity that has improved our collaborative efforts on behalf of students.*

It is even more important to have a critical friend during times of hardship and adversity, when you may feel a natural tendency to close ranks and isolate. As Richard F. Elmore (2004), the Gregory R. Anrig Research Professor of Educational Leadership in the Harvard Graduate School of Education, advises, "Isolation is the enemy of improvement" (p. 67). To improve and grow, leaders must be willing to embrace vulnerability and expose themselves to a critical friend to receive authentic feedback. Recognized author and researcher Brené Brown (2012) further emphasizes the need to embrace and cultivate vulnerability and mutual trust:

> Vulnerability is not weakness, and the uncertainty, risk, and emotional exposure we face every day are not optional. . . . Our only choice is a question of engagement. Our willingness to own and engage with our vulnerability determines the depth of our courage and the clarity of our purpose. (p. x)

Public speaker and author Stephen M. R. Covey (2006) defines *trust* as a "function of two things: character and competence. Character includes your integrity, your motive, and your intent with people. Competence includes your capabilities, your skills, your results, your track record. And both are vital" (p. 30). Leaders need critical friends who have both the integrity to give meaningful and constructive feedback and the competence to coach correct principles. Finding the right person (or people) to fulfill this role is imperative—be discerning. Look for someone who will do the following.

- Tell you the truth.
- Challenge you.
- Ask tough questions.
- Provide criticisms when appropriate.
- Build you up.

The purpose of a critical friend can never be to demean or demoralize. This trusted sounding board offers feedback to assist in growth and getting better. If your goal is simply to hear praise and affirmation, don't bother. Though it might feel good, it won't help you build your capacity and expand your impact.

--- *Reflection* ---

What is your system for getting feedback?

How do you know if the feedback you receive is building your capacity?

Believe In Your Talents

To be successful, a certain degree of modesty and humility is critical. In our experience, people have little interest in following someone who is arrogant and egotistical. However, effective leaders must also exude a degree of confidence and belief in themselves. A blend of confidence and humility is key. As coauthors Kerry Patterson, Joseph Grenny, Ron McMillan, and Al Switzler (2012) explain in *Crucial Conversations*:

People who are skilled at dialogue have the confidence to say what needs to be said to the person who needs to hear it. Confidence does not equate to arrogance or pig-headedness. Skilled people are confident enough that they have something to say, but realize others have valuable input. They are humble enough to realize that they don't have a monopoly on the truth nor do they always have to win their way. Their opinions provide a starting point, but not the final word. (p. 133)

Achieving this blend of confidence and humility is challenging but can have a tremendously positive impact, as Jason learned from a friend and colleague with an impressive record of achievement:

> Maureen "Mo" Donahue rose to the level of the president of the New York State Council of School Superintendents, representing leaders from more than seven hundred diverse school districts, and serves as a faculty member in the state's superintendent development program for aspiring district leaders. Mo models the balance of confidence and humility perfectly. She articulately, clearly, and concisely shares her perspectives. She is not, however, the first or most frequent speaker. When she does speak, others listen. The whole room perks up a bit. She shares her stories and perspectives clearly, and often passionately, with a strong focus on her purpose—student learning. At the same time, Mo is an incredible listener who gives everyone the sense that they have her undivided attention, because they do. She asks questions and always seems to empathize with what they have to say. She will often reach out to check in days or weeks later. Her humility, approachability, and genuine interest in others, balanced with valuable experiences and knowledge, make her a leader whom others regularly seek out as a trusted sounding board and resource. And she accomplishes this all quietly and without seeking the spotlight.

We encourage you to seek models of confidence like Mo, who balances offering her input and views with listening to and learning from others. Striking this blend will serve all leaders well.

Such confidence and comfort in one's self comes from self-efficacy. Psychologist Albert Bandura (1997), widely regarded as the foremost authority on *self-efficacy*, defines this critical attribute as "a judgment of one's ability to organize and execute given types of performances" (p. 21). Leaders who do not believe in their own abilities cannot reasonably expect others to believe in them. To develop self-efficacy, first work on building a strong network of peers who model the behaviors you seek to replicate. Observing those who model self-efficacy can help you build it in yourself. Second, celebrate success. This positive reinforcement of accomplishment assists in building confidence for future success. Finally, as we previously stated, seek feedback. Self-efficacy and subsequent task performance improve after receiving more detailed levels of performance feedback (Beattie, Woodman, Fakehy, & Dempsey, 2016).

Another aspect of confidence reflects this advice: *if someone opens a door for you, walk through it.* It is important to have the confidence to take advantage of the opportunities that present themselves. If you wait to have all the experiences and skills you perceive necessary in preparation for a leadership role, you may miss an incredible opportunity. We acknowledge men are socialized to have this confidence more so than women. As an expert on women's leadership, Tara Sophia Mohr (2014) describes a well-known Hewlett Packard internal report that finds "Men apply for a job when they meet only 60% of the qualifications, but women apply only if they meet 100% of them." In her own survey of professionals, Mohr (2014) finds that many women decline to apply, saying things like, "I didn't think they would hire me since I didn't meet the qualifications, and I didn't want to waste my time and energy." Awareness of the fact "not everyone is playing the game that way" may help you feel more comfortable taking a chance on opportunities that might be stretches for you (Mohr, 2014). We have worked with many incredibly talented women who could have successfully fulfilled leadership positions, but simply did not view themselves as qualified. For Bob, Kim Monkres is the epitome of stepping up despite not feeling 100 percent certain about the outcome. Although an accomplished state and school leader, and educational consultant, Kim has had her share of disappointments. In spite of this, she persists, because the rewards far outweigh the risks. She states:

> I don't know if anything I apply for or attempt in a school is going to work out—it's a risk. But I do know that regardless of the outcome, I will gain more skills, learn lessons I might not have learned, and get to meet new people. I'm not going to know until I try! (K. Monkres, personal communication, December 27, 2021)

So, if the door appears to be open, we hope you will walk through it—and if necessary, even push through it—and not underestimate your ability to rise to the challenge.

A final element of confidence is using your intellect to take intelligent risks. According to Ryan MacDonald (2017), program associate at the Innovation Lab Network of the Council of Chief State School Officers, school leaders must "be willing to take that risk and develop a culture where educators and students feel comfortable taking necessary risks." Leaders must leverage their intelligence and confidence to take measured risks and inspire action among those they lead. We do not suggest leaders blindly gamble, but rather, utilize their significant skills and abilities to courageously lead others to places they might not otherwise go. As leaders take intelligent risks, they should consider a few valuable suggestions consultant Adam Sicinski (n.d.) offers.

- **Transform your perspective:** See risk as a journey of personal self-discovery or as an exploration of your desired outcomes.

- **Commit fully:** If you hesitate while taking risks, you are more likely to fail. Avoid this pitfall by committing yourself wholeheartedly to the attainment of your desired outcome.

- **Be willing to lose:** Be willing to lose, but also be willing to learn and adapt your approach the next time around.

- **Fail forward fast:** All the lessons successful people need to learn are packed into their failures and mistakes. The rewards always go to those who *fail forward fast*—who learn their lessons quickly and then take the necessary risks to take advantage of opportunities that come their way.

- **Cultivate optimism:** Cultivate optimism, excitement, and faith that things will eventually work out no matter what you might be dealing with in the present moment. Any obstacles or setbacks you face are simply lessons.

Leaders and prospective leaders who practice taking intelligent risks, model humble confidence, and motivate others to take action will not only be successful but will also serve to inspire the vulnerability and creativity schools and districts need.

―――――――――――――― *Reflection* ――――――――――――――

How can you simultaneously exude both confidence and humility?

How do you approach taking risks?

Conclusion

When invited to contribute to *Women Who Lead*, we were humbled for many reasons. To share the pages with the coauthors of this book, educational all-stars and women whom we deeply admire, is nothing short of special. Their shared experience and incredible wisdom are inspiring, and all leaders should emulate them. Along with this, we were both eager to share lessons we have learned from women who lead. As male leaders, we have learned (and continue to learn) many valuable lessons from powerful women leaders. We know we are better leaders because of them. Those lessons have helped develop and refine our leadership skills and put us in positions to assist the next generation of women leaders.

We are extremely indebted to one of the most inspiring women leaders we were fortunate enough to learn from—Rebecca DuFour, who embodied strength and grace, inspired each of us to be better, taught us the value of relationships, and modeled the warmth, passion, and authenticity we continually aspire to emulate. Educational leadership is tough, complex, demanding work. It is our observation that effective educational leaders understand the value of relationships and a clear purpose that drives the work of the organization. They are confident, humble, and remain perennially eager to learn while committing to the right work.

We conclude with this parting thought to our own daughters and women everywhere who lead or aspire to lead: believe in your many skills and talents, develop and nurture valuable relationships, be fiercely compassionate and patient with yourself, and go make a difference in a world that desperately needs you right now. This is your time!

--------- *Reflection* ---------

Which of the lessons in this chapter have you successfully
applied in your career?

Which lessons are most challenging for you?

References and Resources

Bandura, A. (1997). *Self-efficacy: The exercise of control*. New York: Freeman.

Beattie, S., Woodman, T., Fakehy, M., & Dempsey, C. (2016). The role of performance feedback on the self-efficacy–performance relationship. *Sport, Exercise, and Performance Psychology, 5*(1), 1–13.

Brenneman, R. (2016). *Challenges faced by women in school leadership discussed in conference panel*. Accessed at https://rossier.usc.edu/challenges-faced-by-women-in-school-leadership -discussed-in-conference-panel on October 11, 2021.

Brown, B. (2012) *Daring greatly: How the courage to be vulnerable transforms the way we live, love, parent, and lead*. New York: Gotham Books.

Burns, T., Huang, J., Krivkovich, A., Rambachan, I., Trkulja, T., & Yee, L. (2021, September 27). *Women in the workplace 2021.* Accessed at https://mckinsey.com/featured-insights /diversity-and-inclusion/women-in-the-workplace on December 16, 2021.

Cimpian, J. (2018, April 23). *How our education system undermines gender equity: And why culture change—not policy—may be the solution* [Blog post]. Accessed at https://brookings .edu/blog/brown-center-chalkboard/2018/04/23/how-our-education-system-undermines -gender-equity on October 11, 2021.

Covey, S. M. R. (2006). *The speed of trust: The one thing that changes everything.* New York: Free Press.

Cuomo, M. R. (Ed.). (2012). *The person who changed my life: Prominent people recall their mentors.* Emmaus, PA: Rodale.

DuFour, R. (2004). What is a "professional learning community"? *Educational Leadership, 61*(8), 6–11.

DuFour, R., DuFour, R., Eaker, R., & Many, T. (2010). *Learning by doing: A handbook for Professional Learning Communities at Work* (2nd ed.). Bloomington, IN: Solution Tree Press.

DuFour, R., DuFour, R., Eaker, R., Many, T. W., & Mattos, M. (2016). *Learning by doing: A handbook for Professional Learning Communities at Work* (3rd ed.). Bloomington, IN: Solution Tree Press.

DuFour, R., & Fullan, M. (2013). *Cultures built to last: Systemic PLCs at work.* Bloomington, IN: Solution Tree Press.

Elmore, R. F. (2004). *School reform from the inside out: Policy, practice, and performance.* Cambridge, MA: Harvard Education Press.

Fielding-Singh, P., Magliozzi, D., & Ballakrishnen, S. (2018, August 28). Why women stay out of the spotlight at work. *Harvard Business Review.* Accessed at https://hbr.org/2018/08 /why-women-stay-out-of-the-spotlight-at-work on December 16, 2021.

Glass, T. E. (2000). Where are all the women superintendents? *AASA.* Accessed at http://aasa .org/SchoolAdministratorArticle.aspx?id=14492 on October 13, 2021.

Glass, T. E., Björk, L., & Brunner, C. C. (2000). *The study of the American school superintendency, 2000: A look at the superintendent of education in the new millennium.* Arlington, VA: American Association of School Administrators.

Goodwin, D. K. (2008, September 14). The secrets of America's great presidents. *Parade,* 4–5.

Hill, J., Ottem, R., & DeRoche, J. (2016). *Trends in public and private school principal demographics and qualifications: 1987–88 to 2011–12.* Washington, DC: National Center for Education Statistics. Accessed at https://nces.ed.gov/pubs2016/2016189.pdf on October 13, 2021.

Ibarra, H., & Hansen, M. T. (2011). Are you a collaborative leader? *Harvard Business Review, 89*(7–8), 68–74.

Lakshmi, P. (2020, March 8). *90% of people are biased against women. That's the challenge we face.* Accessed at https://cnn.com/2020/03/08/opinions/women-gender-bias-padma-lakshmi /index.html on October 13, 2021.

MacDonald, R. (2017, April 21). *Risk, trust, collaboration: Leadership for personalized, learner-centered environments* [Blog post]. Accessed at https://blogs.edweek.org/edweek/learning_deeply/2017/04/risk_trust_collaboration_leadership_for_personalized_learner-centered_environments.html on October 13, 2021.

Machida, M., & Schaubroeck, J. (2011). The role of self-efficacy beliefs in leader development. *Journal of Leadership and Organizational Studies, 18*(4), 459–468.

Madsen, S. R. (2019, March 8). What women want from men—a sponsor. *The Salt Lake Tribune.* Accessed at https://sltrib.com/opinion/commentary/2019/03/08/susan-r-madsen-what-women on February 7, 2022.

Mohr, T. S. (2014, April 25). Why women don't apply for jobs unless they're 100% qualified. *Harvard Business Review.* Accessed at https://hbr.org/2014/08/why-women-dont-apply-for-jobs-unless-theyre-100-qualified on October 13, 2021.

Morrison, N. (2018, April 12). White men are still over-represented in school leadership. *Forbes.* Accessed at https://forbes.com/sites/nickmorrison/2018/04/12/white-men-are-still-over-represented-in-school-leadership/#1032bfb36019 on October 13, 2021.

National Center for Education Statistics. (2020). *Characteristics of public school principals.* Accessed at https://nces.ed.gov/programs/coe/pdf/coe_cls.pdf on November 21, 2021.

National Center for Education Statistics. (2021). *Characteristics of public school teachers.* Accessed at https://nces.ed.gov/programs/coe/pdf/2021/clr_508c.pdf on November 21, 2021.

New York State Council of School Superintendents. (2015). *Snapshot IX: The 9th triennial study of the superintendency in New York State.* Accessed at www.palmaccsd.org/docs/district/superintendent/snapshot%202015%20web%20version%20final.pdf?id=270 on March 3, 2022.

New York State Education Department. (2019, December). *Educator diversity report.* Accessed at www.nysed.gov/common/nysed/files/programs/educator-quality/educator-diversity-report-december-2019.pdf on March 3, 2022.

The Obama Foundation [@ObamaFoundation]. (2017, March 8). There is no limit to what we, as women, can accomplish.—*@MichelleObama #InternationalWomensDay* [Tweet]. *Twitter.* Accessed at https://twitter.com/obamafoundation/status/839493848816570369?lang=en on October 13, 2021.

Patterson, K., Grenny, J., McMillan, R., & Switzler, A. (2012). *Crucial conversations: Tools for talking when the stakes are high* (2nd ed.). New York: McGraw-Hill.

Ramaswamy, S. V. (2020, February 20). School superintendents are overwhelmingly male. What's holding women back from the top job? *USA Today.* Accessed at https://usatoday.com/story/news/education/2020/02/20/female-school-district-superintendents-westchester-rockland/4798754002 on November 21, 2021.

Scott, K. (2019). *Radical candor: Be a kick-ass boss without losing your humanity* (Rev. & updated ed.). New York: St. Martin's Press.

Sicinski, A. (n.d.) *How to take intelligent risks in the pursuit of your goals* [Blog post]. Accessed at https://blog.iqmatrix.com/intelligent-risks on January 6, 2022.

Superville, D. R. (2016, November 15). Few women run the nation's school districts. Why? *Education Week*. Accessed at https://edweek.org/ew/articles/2016/11/16/few-women-run-the-nations-school-districts.html on October 13, 2021.

Symbiosis. (n.d.). In *Merriam-Webster's online dictionary*. Accessed at https://merriam-webster.com/dictionary/symbiosis on December 26, 2021.

UN Women. (2021, January 15). *Facts and figures: Women's leadership and political participation*. Accessed at https://unwomen.org/en/what-we-do/leadership-and-political-participation/facts-and-figures#_ednref1 on December 30, 2021.

Epilogue

Women face many obstacles that could prevent them from advancing in their careers, and these obstacles result in the gender gap in educational leadership positions. The purpose of this book is to provide insights, inspiration, and guidance to women so we, as leaders, can help them grow as educational leaders. Our first theme was discussing the importance of leadership to help women become stronger leaders. Yvette Jackson, Carmen Jiménez, Joellen Killion, and Janel Keating discussed the necessity of cultivating confidence, leading change, and leading with compassion and insight. Our second theme was addressing the obstacles women face. Julie A. Schmidt, Suzette Lovely, and Heather Friziellie discussed a variety of challenges with strategies to navigate common obstacles. Our final theme was centered around self-growth. Jessica Kanold-McIntyre, Jasmine K. Kullar, Tina H. Boogren, Bob Sonju, and Jason Andrews discussed the importance of seeking a mentor, how to prepare for a promotion, the value of self-care, and finally, learning from other women leaders.

Leaders need both aspiration and inspiration. As you engage with the daily challenges of life, it's easy to forget others are watching you. Potential leaders, new leaders, and even experienced leaders are watching and learning from you. Are you modeling what *you* would find inspirational? Are you prepared to commit yourself to being the kind of leader that others seek to emulate? As singer and songwriter Dolly Parton says, "If your actions create a legacy that inspires others to dream more, learn more, do more and become more, then, you are an excellent leader" (Goodreads, n.d.). Together let's push one another, grow one another, and support one another so we can all become the best we can be. Let's be the role models for the next generation of women, our own daughters, nieces, and granddaughters.

Ultimately, the question is: What will you do to enhance the capacity and efficacy of yourself and of women leaders around you? Our effectiveness as leaders is enhanced when we join together in *collective* support of one another. We must join together in multiple ways, leveraging networks, support groups, social media, and so on. You bring your own unique talents and perspective to leadership. We need that. We need you. We need representation not just of women, but of women of color in leadership roles everywhere. Our capacity to enhance the role of women as leaders requires more than our individual efforts. Will you provide the support and encouragement needed to increase the number of women in leadership positions? Are you prepared to be that go-to pillar of support for those who are undertaking more challenging leadership responsibilities? Or will you be someone who closes the door behind you once you are securely inside? There is plenty of room at the top for all. Make a commitment not just to hold the door open for those who are seeking to enter but also to reach out a hand and lift them up.

One final word. The world needs more kindness. You can be a strong leader and *also* be kind.

Be kind.

References and Resources

Goodreads. (n.d.). *Dolly Parton quotable quote*. Accessed at https://goodreads.com/quotes/391 82-if-your-actions-create-a-legacy-that-inspires-others-to on February 16, 2022.

Index

Step In, Step Up
Jane A. G. Kise and Barbara K. Watterston

Step In, Step Up guides current and aspiring women leaders in education through a twelve-week development journey. An assortment of activities, reflection prompts, and stories empower readers to overcome gender barriers and engage in opportunities to learn, grow, and lead within their school communities.

BKF827

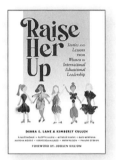

Raise Her Up
Edited by Debra E. Lane and Kimberly Cullen

This anthology presents a collection of powerful stories written by women whose backgrounds are as diverse as their leadership roles. Readers will discover a sense of community among the pages, as well as practical guidance on how to develop the skills and character to achieve success.

BKG045

180 Days of Self-Care for Busy Educators
Tina H. Boogren

Rely on *180 Days of Self-Care for Busy Educators* to help you lead a happier, healthier more fulfilled life inside and outside of the classroom. With Tina H. Boogren's guidance, you will work through thirty-six weeks of self-care strategies during the school year.

BKF920

Connecting Through Leadership
Jasmine K. Kullar

The success of a school greatly depends on the ability of its leaders to communicate effectively. Rely on *Connecting Through Leadership* to help you strengthen your communication skills to inspire, motivate, and connect with every member of your school community.

BKF927

Solution Tree | Press

a division of
Solution Tree

Visit SolutionTree.com or call 800.733.6786 to order.

Wait! Your professional development journey doesn't have to end with the last pages of this book.

We realize improving student learning doesn't happen overnight. And your school or district shouldn't be left to puzzle out all the details of this process alone.

No matter where you are on the journey, we're committed to helping you get to the next stage.

Take advantage of everything from **custom workshops** to **keynote presentations** and **interactive web and video conferencing**. We can even help you develop an action plan tailored to fit your specific needs.

Let's get the conversation started.

Call **888.763.9045** today.

SolutionTree.com